LONG TRAIN RUNNIN'

LONG TRAIN RUNNIN'

OUR STORY OF

The Doobie Brothers

TOM JOHNSTON AND PAT SIMMONS

WITH CHRIS EPTING

St. Martin's Press
New York

First published in the United States by St. Martin's Press, an imprint
of St. Martin's Publishing Group

www.stmartins.com

Designed by Meryl Sussman Levavi

Endpaper photograph © David Warner Ellis / Getty Images

The Library of Congress Cataloging-in-Publication Data is
available upon request.

ISBN 978-1-250-27005-4 (hardcover)
ISBN 978-1-250-27006-1 (ebook)

Our books may be purchased in bulk for promotional, educational,
or business use. Please contact your local bookseller or the Macmillan
Corporate and Premium Sales Department at 1-800-221-7945,
extension 5442, or by email at
MacmillanSpecialMarkets@macmillan.com.

First Edition: 2022

10 9 8 7 6 5 4 3 2 1

CONTENTS

CAST OF CHARACTERS

Tom Johnston—founding member of the Doobie Brothers

Pat Simmons—founding member of the Doobie Brothers

Tiran Porter—longtime bassist for the Doobie Brothers

Ted Templeman—Doobie Brothers producer

Michael McDonald—longtime Doobie Brothers singer/song-writer/keyboardist

Bill Payne—Little Feat keyboard player, former touring member of the Doobie Brothers, and frequent session player

John McFee—longtime guitarist/vocalist for the Doobie Brothers

INTRODUCTION

It's hard to believe it's been more than fifty years since we first met and this thing called the Doobie Brothers was created. We have been through a lot together, and the fact that we are still playing today is something we are deeply thankful for. In the course of putting our book together, we decided it would be cool to allow some other voices to join us on the page. After all, the Doobie Brothers have always been sort of like the ultimate musical brotherhood with all the great players who have been part of this band. It really is an extended family and we thought that having a few family members offer their own words would just be a nice way to help tell the story. We thank them, and we thank you as well for picking up our book and for listening to the music. We couldn't have done this without all of you.

PAT AND TOM

LONG TRAIN RUNNIN'

NATURAL THING

Tom

In some ways it feels like a long journey. But in others it seems to have just raced by. For me, it starts at the beginning, in the small town of Visalia, in Central California. *Grapes of Wrath* country. My parents came out to California in 1933 from a little town outside St. Louis, Missouri, driving a '33 Ford, and whatever they had was packed in the car. My dad got his aeronautical engineering degree in L.A. and began working at the Burbank Airport. My brother was born in 1938 and my sister in 1941, both in L.A. Then my parents moved up to Visalia from L.A. so my dad could work at Tex Rankin Field. He was an aircraft mechanic in World War II for the Army Air Force. I was born in 1948. My dad later started his own aircraft shop in the neighboring town of Tulare, working mostly on crop dusters as well as a few private planes. This is where I would spend every summer working from about the age of eleven or so till I was eighteen. It was hot and repetitive, and I wasn't that mechanically inclined, so I worked under supervision most of the time, working in everything from the engine shop to the parts department. I did love the Word War II fighters that would show up occasionally and do some aerobatics over the runway before landing and taxiing to the hangar, where they'd get converted for firefighting. And my dad's shop occasionally worked on World War II torpedo bombers that were being converted for the same reason. But the rest was mundane to me. The one thing that made it bearable was listening to music on the radio and smoking the occasional cigarette I'd "borrow" from one of the guys working there. I'd sometimes get to put on the radio station that had *Happy Harold's House of Blues* from a little town up by Fresno. He played nothing but blues and it was killer!

My folks were pretty religious and belonged to the Methodist church in Visalia. This became a sore spot with me and caused friction because I just didn't fit in and wasn't into it. By the time I was twelve, they finally gave up on it. Meanwhile, my older brother was into some great music and brought home records starting when I was about nine. Guys like Little Richard, Bo Diddley, Jimmy Reed, Elvis, and Jerry Lee Lewis; those albums in the mid-1950s that he brought home were like magic for me. He was kind of a James Dean–style hot-rod enthusiast. Lots of girlfriends and a few troublemakers hanging around. I think that's why I looked up to him. I was a rebel in waiting.

This all happened when we lived on Myrtle Street, which was in town and located around a lot of the schools I went to. The high school I would eventually attend was right behind the house. My brother had already gone to UC Berkeley and ended up living in L.A. for a while and getting his aeronautical engineering degree, just as my dad had, before getting married and moving back up to Visalia to work at my dad's shop, eventually taking over running it. My sister was going to college at Cal Poly in San Luis Obispo, after which she moved up to Santa Clara to work at the Santa Clara County Hospital as a med tech. My brother and sister were both quite a bit older than me so they were both out of the house by the time I was about eleven and we moved to S. West Street, which was more out in the country.

The Central Valley was basically all agricultural, with walnut, almond, peach, nectarine, and plum orchards, and cotton fields around the house we moved to after I turned eleven. There were also cattle ranches out on the "west side" as it was called, which was out by Firebaugh, west of Visalia. My friends and I would spend a lot of time hanging out in the orchards, and in the summer we'd float on inner tubes down the big irrigation ditches that ran through them. We'd also cruise the main drag in town once we were old enough to drive, usually in someone's parent's car—or if someone actually had a car, that was even better. Gas was about twenty-five cents a gallon, so you could hang out all night for pretty cheap. It was like a scene out of *American Graffiti*. We even had a Mel's Diner with girls on roller skates to take your order at your car window, same with the A&W root beer place. Another pastime on summer weekends during high school and junior college was to drive up to Three Rivers in the foothills and tube down the river. Three Rivers was a gathering place for all the kids my age, a lot of whom I went to school with. And it was kind of a party scene with lots of beer, but a lot of fun in the summer because it was always so damn hot!

During the time from when I was about nine till I was fifteen, we would take trips to Missouri to see relatives in the small towns outside St. Louis, where my parents had come from. Early on, we would drive, which took about two and a half days, but by the time I was twelve or so, we started flying in private planes my dad would either borrow from friends or, I guess, rent. It could take up to two days to fly to Missouri, flying many hours a day. If we used the Navion, which topped out at 145–150 knots, it would have been the two full days. We only stopped for fuel and at night to sleep. Other planes, like the Bonanza, were a little faster. One trip was in an Aero Commander which was a twin engine plane and flew pretty fast for a private plane in that era. Generally, these planes were small inside, just big enough for four people, and after a couple of days or so it would get pretty boring. So I would get to find all the radio stations broadcasting between California and Missouri as a way to keep track of where we were during the trip. But probably more to keep me occupied. But that at least afforded me the chance to keep up with the music that was popular at the time.

Missouri trips were such a departure from living in California, and I really enjoyed the experience, whether exploring my mom's parents' house, wandering in and around the town of Bourbon, or visiting relatives on my mom's side in Farmington, or hanging out with my dad's family in Sullivan, which was right up Route 66. I remember a lot of trains in both areas, which was in rural Missouri. The train was about two hundred feet across the road from my grandparents' house in Bourbon, and I loved watching the long freight trains go by. Going to my aunt and uncle's (on my dad's side) cabin on the Merrimac River outside Sullivan, where they lived, was a gas. We'd drive out to the river in my uncle's '52 Chevy pickup, usually with one or two of my cousins and my brother and sister, depending on the year. Once we got close to the river, we'd hop out and ride on the running boards through all the tall grasses and woods that were out by the river. Lots of fireworks, fishing, and boating up and down the river, and cookouts. And when I was back in the town of Sullivan, my granddad (my dad's father) had a leather shop that made everything from saddles to harnesses for horse teams. And this sat right by an old-time soda fountain . . . heaven! This is when I was pretty young. As I got older and was hanging around with my older cousin, I got to be the test driver for the scooters and go-carts he would make from lawnmower engines and whatever else he could scrape together. It was the all-American dream for a kid at that age. One summer we made cherry bomb cannons out of plumbing pipe that would shoot D-cell batteries. This was a little crazy. You could sink a boat or tear limbs off trees with those things. That lasted for one summer. After these trips, which sometimes had my brother and sister along and were about ten days long, we'd head back out to Visalia and pick up our daily lives.

I started playing guitar at twelve, learning as many blues, R&B, and rock and roll songs as I could. My early inspirations were Little Richard, Jimmy Reed, and Bo Diddley, and a couple of years later the "Three Kings of the Blues," guitarist-singers Albert, B.B., and Freddie King. No relation, of course, but all rock and roll royalty! As a sophomore in high school, I started playing in bands with other kids in school, playing all over the area, covering everything from the Beatles and other pop music to Wilson Pickett and James Brown. We played school dances and civic centers like the Tulare Veterans Memorial Hall (not to be confused with the Tulare County Civic Center) and bars in Tulare, Porterville, Lindsay, Farmersville, Exeter; this continued through junior college (at College of the Sequoias) in Visalia. So I played over about five years with quite a few different players. When I was seventeen or eighteen, I'd some-times get gigs on the fly after getting a phone call saying, "hey man you wanna make five to ten bucks tonight, we're playing at . . . ," and then you could fill in the blanks of a number of bars in and around Visalia. By the time I was at College of the Sequoias in '67 through '68, I had already done a recording trip in L.A., had a blues band of my own, and played in Mexican wedding bands and a soul band in Tulare called the Charades. This band was my first experience playing specifically soul music and singing backgrounds and a couple of lead vocals on songs I wrote with the band for all-Black audiences. It was an education and experience you couldn't get in Visalia. I had a ball, and so did the crowds! The band's leader, Ray Baradat, was the only other white male singer in the band and did all their business—like booking, recording, travel, and so on. We mostly played in Tulare at the Black Elks Club but also did a couple of gigs in Hanford and Visalia, even Fresno.

The pickup gigs were all interspersed in and around the wedding band, Charades, and the blues band. So I was playing a lot, which I loved. So many different kinds of music and musicians, and some of these guys were really good, like the B3 player for all the wedding gigs. He was at the Jimmy Smith level. At some of the pickup gigs, it got a little crazy some nights. I remember that one night in a Porterville bar, some rednecks didn't like us because we didn't play any country (we didn't know any), only R&B and rock tunes that everybody knew, so they decided to try to physically pull us off the stage until the bartender chased them out with a shotgun. A year or so later, and through the late sixties, I was heavily influenced by John Mayall's 1966 album *Blues Breakers,* as well as by Clapton, Cream, and Jimi Hendrix, whose playing style and guitar sound was different from anything I'd heard, and the heavy rock sound of Mountain. I was mesmerized by Hendrix and by Leslie West's huge guitar sound as well as Clapton's take on blues and blues-rock. Phenomenal! This was the same time I got turned on to the *Born Under a Bad Sign* album by Albert King on Stax Records. The tune "Crosscut Saw" was a great example of what Albert brought to the blues. What a unique style of playing! The Doobies would get a small tour with Albert in '72, but that of course was a ways off. There was so much amazing music being made that I was getting ready to leave Visalia and go find where it was really all happening up in the Bay Area. But before I left, I cut another single in Fresno as a solo artist using a couple of musicians from the Charades for drums and bass. One song I wrote on piano was a blues tune called "Sittin in Prison." We cut the basic track with piano, bass, and drums, and then I did the vocal and lead guitar fills on separate tracks. The flip side was a Hendrix-style rock tune called "Burnin" which was rhythm guitar, lead guitar, bass, drums, and the vocal. My friend Iggy played drums on the tracks, and he and I went to L.A. to try to get a deal, which was a waste of time other than the experience of doing it. I was offered a thirteen-year contract at some funky label on Sunset Strip, but that seemed like a bad idea, so I said no thanks and we drove back to Visalia.

As a freshman in high school, my life changed when I saw James Brown and the Famous Flames in nearby Fresno at the Fresno Civic Auditorium in the early sixties. It was a classic-soul revue show. Something I'd never seen before and I was knocked out! He was electrifying! It was a professional show in size and intensity, and that was unusual for the acts that came through the valley. He was touring on the first *Live at the Apollo* album when I saw him, and I remember it like yesterday. His live show had a built-in work ethic and energy output like nothing I'd ever seen. He had a huge band with two drummers, two guitar players, bass, and keyboards. And an announcer who sat on a platform in the back corner of the stage. First, there was a female vocal group to open the show, and they would do some background singing later along with "the Famous Flames." That was followed by James coming out and playing B3 for about twenty minutes before a small break. Then came the main show, and that part was a life-altering experience. It was beyond my comprehension that somebody could move and sing like he did: all the moves with the mic, the dancing (the good foot), the dropping on his knees (with a guy throwing a cape on him for "Please Please Please"), his screams like I'd never heard—he was in constant motion for the whole show! The crowd went crazy! He just never stopped dancing, singing, working the audience into a frenzy! And the crowd was a mix of whites (mostly women) and Blacks of all ages. It was something else for a young kid from Visalia! A friend with whom I went to school and played in bands (Bob Duarte) is the one who turned me on to James Brown to begin with, driving us to the concert at the Fresno Civic. Thank you, Bob!

Pat

Both of my parents were from Washington State. My mom was from a little town called Twisp in the Cascade Mountains near the Canadian border, and my dad was from Wenatchee, about 150 miles from Seattle. I was born in Aberdeen, and that's where I lived as a youngster. Both of my parents were teachers. My dad had been in the navy during World War II, and when he got out of the service, under the GI Bill, he went to college. My mom studied nursing, and they met when they entered school at Eastern Washington State College near Spokane, where they went to get their teaching degrees. When my folks got married, my mom already had two daughters from a previous marriage: Joyce and Julie, who were five and seven years older than me, but as far as I was concerned they were simply my sisters. My dad was actually the principal of my school when I was in kindergarten, which was kind of weird. I mean, we all know how we feel about the principal when we're little kids. But my dad did a good job, and everybody seemed to like him. It wasn't like other schools I would go to later on, where the principal seemed to be feared by everyone. My memories of living in Aberdeen can be summed up in one word: rain. I swear it seems like it rained virtually every single day of the year. The gray clouds were just like an ominous blanket covering the town at all times. This is the town where Kurt Cobain would be born and raised, and I always suspected that the powerful music that he and his band Nirvana made was a reflection of the dark and bleak mood that seemed all-consuming. We are talking about rain like three hundred days a year. Overcast almost every other day. Literally hardly a dry day in the year. There was something so depressing about that. Honestly, I didn't like it. But what I loved was that each summer we would head up north to see my grandparents, where it was nice, warm, and dry. There were wonderful rivers and lakes where you could swim and fish. Just some of the most beautiful country I'd ever experienced. I would get lost in the sunshine of the day and the long beautiful nights, which featured thousands of stars and lots of good food and company. Summers were just wonderful. And then would come that fateful day when we would have to pack everything up, get back in the car, and drive back down to Aberdeen, which, honestly, I dreaded. It felt like the second you crossed over the county line, it just got rainy, gloomy, dark, and horrible. It was pretty depressing. Still, I loved going to school. It was kind of a redneck area, very hardscrabble, and so the kids were tough. I proudly come from a long line of rednecks, ranchers, loggers, farmers, fishermen, horse people, and hunters. That's logging country up there, and so everything is kind of rough to begin with, and I got along well with the local kids. I loved comic books, which I collected endlessly. This was probably the beginning of a lifetime of collecting. I went from comic books to collecting postage stamps, baseball cards, musical memorabilia, books, guitars, Civil War memorabilia, black powder guns, motorcycles, and any two-wheel memorabilia. I'm still active in all these areas of interest. I'm just a collector at heart. As it turns out, there are lots and lots of people out there who are passionate about collecting. As a child, and now as an adult, many of my best friends are those I've met through these hobbies.

When I was five years old, I met a woman who made a big difference in my life. Her name was Lucy Anderson. She was the grandmother of a couple of students who went to my dad's school. Somehow, my father made arrangements for me to stay with her after I got out of my half day of kindergarten class. I would stay with her in the afternoons until my parents finished work and were able to pick me up. The Andersons had a piano in their home. We also had a piano in our house that had belonged to my grandmother, my mom's mom. It had a hole in the side from the discharge of a shotgun that had gone off accidentally while being cleaned. My sisters took piano lessons, so I was familiar with the instrument, and one day I was playing around on the keyboard of Mrs. Anderson's piano. "Do you play the piano?" she asked me. I just shrugged and said, "I don't, but my sisters do." Then she asked, "Would you like to learn how to play? I can teach you. I'm a piano teacher." Well, that sounded intriguing. What a great arrangement, I thought. And so that's how I first got into music. It all started off pretty basic. She taught me sharps and flats and all of the other foundational things like, "every good boy does fine," F-A-C-E to learn the notes on the staff, note values, musical notation, and terminology. I started developing my playing skills and learning how to read music. Such great stuff for a curious little kid to learn. And talk about a crash course. I was there five days a week with her, and every single day she was teaching me piano. But it was more than that. We would work for about half an hour on the piano, and then she would stop me and say, "Okay Patrick, now it's time for cookies and milk, and to listen to the radio." We would go into her parlor, and she would turn on her old-fashioned radio. It would take a couple of moments for it to warm up, but then she would be adjusting the dial to find what she was looking for: the Liberace radio show. "Patrick," she would say to me, "if you want to learn how to play the piano, then you have to listen to the masters play piano. Liberace is a wonderful piano player, and by listening to him it's going to help you become a better player."

When people think of Liberace today, he's probably thought of as kind of a cliché, just a glittery, glamorous showman without much musical substance. But that wasn't the case at all. He had been a child prodigy, the first-generation son of working-class immigrants. At the height of his fame, starting in the 1950s, he was the highest-paid entertainer in the world, and despite all the flamboyant excess both on and off the stage, and his nickname, "Mr. Showmanship," there was a lot of substance behind his piano playing. He was a brilliant technical player but blended that precision with a knack for showmanship.

His radio show would feature him speaking with a variety of guests, but then he would play the piano. Even as a small child, I thought his music sounded wonderful coming through the warm old radio. He was funny and interesting as he described what he would be playing and he could also perform a variety of styles from classical to popular song to ragtime—whatever. As we listened to the shows on the radio, Mrs. Anderson would explain to me, "Listen to what he did just there. Listen to how he played that song." Everything was a teaching opportunity, and I really enjoyed every day with Mrs. Anderson.

2

FEELIN' DOWN FARTHER

Tom

When it came to my early guitar playing, I started on a cracked Harmony Archtop I bought for twelve dollars from Jack Love, with whom I would later be in bands, including the Implicits. I didn't take lessons. I learned everything by ear and experimentation, mostly because I played clarinet and saxophone through my freshman year of high school, which required endless lessons. The saxophone was cool, but I hated the clarinet. It was the wrong image for what I was into musically and otherwise. At the end of my freshman year, I packed that thing up, stuck it in the closet, and told my parents, "I'm not gonna play this thing anymore."

So guitar became my sole focus for expressing myself, and by the time I was fourteen or fifteen, I had moved on to an electric single-pickup Kay guitar and a small amp. I'd become good enough to play in bands and started reaching out to the local musician community. I learned by listening to Jimmy Reed and figuring his style out. Then I got some rhythm chops down by playing along with Bo Diddley. That led to Freddie King and some Chuck Berry. I even played along with Link Wray and some surf music like the Ventures. It was all going in different directions, and that was a good way to learn. My parents had an upright piano that I also spent a lot of time on, trying to figure out tunes I'd hear as well as writing my own. By my freshman year, I knew how to play the iconic Freddie King blues instrumental "Hideaway," which was a necessary tool if you wanted to play in a band at that time. I started playing in bands while at Mt. Whitney High School. The bands I played in did everything from Byrds and Beatles to the Box Tops and the Hollies. By this time, I had purchased a '65 Fender Bandmaster, which I used on early Doobie gigs and recordings, and a Gibson 335 from the local music store just to keep up. Later in junior college I would add a J-50 Gibson acoustic that I would go on to use on every Doobie Brothers album up to and including *What Were Once Vices Are Now Habits*. The other tunes we played were all R&B, like Wilson Pickett's "In the Midnight Hour" and "Mustang Sally," Robert Parker's "Barefootin'," and James Brown's songs—going as far as playing "Please Please Please," complete with knee drop! This was something new for the kids at my school, who had no idea who James Brown was. It was a risky move, but to my surprise they liked it and even clapped and yelled. Mind you, this was all in one set. A pretty crazy musical mixture, but it worked. This was soon after *The T.A.M.I. Show* movie had come out, featuring a lot of popular artists in both pop and R&B.

After doing this for a couple of years, some of the musicians I knew in and out of school formed the Implicits, which consisted of two guitars, bass, drums, and a keyboard player. We played Motown and other R&B songs along with various rock songs that were popular on the radio at the time. We even had a female vocalist for about two months. And that was the band that went to L.A. to record for the first time. The songs, "Give Me Justice" and "She's Alright," which we had written for the occasion, were pretty rudimentary rock, but we thought it was pretty cool at the time. We had been talking with this sleazy "producer," who would come around to some of our practices with her sidekick from L.A., who worked as a janitor at the Capitol Records building. So when we got down there the day before, we cut the direct-to-disk record at some crummy little studio off Sunset, and we got a "tour" of Capitol Records courtesy of the janitor, who claimed to be a bigwig at Capitol. We even got to go in Bobby Darin's office, which at the time seemed like a pretty big deal. I "borrowed" a pack of cigarettes off his desk and kept them for about two years. After the "session," we drove back to Visalia and tried to get the local station to play the songs, but they weren't interested! Still, we felt pretty cool to have a record, even if it didn't go anywhere.

I still have that 45. So that was that, and we went back to playing schools and the same venues we'd been playing like the
Tulare vets' hall and other small gigs around Visalia.

I moved on to B.B. and then Albert King, who was the most
lyrical electric blues player I'd ever heard. That was my early
world. Blues, R&B, and rock and roll. Guitar became my way
of expressing myself, and I spent hours in my room figuring
stuff out by ear, no charts, and that makes it a thing you're
proud of and very personal. Mixed in with what I was already
listening to and also expanding my input to Wilson Pickett,
Jimi Hendrix, Electric Flag, Otis Redding, Aretha Franklin, and
John Mayall with Eric Clapton. In addition to the Charades, I
had a little outfit called the Tom Johnston Blues Band, playing
stuff by Electric Flag; Bobby Bland; B.B., Freddie, and Albert
King; and Little Junior Parker. We played clubs/bars, and even
though most of us were underage, no one seemed to care. I just
couldn't play enough, no matter what the situation.

When I was playing regularly in Visalia and the surrounding area before leaving town for San Jose, my mom was already getting worried, especially after finding weed in my
guitar case. I believe she and my dad thought professional musicians were all potheads and drunks. So when that occurred
they, especially my mom, tried to dissuade me from following
that path but gave up when I basically said, "I can't promise
you I won't pursue this." That was the first time I ever saw
my mom cry. I felt pretty bad, but not bad enough to quit. My
dad and I didn't really communicate a lot by that time, so his
thoughts didn't hold much sway over me.

During the late sixties, my buddies and I became true week-end warriors, cruising up north a couple hundred miles practically every weekend in my friends' '51 Plymouth. That's where we wanted to be. The Bay Area music scene. The first concert I ever saw up there was Quicksilver Messenger Service and the Youngbloods playing in Larkspur in Marin County. This was in 1966, my senior year. Again, different surroundings, different crowd, and very different music. By the next year, we started driving up and hanging out in Haight-Ashbury with all the hippies and just took it all in. There was a huge amount of people up there, and none of us knew our way around San Francisco, but we learned after a couple of trips. And we'd crash at my sister's place in Santa Clara after a day in the Haight. I saw Janis Joplin and the Grateful Dead in the park at "hippie hill." There were Hells Angels, runaways, musicians, and hippies, who were renting Victorians or just living on the street. There was always something going on, on the street and in Golden Gate Park. Constant clouds of pot smoke in the air. And at night there was the Fillmore Auditorium featuring everybody under the sun playing, sometimes in very unusual combinations like Jefferson Airplane, Albert King, and Otis Rush all in the same night. Or Big Brother and the Holding Company with Janis Joplin, the Charlatans, and Muddy Waters. Butterfield Blues Band, B.B. King, and Blue Cheer. Hendrix, Cream, the Grateful Dead, Memphis Slim, Charlie Musselwhite, and on and on. The Dead were regulars in the park as well, playing free concerts to raise money for the Diggers, who tried to feed the people on the street. No easy task! And we were there for the funeral of the Hells Angel Chocolate George, held in the Haight, which was pretty intense. Hells Angels everywhere in the street, and the park. But things mellowed out the next day and got back to the ebb and flow of the Summer of Love. It was like living double lives up there, away from Visalia, where we'd return every Sunday night. I did get to see the Electric Flag and Frank Zappa in Fresno before I moved to San Jose, so that was a great send-off. When I think of that summer of '67, the songs I associate most with it are "Get Together" by the Youngbloods and "Soul Man" by Sam and Dave. Those songs just seemed to be everywhere and represented that whole era, and to this day when I hear them, I flash on what that time was like. That whole scene and everything that went on then could only happen in that little window of time. It will never happen again.

On subsequent trips to visit my sister, she introduced me to the Santa Cruz Mountains scene and the folks living up there at Von Ahnen's family house, which was a regular hangout for a lot of South Bay folks who were into music and the "mountain life." Paul, the patriarch of the family, was a retired IBM engineer, and he and his wife and two kids lived in a rustic house that had been converted from a barn. I met a lot of people my age at their house, many of whom were musicians. And there was always something going on up there, so this really piqued my interest in going to school and living in San Jose.

That summer a friend of mine (Albert Duarte) and I went to see Albert King play, and we also saw the Butterfield Blues Band open for Cream at the Fillmore. I'd seen Butterfield before, and was a huge fan of Paul Butterfield's playing; he was a virtuoso blues harp player, and I was really excited about seeing Cream for the first time. It was their first time playing on the West Coast. Before they hit the stage, though, I had the misfortune of taking the last hit of a joint that had been passed down a long row of folks sitting on the floor in front of the stage. A security guy yanked me up and dragged me into the office of Bill Graham, the famous promoter who ran the place. I couldn't believe it—busted for hitting a joint at the Fillmore? EVERYONE was getting high. I never did figure that one out. But there I was, and Graham started yelling, "Where are you from?" "Visalia," I told him, feeling pretty intimidated. "Then go get high in Visalia!" he yelled, and he literally chased me out the door, and I had to wait about two hours wandering around the Fillmore area till the end of the show, when my friend Albert came out (he had the car) so we could head back to my sister's place in Santa Clara. Man, I was disappointed. A funny story: about four or five years later, after the Doobies had put out both *Toulouse Street* and *The Captain and Me* and had become something of a name, we were playing our first show at Winterland and Bill came backstage to chat us up. I decided to ask him if he remembered a kid from Visalia that he had chased out of the Fillmore the night Cream were playing their first show on the West Coast. He didn't, of course, but he did ask why I wanted to know and I said: "Because that was me!" He laughed till he cried. He thought that was hilarious! After that, we got along well, and he even came to some of my solo shows in '79 that he was promoting. We both lived in

Mill Valley at that time, and I'd see him on his BMW motorcycle with his dog in the sidecar. He was a legend in the business but was actually pretty down-to-earth most of the time. We would go on to play quite a few shows for him in San Francisco, including the SNACK concert, which had Dylan, Neil Young, and a lot of bands from the Bay Area.

Pat

As my first year of school ended, so did my piano lessons. My dad came home one day and announced to all of us, "Everybody, we are moving to California." I had no idea what that meant. But when he told us it hardly rained at all there, I was thrilled. So we packed up the car and made our big move down to Palo Alto, where he was going to be starting a new job.

What was really funny was that this was in 1954, one of the rainiest years in California's history. So when the five of us first arrived, our initial thoughts were, really? This isn't that much better than Aberdeen, at least when it comes to the weather. But then, eventually, the storms passed, the skies cleared, and we fell in love with our new home. It was just so different than Aberdeen. In my young mind, California was where the cowboys roamed the open plains, just like in all of the westerns you would see at the movies. That's not quite what we experienced, but it was very beautiful. And it really was like being out in the country.

Wherever you looked, there were orchards with the freshest fruits and vegetable gardens. We even had a peach tree in our backyard. Up in Washington, it was all about apples and pears. Down in California, it was walnuts, nectarines, peaches, cherries, and many other kinds of produce. My dad got his masters at Stanford in education with an emphasis in mathematics and took a job at a local school, where he did very well. After one year in Palo Alto, we moved to San Jose so he could take an even better job. This is about when I was in the second grade. We lived in an area called Willow Glen, a district of San Jose, which was very comfortable and pretty. There was no looking back from Aberdeen. For me, California was the place to be.

The next year, we moved to a house near Los Gatos. I missed my piano lessons, and so we found a teacher near San Jose, but she wasn't as good as Mrs. Anderson. Still, I learned what I could. We had a little monophonic record player in our house. My mom had a few albums by Mahalia Jackson, Frank Sinatra, and Nat King Cole. My dad was a country guy, who listened to Tennessee Ernie Ford, the Sons of the Pioneers, and Patti Page. But my sisters had both started buying records around this time as well. They just loved Elvis Presley, Bobby Vinton, Connie Francis, and many other hitmakers of the day. Another game changer for me was when a friend of the family came to stay with us. He was the son of an associate of my father's, and when he joined the army and was sent to Fort Ord from Washington State, where he lived, he came and stayed at our house for a short time. What made that special for me was that he brought along his entire record collection. He had every 45 you could imagine: Little Richard, Chuck Berry, the Everly Brothers, Bobby Darin, Elvis; he just had it all, and I would sit on the floor endlessly playing those 45s on our little record player, just falling in love with music. Over and over and over, I would play those records. Those were very influential. When he went to the army for basic training, he left those sleeves of records, and for months that became my musical education. The music excited me so much that I would take the record player up to my bedroom window and blast the music out so that the whole neighborhood could hear what I was listening to. Something else influenced me as a young person: *The Adventures of Ozzie and Harriet* television show. Our family, like many others around the country, would gather around the television set each week and watch this real family live their life right before our eyes. Ricky Nelson was amazing. It blew my mind that there was this guy on TV that I could actually relate to. It wasn't a character like Little Richard or Chuck Berry. He looked like a guy next door. I mean, I could aspire to be that guy. And he was so cool with that flattop haircut. That's what I wanted to be. Watching him play his guitar and singing songs, I was just transfixed. I didn't know what "star quality" was back then, but looking back on it, Ricky Nelson certainly had it. How many other youngsters around the country were watching him, dreaming about what it must be like to be able to pick up the guitar and play such cool songs?

When I was just maybe eight years old and I saw a real acoustic guitar at my friend Ronnie Waltrip's house (his mom and dad played in a local country band), I just had to reach out and touch it. It was sort of mystical; it looked a lot like the one Ricky Nelson played. Ronnie let me pick it up and hold it, and I couldn't believe it—*a real guitar.* He said to me, "Wanna learn a chord?" And right then and there, he taught me a G chord. And that was it. Everything just clicked in that second. I liked playing the piano. I enjoy the repetition and the lessons and everything about it. It was very rational, though. Hitting that first G chord on the guitar was different. This was emotional. All of a sudden, I kind of felt like Ricky Nelson. That first chord literally changed my life. I would spend every day at Ronnie's house learning to play the guitar. He taught me everything he knew until I was able to play songs with him. As I became more proficient on the guitar, we began to play together in public, winning talent contests, singing and harmonizing. I couldn't get enough.

There were more influences around me in addition to the radio and records. Dick Clark's *American Bandstand* was on TV every day and often featured performances by the biggest acts in popular music. Ed Sullivan also hosted a variety show, where up-and-coming acts often made their television debuts, like Buddy Holly and Elvis. In the early sixties there was a TV show called *Hootenanny,* which featured lots of cool music by artists like Pete Seeger, Joan Baez, the Limelighters, Harry Belafonte, Josh White, and Odetta. For me, it felt like a counterculture soundtrack. A sonic uprising. When I was about twelve years old, I took guitar lessons from a lady named Annette. She was kind of an early version of a hippie and inspired me with her bohemian lifestyle. She was probably in her mid-twenties. She was a young mom who had graduated with a music degree from San Jose State and began teaching music when she came out of school. I just loved the environment in her home. This was somebody who, to me, was living an almost alternative lifestyle when you consider how conservative everything was back then. She had the coolest stereo system, something she and her husband put together with separate components that they found in magazines. This was nothing you could just go buy in the store. They had worked to create the ultimate music system in their home. She had speakers that her husband had constructed—these incredible cabinets that were as beautiful as they were good-sounding. At home, you were lucky if your parents had a simple little record player set up. But what she had in that home was incredible. Our records were all mono-phonic, but it was the dawn of stereo, and this was the first time I had ever heard it. It allowed the records to come to life in the room. The whole vibe in their home was special.

In the early 1960s, a musical revolution was taking place in our country. Folk music and socially conscious songs were beginning to take shape, and I loved all of it. But there was a deeper cultural revolution taking place, one that encompassed literature as well. As soon as I started reading poets and authors like Allen Ginsberg and Neal Cassady, Jack Kerouac and Gary Snyder, among others, I felt inspired and transported. Even though I didn't really understand what it was they were writing about, I liked the lifestyle it represented. And it represented a harsh juxtaposition to the conservative, "normal" lifestyle that I had been living with my family. I didn't know exactly what it was I was feeling, but I knew there was a subculture out there that I was curious about. An artist's world that I had a yearning for. I think there might have been a rebelliousness burning inside of me, an itch that I just had to scratch.

Her pad was also the first place I ever heard Bob Dylan. Talk about an earthquake. This wasn't like Elvis Presley or Chuck Berry. Listening to the radio from such an early age, I knew what a beautiful voice sounded like. Like Nat King Cole. Or Johnny Mathis. Or even Ricky Nelson. Elvis, Chuck Berry, and Little Richard may have been rougher and rawer, but they could still sing. Dylan's voice was the opposite of everything. It was nasal and twangy, almost as if he was trying to irritate you or get under your skin. I loved that. I mean, if this guy could sing, I thought, maybe I could, too. Years later, when the punk rock movement happened, the ethos was very much, "Hey, anybody can do this." Dylan kind of gave me that same sensation. Here's this guy with a guitar and harmonica. That's it. Wait, he also had those great songs. There was nothing fancy about it, yet it was still earth-shattering. What he was writing about and singing about sounded like things that mattered. He sang with force and energy. It wasn't pretty. But it was beautiful nonetheless.

My guitar teacher, Annette, also played Joan Baez, Mississippi John Hurt, and other wonderful artists. These artists were different than Bob Dylan, but they still had a lot to say. I loved folk music and obscure Appalachian songs. I absorbed all of that incredible American music as a teenager and decided that's what I wanted to play. She would help me figure out those songs, and she kept turning me on to new music from outside the United States, from Africa and Ireland, appreciating "world music" before the term was even invented. She would send me out to go buy certain songbooks that would have all of these obscure Appalachian folk songs. And then that's what she would teach me. I mean, at fourteen years old, I was becoming an old musical soul. Eventually, she told my parents, "I've taught him everything I know." And that's when I felt I was truly on my way.

A couple of years later, I also started listening to the Wolfman Jack radio show. Wolfman broadcasted from somewhere down along the border in Mexico, and there was just something magical when you would search the radio dial and finally find that signal and hear him howling, literally howling like a wolf, before playing all of your favorite records. Blues and obscure R&B—that was his thing. He played stuff I had never heard before that just knocked me out. It was just such a cool time in so many ways. I was learning about good music, I was listening to music, I was absorbing music in various ways. Very soon after all this, I would go out and start playing music. I knew that was going to be the natural arc of my life. And I didn't want to waste any time.

About a year later at school, I met a guy named Owen Snyder. He heard me play the guitar and, since he too played, thought that maybe he and I might be able to do something together. We found that we had a lot in common musically and began collaborating on songs. We played some events at our high school, and one night at a local coffeehouse in Saratoga, the Brass Knocker, got hired to play our first professional gig.

A mutual musician friend allowed us to do a few songs while he took a break. The owner, Murray Brookman, heard us and hired us on the spot. At the time, this was the coolest club in the area, so we were incredibly lucky. I wasn't old enough to drive yet, but Owen had a car and could get us around, which made me feel a lot older than I really was. At first, we would play free events at our high school. That was a great way to get our feet wet. It also made us seem a lot cooler than we really were. Pick up a guitar and start playing music, things just happen. People look at you differently. From those high school events we then graduated to playing in the coffeehouses around the area. Country blues, folk blues, psychedelic; I was falling in love with all kinds of music. I also had a little group in high school, the Unrelated Brothers, with another guitar player friend of mine, whose name was Joe Weed! Go figure . . . He's a talented musician and continues to be very active in the music community, and has made some great recordings. We still stay in touch after all these years. We were like lots of other groups. We sang songs by the Byrds, the Animals, the Rolling Stones, the Beatles, the Beau Brummels, and other radio-friendly acts of the day, playing cover tunes. I still loved folk and traditional American music, but I was expanding my tastes. My parents totally didn't get it, though. They wanted me to work at a "real" job. To them, music was a great hobby, but they wanted me to go to college and have a career like I'm sure a lot of parents were telling their kids in the early 1960s. I had gotten my first real, paying job at a gas station when I was sixteen and it paid a buck an hour—with twelve-hour shifts. I could play guitar and make about ten bucks in three hours, and so it was a no-brainer for me how I wanted to spend my time.

I always felt that my parents, as smart as they were, didn't experience things in life firsthand. They were more observers. Me? I wanted to taste it all and understand what life was like by actually experiencing whatever I could. My dad, Roy, would always say to me, "You have to go to college and get an education because you'll need something to fall back on when the music goes away." He has since passed away, but several years before he did, I visited him one day, with my son Pat Jr. My dad asked him what his plans were, and my son, who also plays music, replied that he was going to college to get a degree. My dad said, "Well, college is great, but this music thing, you should really hang in with it. You might need something to fall back on." It was so funny how he came around on that one after watching how music had affected my life.

So as for music, my parents just couldn't see it. They were so traditional and conventional. The wedge between us grew deeper and deeper as I continued to play music at school functions and coffeehouses and other events throughout the area.

When I was sixteen, I worked in a gas station/garage, Dick's Union 76. My dad got me the job; he took his car to the mechanic there when it needed work. I was glad to make some money of my own and learn about cars. I had just gotten my driver's license and cruised to and from work in my dad's 1953 Chevy Powerglide. I had already rebuilt the top end of the engine on the old car, with help from Joe, our station mechanic. On Fridays, I worked from ten o'clock at night until I got relieved at ten on Saturday morning. Technically this was against the law. I was a minor working a twelve-hour shift, but in those days nobody cared. This really screwed up my social life for quite a while, until I got some better hours. Both my older sisters had moved out from home, and I lived alone with my parents. That summer my parents had decided to get away, just the two of them, and allowed me to stay home by myself. This had never happened before. I was instructed to lie low, stay at home, keep an eye on the house, behave myself, and specifically "not to drive the car; we're trusting you." While at work, before they left, I mentioned to my buddy Bob and his cousin, who also worked at the station, that my parents would be away for the weekend. "You're shittin' me, Pat. Let's get drunk!" Wow! This had never occurred to me before. What would that be like, exactly? I'd never drunk any alcohol, ever. My parents had plenty of booze around, but I was too paranoid to touch it. "We'll bring the beer," said Bob. That seemed like a pretty good offer, and as long as I cleaned up afterward, what could be the problem? So Friday night, my parents take off. "Come on over, guys—let's party!" They show up with a case of Olympia beer. Twenty-four fifteen-ounce cans. It looked like a lot of beer, but there were three of us, after all. I had just bought this new record album that I was crazy about, by the Paul Butterfield Blues Band. The perfect album to get drunk to for the first time. So we got to it, and sucked down those beers! Yee haw, I was drunk, and so were they! We listened to that album over and over again for the next couple of hours. What a blast! Except, now all the beer was gone, and we needed to get some more. Bob called the new guy working the graveyard shift at the station where we worked. He was the one that bought the case for Bob and his cousin. If we came down and watched the station for him, he'd go get us some more beer. "But I'm not supposed to drive! My dad said so." "Come on, man, don't be a pussy! You want more beer, doncha?" He was right about that. Just a little more, then back to listening to Butterfield testify. I was feelin' the blues, and a few more beers would put me just in the right mood. So we jumped in my dad's car and drove the five miles to the station. The night man got us another case, and we were back in business. We headed out behind the garage and started chuggin' some suds. Ahh . . . no pain, feelin' jus' fine. We finished off most of the beer and piled back into the Chevy. Bob's cousin on the floor, passed out, in the back seat. I started the car and put the Powerglide tranny into drive. Nothing . . . ? Huh? The engine revved, but the car stood still. I put it back into park then drive again. Nothin'. Holy shit! I moved the lever to reverse, and the car backed up. Uh oh . . . what should I do? I had to get the car back home, or my parents would kill me. Well, it works in reverse . . . It seemed logical that if I were careful, I should be able to navigate the five miles home, going backward, and I'd only drunk about three six-packs, albeit for the first time in my life. So off I went, but should I be going backward with traffic, or should I be in the opposite lane, facing the right direction, but moving against traffic? I hadn't counted on having to make such complicated decisions. I opted for backward with the flow of traffic. This seemed to make sense to me, but not to the guy in the car behind me, who started honking and braking to put some distance between us. Meanwhile, Bob is laughing maniacally, yelling, "We're gonna die," over and over, while his cousin is moaning about throwing up in the back seat. I can't really see very good at night out of the back window and am kind of weaving all over the road. I keep forgetting which side I should be driving on. All of a sudden, I'm sitting parked, in front of my parents' house. How did I get here? Was I dreaming? I look out of the car window, and I see Bob's cousin on his hands and knees, crawling across the lawn, alternately barfing, and it looks like peeing his pants. Well, at least he waited until we got here and had the decency to exit the car. Bob is still laughing. "You did it, man. You fuckin' did it—we made it! Let's go finish this beer!" We grab Bob's cousin, head inside, and crank up the Butterfield album. "I got my mojo workin' . . ." Yeah, now that's the blues.

3

CLOSER EVERY DAY

Pat
___

When I would've been a sophomore in high school, I saw and met the guitar player Jorma Kaukonen, thanks to a guy who was teaching me the blues on the guitar, and Jorma was an instant inspiration for me. His ragtime technique, in particular, I found astounding. Jorma was playing at a club in downtown San Jose called the Shelter. Amazingly, he played an early version of "Embryonic Journey" that left a lasting impression on me. He would, of course, go on to play with Jefferson Airplane very soon after this, and trade his acoustic for an electric guitar. I loved that I lived so close to the San Francisco music scene. It was the most happening place in the world at that time. Venues like the Fillmore Auditorium, the Avalon Ballroom, and

Winterland were hosting the most exciting bands on the planet from the Grateful Dead to Jimi Hendrix.

I also discovered smoking pot in high school, and I really liked that. It just opened my mind in ways I never thought possible. I started growing my hair long and dressing in a more rebellious manner. That really got under my parents' skin. But it was just who I was. I realized soon that I had to leave the house. Even though I still had not graduated high school, we just weren't getting along at home and I needed to make a move. There was a guy that I knew in grade school and then later in high school who was really smart when it came to all things mechanical. At about seventeen, I learned that he, Larry, was living on a property up in the woods above Los Gatos. He lived there free of charge and just helped work the land. He was always pruning the owner's apricot trees and driving a tractor all over the place, cultivating, dozing roads, doing general maintenance. The guy he worked for lived on this large acreage, and Larry lived in a cabin on the property. His parents were fine with it. He would chop wood for his stove, and for all I knew he was hunting his own food out there. He knew how to live off the land, it seemed. On Christmas Day of my junior year, I stuck my thumb out and hit the road up to that cabin in the woods, showing up at his front door. My parents had basically thrown me out that afternoon, because of a disagreement about the length of my hair. He asked me if I needed a place to crash, and I took him up on the offer. I just wasn't happy at home.

I stayed in his cabin on the floor in a sleeping bag. In that little twelve-by-twelve room, we would smoke pot all night and just talk. He turned me on to the writer Ken Kesey, whom I just loved. I stayed up there for about a week or so. Larry was still going to high school, and the two of us got up every morning and went to classes. I always wondered why he looked so scruffy, like a mountain man at school; now I understood. We both smelled like smoke, and it was nice to be able to use the showers in the boys' locker room. Eventually, my parents told the school authorities what I was up to, and I was forcibly returned to their home under threat of expulsion. By the way, later in life, I'd write a song in honor of him called "Larry the Logger."

In high school I was playing in bands, covering everything from folk blues to electric psychedelic. Then there was the British Invasion at that time and so we played all the British stuff like the Beatles, Zombies, Dave Clark Five, and more.

Because of how conservative my family was, I was not allowed to play in rock and roll bands, so I had to sneak out to do it. My parents were "thinkers," but they were afraid of the cultural shift going on around them. They were conservative and religious. The psychedelic revolution, long hair, and the hippie movement scared them to death. It was obvious we were on separate paths.

I ran away from home the following summer and stayed for a couple of months with another friend of mine who lived way up in the Santa Cruz Mountains. He let me sleep in his tree house in a tall oak tree outside his mother's house. He was friends with a local band called the Chocolate Watchband.

They were kind of like one of the stars of the San Jose scene, with this great British Invasion kind of style. They combined psychedelic and garage rock components, more in the style of the Rolling Stones than the Beatles. In 1966 they had released a single called "Sweet Young Thing" that was played all over local radio in the Bay area. They never really broke out from Northern California, but at that moment in time and at that place around San Jose they were just huge and had a fierce, loyal following. My buddy took me to the house where the band rehearsed, and I got to meet them. One night, they invited us to the famed Fillmore in San Francisco, and away we went. That night on the way into the city, the guys in the band gave me a hit of Purple Owsley, the infamous LSD developed by Owsley Stanley, the "artisan" of LSD. It was my first trip. I had recently read an article in *Life* magazine about what to expect when dropping acid, but it wasn't even close to capturing what I was about to experience.

Just outside the Fillmore, the acid kicked in, and the sidewalk began rippling like a stream. I thought I was losing my mind. *Whoa!* When I got into the theater, I wasn't sure if it was the Joshua Light Show light bleeding and pulsating colors all over the walls or just my brain playing warped tricks on me. Nothing seemed real. I bumped into Jorma, who was playing on the bill that night with the Airplane, and I said to him, "I'm so fucked up. I took a hit of acid." And he said, "It's cool, man. Everything will be okay." Calm as he could be. That was Jorma.

That night, as I walked into the venue, the Grateful Dead was onstage playing. Between the light show, the strange-looking guys onstage, and the surreal-sounding music emanating from the speakers, I felt like I had died and was now relegated to spending an eternity in some strange Tibetan hell-world! All night long, whenever I bumped into one of the guys I'd come with, we'd look at each other and mutter, "What's happening, man?!" That was my introduction to San Francisco music, and it blew my mind. I knew the Airplane because of Jorma, but Quicksilver and the Dead were new to me. After the Dead's set (which blew my mind) I wandered up on the Fillmore stage, still floating a bit from the acid, in a bit of a trance, and I hit one of the keys on Pigpen's organ, which was still powered up. Holding the key down, I could hear that one, endless note filling the entire room. I could feel it. Hell, I could *see* it. Suddenly an arm brusquely grabbed me and a voice barked at me, "Get off the stage! Beat it!" Snapping me out of my hallucinogenic bliss was my introduction to the pugnacious promoter Bill Graham. Little did I know the history he and I would eventually have, but that was a few years away. That was such a crazy night. I roamed around the Fillmore tripping my brains out. Finally, I somehow wandered into Bill Graham's office. "You again! That's it, you're outta here," and with that, I found myself outside the venue. I walked down the stairs in front and opened the back door to a San Francisco Police Department cruiser that was parked at the curb, got in, and closed the door behind me. The two cops in front turned around and gave me a puzzled look. "Uh, is there something we can do for you?" "Jeez, I'm sorry, guys. I took something, and I'm having a really hard time." "Was it a sugar cube, LSD maybe?" "Yeah, I'm afraid so. . . ." "We have a lot of experience with this, would you like to just drive around with us while we make our rounds, see how you feel after a while? Try to come down?" This is San Francisco in the sixties, how cool is that? I drove around with them for a couple of hours. Finally, I started coming down, told them I felt better, and they offered to drop me off at the Greyhound bus station. I must have looked like a poor, sad kid. Some sailor saw me and asked me what was up. When I told him, he said, "Yeah, I'm a pharmacist mate on a ship docked here. I know about acid." In my psychedelic ecstasy, I had thrown all my money away. He generously bought me a bus ticket back to San Jose. Angels were everywhere in those days.

Soon after that, I ended up back at my parents' house and tried to hold it together, but I finally got busted for possessing a little marijuana and LSD when I was a senior in high school and eventually did a bit of jail time. The school decided to lower all my grades to teach me a lesson. My straight As that I'd achieved were all lowered to B minuses. Was that even legal? I lost my college scholarship, so I went to work and saved money for college. The next fall, I enrolled at San Jose State University. I even joined a frat, Theta Xi. I was "1-A" in terms of the Vietnam draft, which meant if I kept my C average I would be safe from the draft. The fraternity was kind of a ruse. My parents thought fraternity guys were good solid citizens. In actuality, my frat brothers were some of the wildest people, to this day, I have ever met in my life. Totally out of control and wild in ways that's hard to imagine even by today's crazy standards.

Tom

I eventually landed in San Jose full-time, where I was attending San Jose State, studying graphic design. The school atmosphere was so different from anything I'd been through in Visalia that I was just happy to be there. Classes were scheduled far apart, and I had completed all my requirements in junior college, so it was all about art all the time. This was at the time of the SDS riots in San Jose State and other colleges, and I spent a semester attending Alan Watts's lectures on campus. At the time, I was reading *Siddhartha* and *Damien* by Herman Hesse, very mind-expanding stuff. But though I gave school a good shot and enjoyed my art classes, I kept playing music as much as possible. After taking stock of the competition I was up against, I didn't think I'd make a living as a graphic designer. While at San Jose State, I got to see Jimi Hendrix, the Steve Miller Blues Band, Loading Zone with Linda Tillery, and several other local bands like the Sons of Champlin at these annual fairground shows. Usually coming back to the house pretty stoned! I even saw Lee Michaels with Frosty on drums at the San Jose State Student Union one night. Maybe the loudest I've ever heard a band play! But they were killin' it!

When the summer came, I'd get whatever jobs I could to keep from having to go back to Visalia, because I was on my own dime if I stayed in San Jose, and that was where I wanted to be. So I got a job at a cannery in San Jose, working from 6:00 AM till 2:00 PM, and did that till I got a job in construction, which paid way better (and had me working all over the Bay

Area). Steve, a friend with whom I had moved to San Jose and shared an apartment on North Eighth Street, had moved into a room in a house at 285 Twelfth Street in San Jose (I was living in a town house with some other folks I knew from school). He got ahold of me and said there was a room opening up, asking if I wanted it, and I jumped: it was really close to the San Jose State campus. That house is where my life as a musician in San Jose began. Just forty bucks a month, and I had my little spot, tucked in among halfway houses and part of the "student row." But I was happy as hell. That house was like the center of the local musical universe, and I started playing with a bunch of different musicians in the area. It's hard to describe what went on in there, aside from all the craziness mixed in with school and music you'd expect. Musically, some of the best players hung out there, and we'd have full horn sections in this tiny little basement where the walls would literally sweat from the heat, dripping with humidity. That house was just an intense place. A lot of students in a lot of bands were living in the neighborhood. I would play music wherever I could, including playing acoustic gigs in Los Gatos at the Wine Cellar, which was a local hang. What's funny is that I was totally out of my element and knew hardly any "folk" type tunes, but I would get up there with my acoustic and just fake it. Make up songs and lyrics on the spot. People would request songs, and I would try to fake it, which didn't work, or I'd just say I didn't know that one. But for whatever reason, they didn't get pissed off; they just accepted what I was playing and kept drinking.

Before Twelfth Street when I lived on North Eighth, a couple of guys I had met through my sister would come hang out with my roommate and me. They were older than we were and kind of wild! One had a flute he played constantly and the other had a bread truck all rigged out with a sound system and rugs in the back. We would go for "journeys" all over the Santa Cruz Mountains, Santa Cruz, Aptos, Big Sur, and the party was on from the minute we got in the truck. Red Mountain wine and weed were the order of the day. This was around 1969— it was really crazy up there in the Bay Area. Everybody was into all these crazy parties and road trips. Just basically living on wine and dope driving around in the van. Crashing out in places like Esalen Institute in Big Sur or at the house of Andy (who owned the converted bread truck) in Aptos and playing music wherever we went; I always had my acoustic guitar. It was a total hippie scene, music being played by the folks at the "gathering," pigs roasting in pits, drinking homemade wine, smoking lots of dope—lost-weekend kind of thing. I remember the Rolling Stones album *Let It Bleed* blasting in Andy's van basically being the soundtrack for a lot of those times. What a great fucking album that was! I loved the tracks and Mick Taylor's lead playing—phenomenal!

I played in a couple of bands up there, one of which was called South Bay Experimental Flash. They were a pretty good band that had a great B3 player who would sometimes leave his organ in the basement of the Twelfth Street house. I probably would've stuck it out with them, but their front guy decided I had to go, so they fired me. Looking back, I guess that worked out for the best.

Pat

While in college, in 1968, some of my frat brothers and I went to see Jimi Hendrix at the legendary San Francisco venue Winterland. This time one of my fraternity brothers supplied the acid, and it was a much better, mellower trip than my first one at the Fillmore. Waiting in line to get in, I bumped into the writer/psychologist/professor/acid expert Timothy Leary. He was with some cute little blond hippie chick. He was actually trying to bum money to get in and see the show. I had spent all afternoon working at my job for a vending machine company, scraping together the few dollars to see Jimi, and was living on the financial edge in those days. Money was tight. "Uh . . . aren't you Timothy Leary?" "Yeah." He smiled at me with, it seemed to me, a smug, "ahh, fame" expression. (Probably the acid . . .) "Gosh man, I'm sorry, but I don't have any extra cash. I actually worked today so I could come here. Aren't you a college professor? Pardon my saying it, but I'm a little surprised to see you panhandling here. Maybe you should get a job!" Oh man, regret flew across my wasted brain: that was really Timothy Leary, you dumbass! Too late, Leary had turned his back and was walking away. "Fuckin' uptight asshole," he said to the embarrassed blond girl. My buddies looked at me like, "Wow, did that really happen?"

I was so starstruck once we got inside. I saw Jorma hanging out, Buddy Miles talking with Mike Bloomfield—wow, *Bloomfield*? One of my musical heroes after I heard the *Paul Butterfield Blues Band* album. I was pinching myself to be this close to such a special musical bubble. The San Francisco music royalty was turning out in full force to watch Jimi. I followed the musicians to where the backstage door was. They entered the magical space, and I lingered outside, dreaming of what the scene may have been like inside that mystical realm. I was talking to one of my frat brothers, and I felt a tap on my shoulder. I turned and in the purple haze of the environment, someone was offering me a joint. I took the joint and did a double take when I saw that it was Jimi Hendrix himself passing it along. I was pretty stoned, but this was real. He was wearing that now-famous black hat, banded with silver conchos. "Want a hit, man?" Hendrix asked with that illuminating, unassuming smile. I couldn't believe it. I nervously mumbled how much his playing inspired me and took a hit off the joint. Hendrix thanked me, and then my frat brother, far more boisterous than me, leaned over in Hendrix's face and said, "Hey, man, my friend Pat here is a great guitar player, and he's going to be playing here someday!" I think Jimi took him literally and said to me earnestly, "Oh yeah, man? When are you playing here?" "Don't listen to him," I said, "he doesn't know what he's talking about."

There was nothing like the San Francisco scene in the late 1960s. The musical Renaissance was palpable, even revelatory. There was an uprising taking place, and I desperately wanted to be a part of it.

4

SITTING BY THE WINDOW
(MOBY GRAPE)

Tom

One day my sister, who then worked at Santa Clara County Hospital but also hung with a lot of artists, called me and said, "Hey, there's this guy I want you to meet. His name is Skip Spence." Well, she didn't have to tell me who Skip Spence was. Of all the records that came out in the late 1960s, the Moby Grape album was one of my absolute favorites. That band was just so different from anything else at that time. They were formed in 1966 in San Francisco by Skip Spence and Matthew Katz. Both of those guys previously had been associated with Jefferson Airplane. Skip had been the band's drummer, playing on their first album, and Katz was the Airplane's manager. After they both got fired, Katz told Spence he should form a band similar to the Airplane, incorporating a number of guitar players, songwriters, and lead/background vocalists. They got their name from the punch line in the old joke, "What's big and purple and lives in the ocean?" Like Buffalo Springfield, they were a three-guitar band, which gave them a really unique sound. Skip's rhythm guitar playing was energetic, and Peter Lewis was really good at fingerpicking. Jerry Miller was the third guitar player, a hell of a lead player, and the "collage" they made with those three sounds was just incredible. The lineup included Don Stevenson on drums and vocals (also a good singer) and Bob Mosley on bass and vocals, which added a whole other R&B element vocally. And, like the Airplane, all band members wrote, and everybody had a chance to sing both lead and backup vocals. One of their first performances was the Mantra Rock Dance in San Francisco. Moby Grape performed at that show, along with members of the Hare Krishna Temple, the Grateful Dead, Allen Ginsberg, Janis Joplin, and several other performers. They also appeared at the Monterey Pop Festival and blew people away. They released another album in 1968 called *Wow/Grape Jam,* which was good, but nothing like the first album.

They started catching on in the United Kingdom, but just as things started to click commercially, Skip's erratic behavior took over. He did a lot of drugs, a lot of LSD, and eventually a lot of heroin. There was a crazy incident in New York City at the hotel where the band was staying: he took an ax to the room door of one of his band members. He got thrown into the infamous "Tombs" jail in New York and was then committed to New York's Bellevue Hospital, where he spent a couple of months under psychiatric care. He never really got it together after that. He started getting crazier and crazier and eventually was pushed out of the band. In the late 1960s and early 1970s, they kept playing, but without Skip. Their legacy was just remarkable. The way they blended harmonies, the way they blended acoustic and electric guitars—little did I know how much that would influence what ended up being the Doobie Brothers.

That debut album was "the" album the band was best known for: thirteen songs clock in at just thirty-one minutes. There wasn't one wasted second on that record. It's perfect. Tunes like "Hey Grandma" and Skip's anthemic "Omaha" hold up today as some kind of grungy garage classics. But then they turn the corner and slow it down on things like "8:05" and "Sitting by the Window," a couple of the prettiest country rock songs of the era.

And it's interesting because a lot of guys that would eventually be in the Doobie Brothers, like John Hartman, myself, Pat, Tiran Porter, and Michael McDonald, all had the same kind of adoration for Moby Grape. It was just something about that band. So when I met and hung around with Skip, it was a time like no other I had experienced. When we met, he was kind of out of control, clearly doing a lot of drugs, but he could still play. And he started hanging out at Twelfth Street (he lived about a block away) and would be there jamming at any time day or night, as well as just hanging out, which could get pretty out there. He had so much energy, fueled both by chemicals as well as his mental makeup, which was slowly degrading. But nobody cared; it was just part of hanging with Skip. He would eventually bring the whole Grape band together at the Twelfth Street house to plan out where they were headed with a "new" album called 20 *Granite Creek*, which was a crazy event, with all of them pretty lit, but it was damn entertaining to watch and listen to. And the early Doobies played a gig with them at a funky, woodsy club in Boulder Creek, for which they didn't even get together to practice, just got up and played. This was right after Bob Mosley had just gotten out of the marines. Well, it sounded pretty rusty, but because they were Moby Grape, we didn't care.

Pat

I first got turned on to cocaine in the late 1960s by a friend who told me it was a "musicians' drug." I had smoked a lot of weed up until then, but I never experienced anything like this. I was playing a little place in Half Moon Bay, and the owner of this club gave me a couple of lines before I went up onstage at eleven o'clock that night. I think I played till about 2:30 AM! Honestly, I loved it. A gram was only about ten bucks. I worked for two bucks an hour, so in five hours I could get what I needed. It was cheap. I mean gas was about thirty cents a gallon. I did coke for a couple of years. As much as I liked it, I also knew it was scary and would eventually take over.

By this time, I had been living on my own for a couple of years. My parents had, for all intents and purposes, disowned me. I was supporting myself by working part-time, playing gigs whenever I could, and was receiving some public assistance. I stuck with school until the start of my senior year; then the draft changed, and a lottery system was instituted. I lucked out and got a high lottery number, which allowed me to avoid the draft. I decided it was time for me to take a break from school. Turns out my education was just beginning. During my last year at San Jose State, I found some guys that had a duplex with an extra room. My third of the rent was $33.33. I was playing gigs whenever I could and going to college and then this musician friend of mine said to me, "I have a class I'm teaching that's associated with the college." It was a kind of esoteric thing where he would bring together songwriters and musicians in the round, meet once a week, and then share musical ideas. You could play your own songs or you could play cover songs, whatever—it was just a loose assemblage of people who learned music under the guise of a college course. Anyway, this guy says to me, "I've gotten really busy, can you take over the class for me?" I didn't really have time, but I couldn't figure out a way to say no, and so I agreed to do it. A few days later, about ten people were sitting in my living room, and I was like the moderator. We would go around the circle, and I would call on people to play some music and talk about their influences. There was a guy named Dave Shogren in the group one time. I had gone to high school with him but didn't really know him. He played a new Neil Young song, "Down by the River." I never really knew he was a musician before, but he was pretty good. Little did I know that Dave was also playing in some jam sessions over on Twelfth Street at a guy named Tommy Johnston's house. Our paths would all cross soon.

5

GROWIN' A LITTLE EACH DAY

Tom

So there was this guy out in Falls Church, Virginia, a drummer named John Hartman. And he just loved Moby Grape. In particular, he was a Skip Spence freak. Obviously, I could relate to that. He went to see Moby Grape play, and it was a life-changing experience for him. Totally rocked his world. He couldn't believe the harmonies, the blending of the guitars, just the diversity of the music. John had a band and was getting ready to graduate from high school, but he didn't want to go to college. He wanted to be a musician. And more than that, he wanted to connect with Skip because he felt like Skip had the power to make his dreams come true. Now, most people that loved Moby Grape might buy the album or go see a show and just leave it there. But Hartman had a different take on it. This is what makes him special. He picked up the phone and called Columbia Records, which was Moby Grape's label. He started calling them to try to get a number for the management or something that would get him one step closer to Skip. But the switchboard operators at the record label were not buying it. But he didn't give up. Somehow or another, he finally managed to get a phone number out of somebody at Columbia. He dialed that number, and who picked up the phone but Skip Spence. Skip had already gone kind of crazy at that point, but he liked the fact that this young fan had tracked him down, and then he actually encouraged Hartman to come out to California—literally told him to pack up his life three thousand miles away and make the move to San Francisco. Well, John was, of course, all for this. He had connected with his musical hero, and his fortunes were about to change. John had a bass player friend named Greg Murphy, who also got to come along on this magical ride, and off these guys went to California. It's a pretty big moment for all of us because once Hartman and Murphy arrive, Skip, maybe regretting his encouragement because he has nothing for them to do, suggested they give me a call. He knew I was looking to connect with some like-minded musicians. And hey, what's the common thread? Moby Grape. I mean seriously, Moby Grape was the part of the musical DNA that connected all of us. So I got a call from Hartman, who was with Skip, and they asked me if I could head into the city with somebody's van to pick the guys up and their stuff and bring them out to the house on Twelfth Street. I remember thinking, what the hell? But I went ahead and did it. And that's how Hartman and I connected.

Once we got to the house, Hartman and Murphy brought all their stuff down to the basement, and that's where they decided to camp out for a while. But first we set up John's drums and Greg's bass amp in the living room upstairs, and we started jamming. And it was LOUD!! But we all dug it, and it was the perfect musical arrangement. We were down in the basement making music most of the time, anyway, and now we had some new blood. We started jamming every afternoon until late at night. We started getting tighter, and this idea of the trio started taking shape. Eventually, we became a trio called Pud that started gigging in the area. We played hard rock, a little R&B, and whatever else you could do with three players. We sometimes used a horn section, usually led by a sax/flute player named Tim from school. He was really a good player and allowed the band to stretch out in some different directions. We would also use some local girls singing background vocals. This provided an even wider musical direction. Always something new. One gig would be a hard rock trio; the next would be with the horn section playing jams loosely based on R&B. It didn't matter—it was all good and a lot of fun!

One day Hartman comes running into my bedroom on Twelfth Street and he's really amped up. I'm thinking to myself, uh-oh, what's happened now? Hartman was such a character that you just never knew what he was going to do next. "Skip just called! He's at a studio in San Mateo, and he wants us to get over there right now!"

"For what?" I asked.

"He's got a bunch of bands over there working with some guys to try and get some label interest. And he wants us to go over there. It sounds like someplace we ought to be."

Well, that sounded okay to me. I mean, there really wasn't much else going on. If nothing else, it was a chance to play in a studio, which was a first. So we got all of our gear together and we drove over to the studio in Dave Shogren's van (he was the new bass player, as Greg Murphy had departed by then), and there was Skip behind the console. This guy named Marty Cohn was engineering, and several other bands were there ahead of us. So we just had to wait for our turn. Problem was, the rest of those bands were really tight and had been playing together for a while. As an aside, two of the bands had future drummers for the Doobies: Keith Knudsen in Mendlebaum and Mike Hossack in Morning Reign. I mean, our little trio was nothing like that. We could rock pretty good, but we were nothing like these other bands. Also, we had never been in a studio before, and so we were learning what the hell we were supposed to be doing on the fly. When it came to our turn, Marty and Skip helped get us set up, and we played a few songs. Who had any clue if this would lead to anything? Honestly, this was just a way to kill an afternoon. And to John's point, Skip wanted us there, so . . . No matter how crazy he had become, he was still the most charismatic guy in the room. That was the thing with him. I saw him get so fucked up so many times, but it never changed the fact that people responded to him and always wanted to be around him. When he called you and asked you to come over, you usually did. When the session was all done, we packed up our gear and headed back to Twelfth Street. I didn't think anything was going to come of it. But I have to say, I had a good time meeting all the other players and listening to their bands. It was cool being in a studio and taking direction from a couple of guys behind the console glass. And we got to go into a professional studio and see what that was actually like. A structured environment where people go to work and create things—that was eye-opening. The fact that you could literally make a living playing music started sounding like a pretty good idea. Was it even possible? It was very hard to say at that moment. But the experience was cool. I liked being in the studio.

Pat

I remember the very first night I met Skip Spence in person. I was playing at the Brass Knocker, a coffeehouse in Saratoga. That's actually where I played my first professional gig when I was fifteen. I would do some folk, blues, and traditional music along with some original tunes. Well, one night, who should be in the place but Skip Spence? He was bigger than life to me. I was such a huge Moby Grape fan, and it was surreal to see him in person. This was before all hell had broken loose. Soon, he would be going through a lot of rough things. He would leave Grape and record a solo record, *Oar,* which unfortunately would not be very good. And he would also break down a bandmate's hotel room door in New York with a fire ax. There would be tons of stories about how delusional he was becoming under the influence of LSD, heroin, and lord only knows what else. But that would come later. For now, he was just the legendary Skip Spence. He got up that night to play, and the charisma that he had was undeniably in evidence. He had this really cool guitar and a ton of style, and he started playing these songs that sounded normal at the beginning, but the more he played, the more confusing they sounded. He seemed to be simply improvising, which was adventurous, but after a while was, unfortunately, less than compelling. But it was Skip Spence, and I felt I had somehow witnessed something worthwhile. As I reflect on it now, I suspect this was early evidence of the mental illness that would overtake Skip's life. An incredible talent that was destined to fall into obscurity.

Fast-forward a couple of years later. While I was a sophomore at San Jose State, one night I was at a laundromat waiting while my clothes were drying. The door swings open, and in walks Skip Spence. I was awestruck but still mustered the courage to say hello to him and tell him how great I thought he was. I had just purchased his solo album, *Oar*. It was very strange, and I hadn't really figured it out yet. My first impression was that it was somehow ill-conceived. There were flashes of Skip's ability as a writer, but to me the record dissolved into a nebulous, muddled vision that was hard to comprehend. I wanted it to be good, and I listened to it many times, hoping there was a hidden brilliance that would reveal itself to me.

Sadly, that would never happen. Once again, I now recognize how Skip's illness was interfering with his ability to pursue his creative work. He said to me, "I'm living right next door in the duplex with my wife and kids." The universe is such a random place. I say this because my friends happened to be living in the other half of the duplex. I couldn't believe it. "I'm there all the time," he said, smiling, and once I told him I played guitar, he told me I could stop over whenever I wanted. Really? So a few days later, I took him up on his offer. I gently tapped on the door, which was half open, and inside I could see him sitting on a mat in the middle of the living room like he was meditating. It was a tiny place, a typical college crash pad. I walked in quietly, and at first he didn't say anything to me. But then he looked at me with a very intense glare. Then a smile. He kept alternating those two expressions. I couldn't really figure out what was going on, and after a while I introduced myself to his wife, who had come into the room. We all smoked a joint, and then he relaxed and seemed to come out of his trance. And then I started going over there every so often. I always had my guitar, and we might play a little bit, but he was never really in very good shape. The last time I went there, he was sitting on the couch shooting up heroin. I thought to myself, I don't really want to see this. I can't watch this fabulous talent throwing it all away with his wife and kids right there. It was heartbreaking. I wasn't sure if I would ever see Skip Spence again, and wouldn't you know it, about a year later I was playing a gig with my then partner Peter Grant at the Gaslighter Theater in Campbell. (Peter was great—he later became Hoyt Axton's steel player and appeared on "Doin' That Rag" on the Grateful Dead's *Aoxomoxoa*). We were going to open for Hot Tuna, but then we were told they couldn't make it because of a conflict, so instead Skip Spence was coming in with a band. When he saw me, he came right over. "I want you to meet somebody," he said. Skip was playing that night with Tom Johnston and John Hartman. "Meet these guys; you will like these guys," I said hello to Tommy and John and then watched them play. I don't think Skip's guitar was even plugged in that night, and he was acting very weird onstage. But Tom was really good. Great guitar player, great singer; I was very impressed. Tom had an original style, distinctive voice, and interesting songs. Confident and charismatic. Little John Hartman was such a badass drummer and ultimate showman. I loved the bass player, too: Greg Murphy. It wasn't necessarily my kind of music; I was way more into traditional acoustic music at that time. These guys had a much bigger sound, but I could still appreciate how talented they were. I spoke with them when they were done, and they asked if I would be interested in this other band they were thinking of putting together with two or three guitars and a lot of vocals. I said I was committed to these other projects at the time but that we should stay in touch.

Tom

I was really impressed by Pat's playing. It was the first time I'd really watched somebody who had fingerpicking down cold.

He was into a very different style than what I was used to, which made his playing that much more interesting and somewhat exotic. There was nobody like that playing in our circle. It's like he was tapping into something we didn't even know about. He was so connected to so many purely American musical forms from folk to blues.

Hartman and I both looked at each other, and I know we were thinking the same thing: this is the kind of guy who could make us a full band. Pat would bring that acoustic element/picking style and another vocal, which would get us a cross-pollination of rock, blues, country rock, and Americana; he seemed like the perfect guy to bring into the mix. And he had a great voice! He obviously was going to be a key component of whatever the hell we were putting together. We never had a plan for anything. I'm not sure we even have one today, to be honest with you. We just wanted to keep playing music. There was never any strategy or master formula for what we were doing. I mean, really the only thing that was pushing us was this idea of getting a sound together that kind of felt original and professional. As far as being commercial, we didn't really think about it that much at the time. But it was on Hartman's mind, and he was driven to get us signed. And none of us would have been against that, because in order to keep playing better gigs, you had to elevate your status in the people's eyes. Looking back, I really have to give John a lot of credit. He had a fire inside of him that was very focused and disciplined. This probably got the rest of us thinking more along those lines. So it worked out for the best.

We invited Pat to come over and jam, and he eventually did. He had other commitments to a band called Scratch and other things he was involved in, so it didn't happen right away.

Pat

There was a guy named Dennis I knew, who coincidentally lived in the duplex next to Skip. He was a guitar player that I had met in a class I was taking at San Jose State. He wrote songs and was always trying to impress his roommates and anyone else who was around. His roommates thought he was great. I just didn't get it. The songs were corny and sophomoric to me, but I always tried to be encouraging. Unfortunately, he wasn't interested in returning the favor. He demanded you pay attention when he played but the minute you picked up the guitar, he would leave the room. Anyway, he put together a band that I didn't really think was that good. The lead guitar player in the band had inherited a bunch of money from his parents and decided to make himself the leader and lead guitar player. They performed Dennis's corny songs, and the lead player, Larry, noodled these corny solos. Still, they got gigs, so what did I know? One of the singers in the band, Mary Lou, was one of my roommates in a house I was living in on Eighth Street in San Jose. She was a surprisingly good singer, and as far as I was concerned, the best thing the band had going for them. One day, Mary Lou and a couple of her band members showed up at our house with a little guy named Marty Cohn.

She introduces me to Marty: "Marty's an engineer, and he's going to get us a record deal." I'm thinking to myself, if these guys can get a record deal, then anybody can! There was another guy with Marty named Paul Curcio who had been the bass player in a band called the Mojo Men. The guys seemed like they were just trolling around looking for the next big band. Later on, I learned they had done demos with Santana, Journey, Tower of Power, and lots of other Bay Area up-and-comers. The Grateful Dead had even recorded *Aoxomoxoa* at their studio in San Mateo, which was called Pacific Recording Studios. Not long after Skip had introduced me to Tom and John, those guys found me and invited me over to jam at the house on Twelfth Street. The house had a very cool vibe, a real party place but lots of music was always being made in there. But I still wasn't quite sure of the music. I went to see them play again at the student union, at the college, only this time they had a horn section and that kind of blew me away. I could see how good they were. I loved that they were not afraid to try stuff and that it was real, no bullshit, and so I basically fell in love with what they were doing. And so I began to hang out at Twelfth Street a lot more. Because I wanted to be a part of it. I remember that one night Tommy and John showed up at a little gig of mine, and Tommy got up and played some guitar and John brought along some congas or something. We had a great time. I even had John come to a session at a friend's studio in La Honda to work on some demos with Tiran and me. The cross-pollination was already beginning to happen. Greg Murphy would soon be leaving

Pud, though, and so they needed a new bass player. That was Dave Shogren.

Tom

Just a month or two after we started hanging out with Pat, we got a call from Skip that he wanted us to come back into the studio and record some more demos. That was a big moment for the Doobie Brothers. That was the crack in the door. Of course, you don't know it when it's happening. You're not thinking that. But with Pat, we were a lot different than the first time we were in there recording. What he brought helped flesh out our sound, and I was very confident going back in.

Pat

We played wherever we could, but the Chateau Liberté was our favorite. It was such a unique place. The name actually means "House of Freedom," and it certainly was. It couldn't exist today. No way. Too many rules. It was essentially off the grid up in the Santa Cruz Mountains. It had its own rules and codes of conduct. From the mid-1940s to the mid-1960s, it was a restaurant and family resort with cabins. People could use the swimming pool and go hiking around the property. It became a music club and hangout in the late 1960s. A lot of bands played there over the years, including Hot Tuna, Jerry Garcia, the New Riders of the Purple Sage, and lots of others. Including us! Some bikers hung out there, including members of the Gypsy Jokers and then later the Hells Angels. But it wasn't a biker bar. It was much more than that. There were so many different kinds of people up there, from students to bikers to everybody in between. You had cowboys and equestrians up there, artists, poets, and even professional people like doctors and lawyers. Everybody respected each other. You might've thought things could've gotten out of control, but it's like if you were up there, you were okay. You understood what the rules were, and you were cool with that. I will tell you, pretty much *everything* went on up there. Sex, drugs, and rock and roll. Lots of it. But it was kind of like Las Vegas today. What happened up there in the Santa Cruz Mountains definitely stayed up there. Years later, a friend of mine called me and said, "Hey, come on out to where the old Chateau is." When I asked him why, he told me he'd been hired to knock it down. A big part of history came down that day. Watching his tractor take the old wooden place down was kind of heartbreaking. A lot of ghosts bit the dust that day. That's probably where our reputation as a "biker band" got started, too. By the way, Skip ended up around there as well. I remember seeing Skip over at Tommy's place on Twelfth Street shooting up heroin or even NoDoz at a certain point. It just got worse and worse for him. So ugly. Eventually, we would see him hanging out up at the Chateau, basically living up there. He was just spiraling deeper into the abyss. He actually started climbing up in the trees around the Chateau, just screaming at people, freaking out, and losing his mind. By this time his wife had left him and taken the kids with her. Such a legend, but in that condition, no one was able to step in and give him the care he needed. Skip did get some professional help later in his existence, which saved his life. Unfortunately, he never really was able to return to his formerly more cognitive state or play music professionally again.

Tom

The Angels liked us. One night they rode their bikes up the steps and in through the front door at Twelfth Street, and they were all pretty high. They parked their bikes in the living room; they woke us up in the middle of the night to do some crazy shit like go play baseball at two in the morning. Our biker following got even bigger once we started playing at the storied Chateau Liberté. It was sort of a bohemian/biker hangout where anything went. It was the most incredible environment. It was earthy and woodsy; I think it had been an old stagecoach stop back in the 1800s. There were cabins scattered around, and I think at one time there had been a bordello there. It was a place where students, hippies, bikers, and musicians were all hanging out together and, for the most part, coexisting. There were no rules, and anything went. Lots of drinking, lots of dope, lots of women, but no real trouble. Everybody was cool with each other. The Hells Angels were up there as part of the scene, and they were pretty cool, too. This was sort of like an extension of the Summer of Love. Cops never went up there, so you knew you were basically free and could let everything hang out. I should add that there was a whole music community that hung around at the Chateau. Bands like Mountain Current (local), Hot Tuna, the Beans (later the Tubes), and others. I think the band Snail was just getting started then and played up there as well. There were a lot of musicians and a lot of jamming every night up there. Every region has its musical hotbed where things crystallize for lots of young, up-and-coming bands. In the Santa Cruz Mountains, it was definitely the Chateau.

Pat

We had a gig at the Chateau and were sitting at the house on Twelfth Street, when we realized we didn't have a name for the band. This would be our very first show together as a band—so we needed a name. Evidently, some of the guys were sitting around the breakfast table one morning, sprinkling pot on their cornflakes, smokin' joints, and bein' crazy. I wasn't actually there. At that time, whenever anybody said, "I wanna smoke a joint," they *always* said, "Let's smoke a doobie." So someone in the room says, "Hey, you guys smoke so many joints, why don't you just call yourselves the Doobie Brothers?" We said, "What a *dopey name*." And that was it. I mean, we thought it was just a joke, but we were gonna use it for the gig and then change it to something better. But it just kind of stuck. So many bands have mysterious stories behind their names, but with us, what you see is what you get. We were destined to be the Doobie Brothers forever.

Tom

If you told me that day that we would be called the Doobie Brothers from that point on, I wouldn't have believed it. We all thought it was a pretty dumb name when our friend suggested it. I was sitting right there at the table, and I think I probably just rolled my eyes. We just needed a name. Once again, we just were not thinking so much about the future or how things were supposed to look. These days when a band starts out, they sometimes have a whole team trying to figure out what it should be called and who it should appeal to. It's like a part of the marketing platform. We were the exact opposite of that. I think we were just too lazy to come up with another name after we played that gig up at the Chateau. What the hell, even if the Doobie Brothers did sound kind of goofy, it didn't seem to bother anybody, and it saved us the trouble of having to come up with something else. Sometimes it's best to not overthink things. That was our thinking in a nutshell, at least as far as the name went. Let the music do the talking.

Pat

Once we played the first gig at the Chateau, we knew we would be back a lot. We just connected with everyone up there. The place had a really low ceiling, and it was cramped and tight like a true roadhouse. Very intimate, with everyone pushed up close. We got our reputation as a biker band since we played at the Chateau all the time. But in reality, I think *everybody* up there really appreciated us. We just connected with the crowd. Right after that, we went to record the next demo for Marty. Tom had explained to me that the door was still open at the studio to do some more demos and asked if I would be interested. I said, "Hell yeah!" They had a few more songs to cut, and maybe about a month later, we went back there. I think Tommy had about five songs ready to be recorded, and I think two of mine got laid down, and that's the demo that started getting really shopped around. A few labels were actually interested almost immediately, including A&M and Warner Bros. We played a little showcase for A&M. Ted Templeman and Lenny Waronker heard our demo and flew up from L.A. to check us out. Lenny and Ted came to the Chateau—very conservative-looking in this raucous biker bar—Lenny in his white cardigan sweater, Ted in his sweater vest and penny loafers. Their eyes were as big as saucers. We did "Jesus Is Just Alright," an early version of "Long Train Runnin'," and "Rockin' Down the Highway"— songs we would be famous for. That night the crowd went crazy; it was a real, old-fashioned, rocking-roadhouse night with the redwood stage shaking like crazy.

Tom

When Ted and Lenny came to see us play at the Chateau, it was pretty funny. They both looked so preppy. By that point, we were well known at the Chateau, and we blew the roof off the place that night. I think they were kind of taken aback. They thought of us as more of a laid-back, semi-acoustic band, but that's not what we were. I mean, we had elements of that, but we kept it rocking pretty hard at the Chateau. I remember thinking, I wonder what Lenny and Ted thought of that show? So they got to see another side of the band from what they had expected, and in a very different environment!

Some background: we learned later that Lenny Waronker was a heavy hitter. He had been hired by Reprise label president Mo Ostin as a junior A&R representative for Reprise and for Warner Bros., which was then run by a guy named Joe Smith. His job was to develop artists who were originally on the roster of Autumn Records, a defunct label Reprise had acquired. So right out of the gate, Lenny produced a bunch of records like the Mojo Men's "Sit Down, I Think I Love You" and Harpers Bizarre's "The 59th Street Bridge Song (Feelin' Groovy)," which he hired Leon Russell to arrange. Both songs got some attention.

Then in 1970 Mo promoted Lenny to head of A&R, where he created a team of soon-to-be all-stars—acclaimed producers and artists including Tommy LiPuma, Ted Templeman, Russ Titelman, Steve Barri, Gary Katz, Michael Omartian, and John Cale. Ted had actually been in Harpers Bizarre, and he was the one who really liked our demo.

Ted Templeman

I had had an early psych group called the Tikis, which was heavily influenced by Buffalo Springfield and Moby Grape. We got our lucky break when Warner Bros. bought the defunct Autumn Records and dumped everyone except the Beau Brummels and the Tikis. Lenny decided that the Tikis needed a change of direction, as well as a name change. With acid rock and the Summer of Love blowing everyone's mind, we were skeptical of the kind of wimpy direction that Lenny wanted to take us in. Really, Lenny? You think this is cool? He had brought a song to us called "Feelin' Groovy," written by some unknown folk rocker named Paul Simon. Let me be clear. I fucking hated it! It got even worse when Lenny wouldn't let any of us play on the record, instead loading it up with strings and Four Freshman–style harmonies. We were now known as Harpers Bizarre, playing off the name of the fashion magazine: trust me, we all hated the record. What we didn't hate was that it became a hit, climbing to number 13 on the charts and launching my career in the record business. By the way, it was not the first time I could not recognize a hit record, as you will learn. As a Warner Bros. artist I did everything I could to learn anything and everything about the business. I started hanging around recording studios, just to soak up the atmosphere and to start figuring out how to make records. The two places I frequented the most were Western Recorders and Sunset Sound. I'll never forget what happened on October 18, 1967, in the lobby at Western. Frank Sinatra walked in. He looked at me and said, "Hey, kid, how do you like my new shoes?" Then he allowed me to sit in with the legendary engineer Lee Herschberg. It was amazing to watch the entire orchestra, including conductor, drummer, pianist, guitar player, bassist, and female background singers, all get into place as Frank began recording the classic "That's Life." I had never seen anything like this. He was awesome. In that three-hour session, I don't think he missed one note. Sinatra was so in tune with everything, and that blew my mind. It's like he was a real musician. If someone played a bad note, you saw Sinatra react. He never missed a beat. I also noticed that when the producer, Jimmy Bowen, made suggestions, Sinatra did not always take them. There was some definite tension happening there. When I left the studio, I was thinking to myself, would that record be better if the producer had been in full and total command and control? That got me thinking. Soon after that, the actress Mia Farrow booked our band to play at a party she was throwing to celebrate her first anniversary after marrying Sinatra. It was the most star-studded event you can imagine. Yul Brynner, Jimmy Stewart, Natalie Wood—iconic face after iconic face. I had one of the greatest times of my life that night. I got to see many other sessions after the Sinatra experience, including Elvis Presley and Ike and Tina Turner. I watched closely to see how producers related to the artists that they were recording. Our band was winding down, and I knew that I wanted to be a producer rather than pursue another band experience. So I started out at Warner Bros. at one of the lowest positions they have, a tape listener for fifty dollars a week. I would just go over demo tape after demo tape making notes and offering up opinions for the powers that be. Just basically sifting through, trying to separate, and looking for that one needle in a haystack. This is where being in Harpers Bizarre, I think, really helped me. Not all tape listeners have played in bands. So I knew what qualities to listen for in order to identify a band that had what I thought it took. And the moment I heard this tape by a group called the Doobie Brothers, I knew there was something going on. I knew I had to meet this band and see them play in person. I loved these guys when I heard the demo. I really did. But Lenny and I weren't quite sure what to do with them. We went up to see them at the Chateau Liberté. I think we stood out like sore thumbs there because it was a real heavy-duty biker bar. But I didn't care about that; I just wanted to hear the music. Tommy had that driving rhythm thing going with his guitar, which was brilliant, and his voice was beautiful, just like Pat's. Those two guys together were very special. Even though it was a band, you could tell those were the guys that were going to make it happen. And there was nothing going on for them right then. Tommy and Pat were basically sharing cans of beans for dinner that night. And we knew we could change that by signing them. I loved them the moment I saw them. They were just such cool guys. They had a great look and a great sound. They were raw and definitely untested. But just a ton of potential. They seemed like leaders. When you're looking at a bunch of young guys like this, you are looking for some leadership, guys that can write and guys that can sing out front and really make things happen. You can call them "stars" or whatever you want. But you need at least one guy like that in a band, and I saw two of them in front of me. I was excited. I didn't really have much on my plate at this point, but I wanted to work with these guys. It was just like this big mound of clay. It was something I thought I could help shape and mold.

Tommy was just crazy in terms of how good a player he was, but he also had this ferocious singing style. He was like a wild, uncaged animal. And I loved the juxtaposition with what Pat brought. Pat was far subtler; he had a quiet power about him. But playing together, they had what you want. You want that unique yin and yang combination. You see it in so many bands, whether we are talking the Rolling Stones, or Led Zeppelin, or many others. A dynamic like that between two people in a band can become a powerful force. And sitting there in the studio that day, that's what I felt. I definitely wanted to work with them. I knew that. What I didn't know was that these guys would eventually help define me as a producer just as much as I would try to define them as a band.

6

NOBODY

1971–73:
Tom Johnston / Patrick Simmons / John Hartman /
Tiran Porter / Michael Hossack

The Doobie Brothers' 1971 debut, like many first efforts, only begins to hint at what is to come. The album, top-heavy with Johnston tunes, established his soulful growl as a signature sound of the band. But Simmons used his lone effort, "Closer Every Day," to plant the seed that his folksy, mellower style was an effective counterpoint. The album failed to attract much attention, but it did set the stage for what was to come the next year. A couple of key personnel changes and one arena-ready anthem later, it was fasten-your-seat-belts time.

Tom

Warner Bros. really was the perfect label for us. They were very artist-friendly. Whenever we would travel down there and once we started recording in Los Angeles after the first album, we would always go hang out at the offices. You never knew who you might run into. I remember meeting Little Richard there, one of my influences early on. And you'd see guys from Little Feat, as well as artists like Bonnie Raitt, James Taylor, Randy Newman, Ry Cooder, Rickie Lee Jones, Neil Young, and on and on. But the "suits," if you want to call them that, were really into music, were approachable, and really understood what was going on. I didn't really go hang out at any other labels, so I can't speak to their environment. But Warner Bros. was different. They had built a really interesting staff there that had people like Mo Ostin, Joe Smith, Lenny Waronker, Tommy LiPuma, Russ Titelman, and Van Dyke Parks, and you'd run into them just walking around with Ted; our careers kind of grew in tandem. It's like he elevated us into a marketable band, and at the same time he'd have other projects like Van Morrison and eventually Van Halen, but there were always people there that you could talk to, like Ed Thrasher from the art department; Carl Scott, who worked on tour setup; and the producers I mentioned, like Lenny Waronker and Russ Titelman. And you could just hang out in anyone's office if they weren't busy and learn a little about artists they were working on and the music business. It was just that kind of place. Very musician-friendly.

In '72 we ended up practicing for tours at the Warner Bros. movie lot on the sound stages. This was pretty cool, as you'd run into all these actors and actresses and movie people in general while wandering around the set and at catering. I can remember *Bonanza* being shot next door . . . crazy.

Pat

I think we got $2,700 apiece when we signed that contract. It was like we were rich. So we went out and got all new gear, guitars, and amps down at Leo's, a local music shop. We were still gigging all around the Bay Area, sometimes with Neal Schon, who was younger than we were and lived in San Mateo. He was always hanging around Pacific Recording (and was still in Santana before he formed Journey), and then there was also a band called the Beans, who would one day be known as the Tubes. The music scene in the early '70s around San Francisco was just amazing—very creative and experimental. We had a great time playing, and you never knew what might happen on any given night. I remember even before our first album even came out, Pete Townsend showed up at one of our gigs one night to play with us. The Who had played the Cow Palace, and he just wanted to jam. He came over to the North Beach Revival, an after-hours San Francisco cabaret that didn't open until 1 AM, where we were playing. He said to us, "I'm just looking for a place to play!" and our drummer John Hartman, who was a Who freak and idolized Keith Moon, was especially thrilled when Townsend started banging his own head on John's cymbals! We also played with John Lee Hooker, Elvin Bishop, Johnny Winter—it was surreal—our heroes actually liked our band and wanted to play with us.

Tom

My memories of recording the first album in San Mateo are that we all thought we were going to get a chance to continue to do what we did onstage on the record. But Lenny wanted a more acoustic and clean electric-guitar style. It is true that we had songs like this written along with all the other tunes we played live, and some of them got played at gigs, but we also did a lot of high-energy, jam-style tunes that resonated with the crowds we were in front of.

We would get up every day and head to San Mateo and start recording around noon. The songs were selected by Lenny and Ted before we started, except for a couple that made it on the album later in the process, like "Growin' a Little Each Day," which I wrote and recorded on piano. The other songs, like "Feelin' Down Farther" and "Nobody," were from the demo that was sent to Warner Bros. We also did a Randy Newman song called "Beehive State," which we cut live with everyone playing and Pat and I splitting the lead vocals. It had a great drum part reminiscent of a Mountain-style song, and Hartman shined on this track! It was his kind of rock! And it was the heaviest rock song on the album. Very different from everything else we recorded.

Pat had a traditional called "Chicago" that we covered, and

we also did a song called "Slippery St. Paul," which we sort of co-wrote in honor of Paul Curcio's questionable business dealings. These were both fingerpicking-based songs. The other tunes I wrote, like "Greenwood Creek," "The Master," "Travelin' Man," and "It Won't Be Right" were all mellower tunes. All the basic tracking was usually done on a clean electric or acoustic guitar, bass, and drums, except for "Beehive State." We'd then overdub guitar parts and lead vocals and harmonies along with harmonica on "Chicago" and "Greenwood Creek." Out of that batch of tunes, the only somewhat upbeat tune was "It Won't Be Right," and it wasn't very edgy either, just a driving acoustic guitar rhythm with a fingerpicking part and harmonies. Pat had written a song called "Closer Every Day" that was also kind of mellow, but in a minor key. It was probably the most arranged song on the album and had a piano track I played behind Pat's guitar (sort of a Neil Young–sounding lick) and was kind of a departure from the other tunes. Cool song.

We had electric solos that were distorted on "Feelin' Down Farther," "Nobody," "Beehive State," and "Closer Ever Day." Listening back to these early albums, I'm struck by how high our voices were!

Both Lenny and Ted were great about giving direction and ideas for arrangements. But Ted did the largest part of the "communicating" with us. And when we finished the album, we were all pretty excited about where we "thought" this was all headed. We had cut our first album on a real label, and we had the single "Nobody" picked out. A couple of months before the album was released, Jim Marshall (of Woodstock and other rock-photo fame) came and did a photo shoot with us starting at Twelfth Street and ending up at the Chateau for more photos—one of which ended up being the cover shot. We all thought this was pretty cool. The sky was the limit . . . until the single stiffed, along with the album. They did release "Beehive State" as a second single, but it didn't do anything either. So at that point, it was time to move on.

I should add that Johnny Winter was hanging around us when we played in San Francisco at places like Keystone, owned by Freddie Herrera (he had two others, one in Berkeley and one in Palo Alto). Other guys like Elvin Bishop and some of the guys from Paul Butterfield's band on the 1969 *Keep on Moving* album were all at the Keystone on the night of our album party, and there was a big jam that went on for a while. Johnny became an acquaintance of our manager at the time and we all were kind of in awe of his playing. He hung out at our manager's house in Diamond Heights in San Francisco right when our first album came out. I don't know why he was there, because Johnny lived in New York. He would later show up at shows, like the one at Nassau Coliseum in New York, dressed in jean shorts, a velvet cape, and a three-corner hat with a feather. Quite the ensemble. When we were in New York, I would go visit Johnny at his apartment over by NYU. He loaned me a Gibson Firebird (of which he had about three or four and played all the time). Since he never asked for it back, it ended up being a great present, and it was a guitar I really liked playing. I had it for about ten years (until it got stolen during a gig in Boston in the early 1980s, when I was playing in a band called Border Patrol).

Shortly after we finished the first album, because I didn't go back for the extra semester to complete my degree, I got my draft notice for Vietnam. My number was a bad one, and I had to report to both the Fresno and Oakland induction centers. This was not fucking good! Warner Bros. hooked me up with a lawyer in L.A., who wrote a huge report on why I wasn't fit for the draft for a number of reasons. It didn't work. The day I was at the Oakland induction center, they took that lengthy report and threw it in the trash along with similar documents presented by several other guys also attempting to avoid the draft. This was at the height of the Vietnam War, and they needed warm bodies to fight the stupid, misguided mistake they'd gotten the country into. I felt bad for the guys who were already stuck over there in Vietnam, and I knew a few guys I'd gone to school with in Visalia who'd gone and didn't come back, or didn't come back "right" upstairs, or had some bad physical problems from wounds sustained in battle.

I proceeded to pass all the physical and mental tests without a problem, which was depressing. And after a full day of bullshit, I was at the last table before getting on the bus to Fort Ord in Monterey. At this point, I figured I was fucked, and I was headed for 'Nam. I was choking on the diesel fumes from the bus engines running outside the last door while they waited for the new draftees.

At the last table before getting on the bus, there was an army doctor who pulled me aside to ask the last questions they had before shipping you off. He wanted to know if I'd had much experience with rifles and so on, and I told him I really hadn't. He then asked me what the bumps on each of my wrists were from. It was really weird, but I hadn't noticed them before going to the induction center, and none of the other army doctors had asked about them all day. He asked if I knew what they were from, and I had no idea and told him so. Then he asked me again whether I could handle firearms with the bumps, and I answered truthfully that I hadn't been around any firearms in years. So he examined both of my wrists and asked if they were painful, which they sort of were, but not in a big way. He then started looking through a field manual of some sort, after which he looked up at me and said that the bumps were swollen ganglions or nerve endings and that I couldn't perform the functions needed to properly use a firearm, so I was 4F! Man, my jaw almost hit the floor! I had just been rejected from service in Vietnam! I couldn't believe that I had gone from heading to boot camp and on to 'Nam to being 4F in about five minutes. And the craziest thing about all this was, as I later found out, that the ganglions were from playing guitar so much that they started to swell! And just as crazy was that the bumps disappeared about a week and a half later, and I never had them again! Call it divine intervention or dumb luck, WHATEVER! I had never been so relieved in my life! Playing guitar had just saved my life and my future in the Doobie Brothers.

So I was free to continue life as I had come to know it and to continue making music with my friends. Amazing!

Pat

Well, at the time the band started getting together, we were all hanging out with various biker types, some in clubs, many unaffiliated. We all had our sights set on buying bikes. A few of the clubs that we played around the San Francisco Bay Area attracted a lot of bikers, and they kind of adopted us as the local biker band, I guess. I know that after we got bikes and rode more and more, we dressed in leather all the time and lived the biker lifestyle pretty much. I'm still, more than ever probably, in love with motorcycling on so many different levels. Our music is full of road references and stories that mirror motorcycling. Our affiliation as a band with Harley and motorcycle events has continued to this day. Well, in the '60s some of my friends had bikes that I was able to borrow from time to time. That started it all. Then around 1969, I got ahold of an old BSA that I had to put some work into to make run, and that really convinced me that I was made for the sport. I got a crash course in motorcycles. Luckily, I had friends who were willing to mentor me through the process a little, but I was the one who had to do all the adjustments and twist all the nuts and bolts. It was my future brother-in-law, Bill Craddock, who really got me into it.

Tom

The people up at the Chateau were the first Doobie Brothers fans. They pushed us. They wanted us to develop and helped us gain confidence by supporting us and cheering us on. I can't say we were the "house band" there, but we definitely played there a lot, and it became a little home away from home for us. I always loved playing up there. But I think there's a misconception about us as a "biker band." The press had a lot of fun with that, and I think it was overstated. Yes, we had fans that were heavy-duty bikers. Yes, once in a while they would hang out with us over on Twelfth Street. But that was kind of it. The Chateau Liberté was kind of a biker bar mixed with students, hippies, and local mountain folk, and because we became popular, everybody thought of us as a "biker band." But we were making music for everybody. We didn't consider ourselves anything other than a band that was growing and developing. That's what I think people forget. Back then you didn't sit around thinking about what kind of band you were going to be or the audience you were going to appeal to. You just got together and played. At that point, it was just about making enough money to be able to keep playing. If you put some food on the table and some gas in the tank, that was considered a success. To be fair, there were quite a few "concept" bands that had success in the '70s and '80s. But back in the late '60s and early '70s, it really wasn't like that. As far as my interest in bikes goes, I did love riding, and I got my first motorcycle in Visalia, a Ducati 250 Diana single cylinder that I ended up pushing more than I drove it. I graduated to a 750 Norton with a loan from my sister after moving to San Jose and wrecked it road racing with a friend who also had a Norton. My next bike, which I bought in '73, was a Harley-Davidson Super Glide that

I had for years. I got a couple other Harleys when the band was compensated with them instead of money for playing shows for the company's anniversaries in Milwaukee. The last one we played was with Kid Rock, Tim McGraw, and Elton John, so the shows were pretty cool. I sold my last bike in 2003 (a Road King) and haven't ridden since. I don't really know why, but I just lost interest in riding.

Pat

I think biker culture with the band specifically started at the Chateau. I would start seeing some other club members at this little restaurant, Jack's Place in Los Gatos, where I had breakfast every day. They knew me from the band, and I would often see them at our gigs around town. They were always nice to me and would acknowledge their admiration for the band and our music. We were writing songs about motorcycles and about the road, so guys in the clubs just gravitated toward us.

7

TRAVELIN' MAN

Tom

As soon as the first record came out, Warners put us out on our first national tour, opening for the band Mother Earth. When you play every night opening for a good band like Mother Earth at decent venues, you learn a lot about touring and you also end up hanging out with players in the other band, which I did frequently with Mother Earth. Karl Himmel was their drummer, and Toad Andrews and Bob Cardwell were their guitar players. Bob and Karl kind of took us under their wing and showed us the ropes both at gigs and in all the towns we'd play, which was all new to us. Also, spending every night watching Tracy Nelson, who could sing her ass off, was eye-opening—what a voice, very soulful, with a lot of gospel influences.

I remember, in particular, our time in the Pacific Northwest and our first time in Nashville, where I was introduced to meat and threes and barbecue. Nashville was so different from what it's become. Back then, it was just a sleepy little town, but very musical. I went with Bob and Karl over to Quadraphonic Sound Studios on what was the early version of Music Row, where Area Code 615 had cut the album of the same name with their hit, "Devil Weed and Me." I don't remember who was working there at the time, but Bob and Karl knew everybody and introduced me around. The bass player, Tim Drummond (who later played with everyone from James Brown to Neil Young), was there. It was like someone's house with a recording studio, which is what most of the early studios in Nashville were like. Such a cool town, back when the King of the Road Hotel (Roger Miller's place) was the big place to hang out and Broadway just had a couple of guitar stores and honky-tonk-style clubs.

The other big memory was being in New York City for the first time, where we stayed at the Midtown Ramada. It was August and hot and humid, which we weren't used to. And there was no air-conditioning. I went to places like the Carnegie Deli and got lost somewhere around Soho with Cardwell and Himmel, just checking out New York. The gig we played was at the Town Hall with Mother Earth and Patti LaBelle, who headlined the show. When we got there, Mitch Ryder (Detroit Wheels) was standing out front yelling about his upcoming gig and new record . . . crazy! Well, the gig was great, and we were all used to hearing each other play by then, but Patti LaBelle took it to another level! She was really killing it up there, doing more of the Aretha style of singing that preceded her work with the band LaBelle and the release of "Lady Marmalade." So classy and really good at working the crowd. And man, she could SING! So the "Mother/Brothers" tour, as it became known, really taught us a lot about being on the road, working on our sound, and a little about showmanship. We also learned on that tour how to abuse the record company's credit card and rack up thousands of dollars in hotel bar bills, among other things.

In August of '71 we were doing some shows in the south with the Mother/Brothers tour and ended up in New Orleans, playing a show at the Municipal Auditorium with Mother Earth and Long John Baldry, and we stayed out by the airport at the Holiday Inn. The next show in Boston got canceled, so we flew back to California and played a couple of shows in the Bay Area. Out of the blue, we were booked to do a show back in New Orleans at City Park Stadium with Black Oak Arkansas, Chuck Berry, and some other groups, and we stayed in town at the Sheraton on Charles Street. The show got rained out. And since this was our second time being in New Orleans and we were closer to town, we started exploring the town and its restaurants and hanging out in the French Quarter. New Orleans has such a vibe about it that it's easy to just get lost trying to see everything, and the music scene is legendary, with all these great artists I'd heard on the radio, like Fats Domino, Lee Dorsey, Dr. John, and Screamin' Jay Hawkins. Little Richard's breakthrough album *Here's Little Richard,* on Specialty Records, was recorded there with local studio players.

I later became familiar with the Meters, Allen Toussaint, Professor Longhair, Dave Bartholomew, the zydeco scene, and on and on. Also, the world-famous jazz/Dixieland that came out of there will forever be part of the American musical lexicon.

By taking the streetcars on Canal and Charles Streets, you could get most anywhere, including a couple of the colorful old cemeteries that were so tucked in among old oak trees with Spanish moss hanging off them. You could get lost for hours wandering around looking at all the mausoleums. Everything has to be buried above ground because the city is below sea level and near the Mississippi River. New Orleans is aptly named the Crescent City because the original town was built at a sharp bend in the river.

The Sheraton we stayed at had a great restaurant that I ate at a lot, and I always had red beans and rice with seafood gumbo! Absolutely delicious, and always served up by Charlene, a waitress there who kind of adopted us, or at least me.

So while we were there with an unexpected day off, I went to a show I was told about at the Warehouse, which was a very cool club/venue down on the Mississippi River. It was just what the name implied, an old warehouse where they used to store whatever came off the barges that were continuously going up and down the river. And you could smell the mildew and old grease from all the years that place had been used. The show was a co-bill with Freddie King and a performance of the album *Mad Dogs and Englishmen*, minus Joe Cocker. I got to go upstairs (one level and open to the stage area) and hang out a little. And there sat Leon Russell talking with Freddie King, along with all the musicians and singers from both bands. Heady stuff for a kid from the West Coast!

Freddie took the stage with his band and proceeded to tear that place up with a killer set that finished with "Goin' Down," which had only come out recently. The band was so damn tight and powerful, and Freddie was on fire both singing and playing, and I remember thinking "I would NOT want to follow that set!" Well, Leon (with his famous top hat) and the other musicians doing *Mad Dogs and Englishmen* took the stage with two drummers, Chuck Blackwell and Jim Keltner, Carl Radle on bass, Don Preston on guitar, Leon on piano and occasionally guitar, Rita Coolidge, Claudia Lennear, and Denny Cordell singing backgrounds, Bobby Keys on sax, Tim Price on trumpet, and Chris Stainton on a B3 Hammond. And, to my surprise, they DID top Freddie's set! I couldn't believe how good they were and wondered where all the energy came from. I guess if you had to follow Freddie, you needed to turn it up a notch! One of the best shows I've ever seen, and right there in that old, funky little warehouse on the Mississippi River. It was kind of a throwback to that James Brown show I saw as a kid, a moment when you know that you are witnessing magic, when someone is playing at a higher level. And it helps you think about what you can do as a musician to be better. It's impressive and also inspiring. There's nothing like being in the audience for a show like that. It's kind of why you get into rock and roll in the first place. Just to be around this kind of great music and musicians. That was definitely a special night.

Pat

Hearing Tracy Nelson, who fronted Mother Earth, sing every night really taught us a lot about singing, too. She was just incredible. And I'll never forget when, on the very first tour, we came back to San Francisco and played the Fillmore. I thought back to that night when I first dropped acid and saw the Grateful Dead on that very stage. Now there I was with my band, the Doobie Brothers. It felt pretty surreal, and I was so grateful for the experience.

Tom

After the first album, not a whole lot changed for us, lifestyle-wise. I was still living in the house on Twelfth Street, and in the days after the first tour, I would sit in my room for hours on end, working on new songs. In fact, I wrote wherever I was inspired. My girlfriend at the time was going to summer school at a college in nearby Stockton, and I'd drive down there in my '69 VW Bug and wait for her to get out of class. I'd sit out in a nearby pasture. Out there in the field, sitting under a tree with my acoustic and the cows watching me, I started to develop my "chunka-chunka" style of guitar playing. In fact, I think I started what would become "Nobody" in that pasture. It evolved from me trying to cover both guitar and drum parts together, backbeat style. This would follow me back to the house on Twelfth Street and is a big part of my playing to this day.

Pat

Rolling Stone wrote about our first album, "The Doobies had a formidable sound, Simmons' deft country-blues picking meshing with Johnston's penchant for thick chord riffing with an R&B bent. Underscored by drummer Hartman and bassist Shogren, it was a powerful rock-pop sound that was buoyant but blistering, mighty and yet melodic. When the first album stiffed despite a splashy Warner Bros.–sponsored Mother/Brothers Tour with Mother Earth, the bewildered band found themselves back among the brawlers at the Chateau Liberté." And that's the truth. The first record only sold about ten thousand copies. We were right back where we started. But it was cool. We loved doing what we did, and we didn't have any huge expectations.

LISTEN TO THE MUSIC

Tom

We had a couple of key personnel changes in between the first and second albums. First, we were playing at Bimbo's 365 Club in San Francisco in June 1971, and John Hartman invited this drummer, Michael Hossack, to come up and jam with us. He added a really nice punch, and it hit us: the Dead and the Allman Brothers had two drummers; we could do the same thing. We'd seen Michael before. He actually had sat in with us before, up at the Chateau. Also, when we were doing our initial demos in San Mateo, he was there with a band called Morning Reign/Roadhouse. We knew he was good and we knew he would bring a lot to the band, which he did.

Pat

Mike Hossack had actually played with us a few times before that gig at Bimbo's 365. He was in a band called Roadhouse, a great band that featured some friends of his from New Jersey. They were also playing up at the Chateau around the same time that we were. We actually played a few gigs with them there. That's where Hartman originally had him sit in with us. I knew he was a fantastic drummer. I mean, I'm talking at the level of a Jim Keltner, Jeff Porcaro—just that good. Very funky, rock, blues—you name it, he could play it. So I was familiar with him and thought he was just incredible. When he sat in with us that night at Bimbo's 365, I think we all knew he would soon be in the band. I mean, all of a sudden, with Mike, we were like the Allman Brothers. He just brought so much to our sound. He lived just down the road from me in Los Gatos, and so we hung out quite a bit. We would have dinner, get stoned, drink a lot, and just basically carry on. A great addition to the Doobie Brothers.

And then you had the situation with our bass player. Dave Shogren really wasn't the guy we needed, so he left the band. As far as a replacement, I thought about Tiran Porter. We had played together as part of the trio Scratch (with Mike Mindel on fiddle). I knew how good Tiran was. Tiran just brought everyone's game up. You would think you were jamming, and then with Tiran you were *jamming*. Tiran and Mike were both studio-quality players. At that time, they could have both been hot studio guys down in Los Angeles. So I'm glad we got them.

Ted really liked the personnel changes, which was great.

At that point, we had blown about twenty thousand dollars in studio time because we were not focused and were doing too much blow, among other things. Our lack of productivity actually got us put on suspension by the label. That's to say, if we didn't deliver soon, we were going to get kicked off. But there were some good songs we were working on, including "White Sun," "Snake Man," and "Toulouse Street," which was inspired by our recent trips to New Orleans. We did some home demos with the new guys, all five of us, and sent it to Ted. He liked it a lot, and that's when we got back on track.

Tom

Pat was really excited about Tiran. He felt strongly about it, and so we were anxious to give him a shot. I don't think you can even call it an audition; he just fit in from the second he walked in to jam, and we knew we had our guy on bass. I had met him before and hung out a couple of times, but I had not really played with him. He impressed me and the rest of the band immediately. He had his own style, and it added a punch and musicality and a different low-harmony sound we hadn't had up to that point. So a definite step up in the band's sound. Great showman, too.

Tiran

There was a guy whom I had been playing some music with in Los Angeles for a few years, and he moved up to the Bay

Area. One day he called me out of the blue and said, "You have to get up here. I'm jamming with this guy named Pat Simmons, and he's an amazing guitar player. A real picker. One of the best guys I've ever played with." Well, that sounded good to me. I was basically broke, and so I headed up to the Bay Area and met Pat. We hit it off right away. Our styles meshed really nicely. We formed a trio and started playing around San Jose and the Half Moon Bay area for about ten months. And then we ran into another trio made up of Dave, John, and Tom Johnston. They called themselves Pud. Well, they stole Patrick away from our little group and that was that. I headed back down to Los Angeles and ended up playing in another couple of bands. Not long after I got home, I became aware of what was now called the Doobie Brothers playing nearby, opening up for a band called Mother Earth and Long John Baldry. I went to the afterparty at the Riot House on Sunset Strip. There was a giant bowl of cocaine on the table, and I thought to myself, "Wow, no wonder they were so energetic up there!" I spent the next couple of hours with them, getting high and yakking into the night. They were a great bunch of guys. Six or seven months later, I got a call from Pat, and he said to me, "Hey, Dave has left the band, would you like to come up and jam?" I wasn't doing anything that important, so I said yes. I went up there and played with the guys and everything clicked. I became the bass player for the Doobie Brothers.

I went back down to Los Angeles, packed up all of my

belongings, and then headed up to San Jose for good. They had a bunch of demos for the second record, which had been rejected by Warner Bros. So things were very much in flux. When I joined them, they were still playing clubs, and I moved into the house on Twelfth Street. What a scene that place was. They had been living and playing there for a couple of years, but for me, it was a brand-new experience. It was kind of like a frat house. Lots of music being played down in that basement. You could feel the history there. The scene on Twelfth Street was really interesting. When I first moved in there, I was bunking underneath John Hartman, who was one of the funniest guys I have ever met in my life. Very smart and very clever and very gracious. I liked him a lot. He brought a lot of personality to the band. What was crazy was that Lindsey Buckingham and Stevie Nicks lived right down the street, and we would have these big street parties where they would be playing at one end and we'd be playing at the other. Can you imagine?

Tom

I'm not sure Tiran was prepared for the scene on Twelfth Street. It was still really crazy, but he took to it pretty quickly and then blended right in. He was more than just a great player; he was a very cool dude who also had a great look. Everybody liked him right away. Sometimes you just find the perfect guy at the perfect time. That was Tiran.

Tiran

I know Tom and Pat didn't think about it a lot back then, but they really were ahead of their time when they brought me in. I mean, they basically let me play up on the frontline with them. There weren't a lot of mixed-race bands at that time, certainly none as big as the Doobie Brothers. Once I came on board, they also let me develop my own bass lines, which always meant a lot to me. I could tell that Tom and Pat were very open and creative, and that allowed for a lot of growth. They didn't have to let me play up front like that. But they did, and when you look back on those video clips today, it gave our band not just a unique sound but a unique look as well. I just loved how much they respected the band Moby Grape. Some of the songs on the first album were just incredible. The Doobie Brothers took their basic template from Moby Grape. Simply made it work. They had a real knack for doing that, for not just staying true to themselves and making the music they wanted to, but also creating songs that connected with a large audience. And their sensibilities were very relatable to a large audience. People picked up on the authenticity of the Doobie Brothers, and I think that's why so many of the songs live as anthems today. They sounded familiar the first time you heard them. They were simple and easy to remember. But they also made you feel good. So many of the songs simply make you feel good. So they were able to take the amazing diversity and creativity of a band like Moby Grape and just translate it to a larger level. It's pretty amazing where it comes from. But when you listen to the Doobie Brothers, what you're hearing is a very original band.

Tom

When we started working on what became *Toulouse Street,* we weren't yet working with Ted as our real producer. We had Marty Cohn engineering and "kind of" producing, but really it was about the early songs we had brought in. We were working at Wally Heider's in San Francisco, which was a happening studio at that time and a sister to his L.A. studio. Brewer and Shipley were working next door, and Jefferson Airplane was recording *After Bathing at Baxter's* downstairs.

I'd have to say that, although we had a couple of tunes, we weren't fully prepared to cut a whole album, and when we sent early tapes to Warners with songs like "Bluejay," "White Sun," "Snake Man," and "Toulouse Street," I remember Warners not hearing any hits and thinking we needed a real producer to rein us in, and they were right! So that was when Ted Templeman began producing the Doobies on his own. And though we did keep "White Sun," "Toulouse Street," and "Snake Man," it was after Marty left that we wrote or covered everything else, like "Don't Start Me to Talkin'." And I'm pretty sure a house engineer named Steve Barncard did the tunes we cut at Heider's with Ted. Following that, we started working at Amigo in Burbank, with Donn Landee engineering, our first experience working with him. Couldn't have been a better pairing! He and Ted worked together seamlessly. And we all loved his engineering.

I had been working on a song while in my room at Twelfth Street. It was pretty basic, but I liked it. The more I built upon it, the better it sounded, and for the first time in my life I started thinking, this feels like something that could be on the radio. It was a hard feeling to describe, because I never thought of songs in terms of being "commercial." I have a better idea now, but it's still "whatever works." But there was something about this little song that I kept coming back to. I started getting excited about it.

I'd sit in my bedroom in San Jose doing what I always do. I had been up playing guitar for hours, and I'd even written the lyric idea and title. It was like two or three in the morning. I had the opening riff to it, and I thought that I had figured out the chorus and bridge chord changes as well. I called Ted Templeman, woke him up, and played it for him over the phone, and he was less than enthusiastic. Probably because I woke him up. But he said, "Well, yeah, it might be pretty good. Needs a couple of changes." I messed with it a little bit more before crashing, and I'll admit that phone call was kind of a buzzkill. But, as I recall, we didn't ever really change anything. It stayed the way it was, the way I had it. The chord changes and everything we recorded are the same ones I wrote in the bedroom. In the studio, the bass part was added by Tiran, drums were added by Mike, and Pat came up with a couple of parts and put in that great banjo part on the ride out. It was really coming together and incorporated so many different elements but kept the straight-ahead feel I'd started with. And I had written all the lyrics, which hardly ever happened until after the track was recorded. And they stayed the same: "Listen to the Music."

That song was based on a somewhat utopian view of the world. The idea was that music could lift humans up— including world leaders, if they were able to sit down on some big grassy hill where the sun was shining and listen to music. Then they would figure out that everybody had more in common than they thought and that no disagreement was worth getting so bent out of shape about. So the world could benefit from the point of view that music could make everything better. Sounds very hippie-dippy, but it's just what I was feeling at the moment. In the studio, Ted warmed up to the song. When I brought it in, I mustered up as much enthusiasm as I could when I played it for everyone. The band liked it. And Ted said, let's lay it down. And in true Doobie style, Tiran came up with a great bass part for it, Ted worked on the drum part with Mike and John, and Pat had a great picking part that ended up being on a banjo for the ride out as well as strumming parts. We started building this song out with the usual guitar, bass, and drums. I ended up layering about three rhythm guitars. One being a clean electric rhythm, another an acoustic track, and a third where our engineer Don took my electric through a direct box, no amp, and miked the strings with a condenser mic just to get the percussive strike of the pick hitting the strings. The vocal and harmonies were laid down. That phasing that you hear in the bridge was something Don created. He and Ted came up with the idea. Having Pat sing the bridge was another great idea Ted had, and it elevated the flow of the song. I think the reason "Listen to the Music" worked so well is because it was the perfect showcase of how we all worked together. Pat and I didn't socialize a lot away from work, but in the studio he always had great ideas for parts on my tunes, and I always tried to repay the favor on his tunes. His playing on "Listen to the Music" fit right in, much like his guitar part on "Long Train Runnin'," which was on our next album, and so many others. And it kind of helped establish the Doobie Brothers sound: two guys singing lead, a really cool brand of electric and acoustic guitar strumming and picking with rhythm, great harmonies from the three of us, and cool drum and bass parts. But we had no idea what was going to happen with "Listen to the Music" once it was done, no matter how good it sounded. And as Ted said, there's a lot of luck and timing involved with a song that gets strong chart attention.

Ted

I remember when Tommy called me one night and said, "Hey, Ted, I just wrote something, and I think it could be a hit!" It must've been three o'clock in the morning. He started playing the song for me on his guitar over the phone, and I said, "Wait, wait, Tommy—wait until I see you in the studio." He was really excited, and for him this wasn't characteristic. Tommy was a low-key guy, so hearing him think he had a hit song was something that got me excited. I hated to say it over the phone, however, but I just wasn't hearing what he was hearing. So we get in the studio and start working on it, and it's still not really happening for me. When we got the track down and had a "work vocal" on it, we decided that Pat should sing the bridge "like a lazy flowing river etc." because it added a really nice counterpoint vocal to Tommy. Pat also added a great banjo part and a couple of guitars. Hossack's idea for the steel drums was brilliant. It was a great team effort, that song. And then there's that phasing thing that goes on during the bridge. Donn Landee and I had used that kind of weird-sounding phasing on one of our Harpers Bizarre records for a track called "Knock on Wood." "Listen to the Music" for me really represents what the Doobie Brothers were all about. The amazing harmony vocals from Tom, Pat, and Tiran and the great teamwork of everybody kind of pitching in, even though Tommy had the original idea. I still wasn't sure that it was going to be a hit record. It definitely came together in a great way that sounded special, though. You can't plan out hit records. It just doesn't work that way. Sometimes, there's a lot of luck that has to happen as well. But I think with a song like "Listen to the Music," which is just a really nice anthem with a basic musical message, it raises the chances that something good is going to happen. And, sure enough, when we put it out, unlike the first album, we had lots of radio stations that were interested pretty early in that song. The guys finally had a hit.

Tom

I know that Ted used some phasing on one of the songs he'd done in Harpers Bizarre, but there was another song called "The

Big Hurt" by Toni Fisher that also used it. Today it seems like no big deal, but in 1972 it was actually a really cool and unique sound and definitely sounded great on the radio. Donn Landee was another huge part of the Doobie Brothers sound. Just a great engineer and very creative with both recording sound and editing songs. He was really into "phasing" effects back in the 1960s; just listen to the track he worked on for Eric Burdon and the Animals, "Sky Pilot." To me, *Toulouse Street* definitely feels like our first album in a lot of ways. The packaging was amazing. For the first time, I felt like we were becoming a professional outfit. So much thought went into everything. I remember driving in San Jose after the album release, and I had the local radio station KFRC on the radio in my car, and "Listen to the Music" came on, and I couldn't believe it. I pulled my Volkswagen Beetle to the side of the road and just sat there staring at the radio. I remember that happening like it was yesterday. "Damn! That's" us! It was a big moment for me. Actual airplay on a major station.

Pat

I loved "Listen to the Music" when Tom brought that in. And it definitely sounded commercial, maybe something good for radio? You can never predict that stuff, but I mean, just listen to that song for the first time and there's something so memorable about it. In the studio, we didn't really write together too much; we brought our own stuff in and then the others tried to add touches.

Tiran

Tom was working on the song "Listen to the Music" when I first moved into Twelfth Street. I would hear him piecing it together bit by bit. There's a lot of disagreement about how that came together, but I distinctly remember coming up with that line, "whoa whoa listen to the music" after Tom's chord progressions. It was when we were in the studio working with Ted. Nobody else remembers it that way, but that's how I recall it, and I'm sticking to my story!

Tom

I know Tiran has said that he came up with the title line for "Listen to the Music," but I remember writing that lyric in my room in San Jose as the catchphrase for what the lyrics were trying to say. Tiran brought a lot to our band and was part of our collective "sound," but he didn't write the chorus. I get it—sometimes we all remember things differently. Sometimes things get hazy. There was a lot of shit going on back then. There are plenty of things that I will second-guess myself on because of how long ago it was. But not that lyric. I remember that plain as day.

Pat

I don't really remember Tiran coming up with that line in "Listen to the Music." My recollection is that Tom already had the chorus and most of the song. If he helped Tom with that, I never heard about it. Stuff like that happens sometimes I guess, but I never heard about it. We worked out the bridge in the studio shortly before we recorded it, I think. Then we just started experimenting with various overdubs, overlaying guitars, vocals, and all the rest. I don't know where the hell I got the idea for the banjo part. I had played with three different banjo players in the years leading up to me joining the Doobies, and I learned a little technique. I just pulled it out of my ass in the studio. I'm glad it worked!

9

JESUS IS JUST ALRIGHT

Pat

Marc Bolan and T. Rex had released an album called *Electric Warrior,* which included a song called "Bang a Gong." That became their biggest hit and really made them a huge band. This was right at the beginning of the glam-rock era, when bands like Slade, David Bowie with his Ziggy Stardust and the Spiders from Mars show, Alice Cooper, and others were really starting to become well known. And T. Rex was right up there. So we were booked to open for them. It was going to be a much more extensive tour than we had done with Mother Earth. This is where we really started getting used to being on the road. It was an eye-opener for us just to be thrown in front of audiences who were there primarily to see what was then the biggest glitter-rock act in the biz. We didn't know it then, but it was the perfect setting for us, and we worked our asses off out there, and the crowds started to respond to us. Plus, "Listen to the Music" was starting to get a lot of radio airplay, and that helped a lot. When you can play something that everybody knows, it has a nice way of winning them over.

Tom

I found Marc Bolan and T. Rex to be a very different kind of musician and musical act. We were all flying commercial on that tour.

He definitely had his own world and was one of a kind, from the way he dressed to his show onstage. He was fun to hang with, and he'd take me aside and show me all his guitars, including an all-aluminum model I had never seen before. Since I had come from a blues, rock, and R&B background, what he was exploring was completely different from anything I had heard or seen before. "Glam rock," as it was called, seemed to be about his physical appearance and the stage show as much as the music he was playing, but it also involved a lot of interaction with the crowd, which was something he took seriously. He and his band were easy to get along with, and that tour was a great opportunity for us. They treated us really well on the road. We always got to sound check. We always got to play our full show, and they totally supported us. It was a very solid experience overall and, yet again, gave us more ideas for performing on the road. Bolan seemed to draw other well-known rock celebs to his shows in big cities—like Mick Jagger, Keith Richards, and Ringo Starr. It taught us to step up our stage show and stage presence. I mean, he was always dressed like a rock star at any time of day! I think at that time we were just a get-up-and-play-your-set kind of band, relying on the songs to get people involved. If anything was learned from touring with Marc, it was the importance of the show aspect like clothes, stage moves, and personal interaction with the crowd, and special effects like smoke, flashier lighting, and so on.

After the last show of the tour, at the Hollywood Palladium, Marc threw a party for his band and ours at the Hyatt Continental on Sunset in Hollywood. The "Riot House," as it was called, was a place we spent a lot of time at during the mid-seventies, and it was always a party atmosphere with lots of musicians all staying there at the same time. And it was usually pretty crazy! You could walk down your hallway, and everyone's door was open with people partying from room to room on pretty much any floor. And there was lots of booze, mirrors, and weed. The air was thick with it.

The next morning, Marc had us come by his room for a champagne toast, thanked us for being a great act to work with and being "solid" onstage every night, and said that he felt it had been a great tour for both acts. And he was right! This was toasted with large amounts of champagne, something he really enjoyed pretty much any time, and I think we all felt it had been a great tour.

And as a kind of a full-circle moment, T. Rex and the Doobie

Brothers got inducted to the Rock & Roll Hall of Fame together in 2020.

I think after that tour Pat, John, and I started spending a lot of time at the rock and roll clothing store Jumpin' Jack Flash on Fifty-Ninth Street in New York City every time we were there. We got to know Cookie, the owner, pretty well, and she would show us everything that had just come in and give us the royal treatment, bringing us all these crazy rock and roll suits, shirts, vests, pants, and hats to try on with a matching pair of outrageous boots. She would also hang out at our shows in New York. Both backstage and out in the audience. One night that stands out is the night we played Carnegie Hall, which isn't a rock hall at all, but the crowd was rowdy. I got pulled off the stage, and some of Cookie's new clothes got ripped off my back! We spent a lot of money on the rock and roll look! Most of her stock was from buying trips she'd make to London at stores around the Kensington Market area (where I later spent a lot of money buying rock and roll duds), famous for their clothes and boots. She then shipped her purchases to her shop in New York. We also got clothes from East West Musical Instrument Co., which made all these great leather suits and vests. Yep, we began "stylin" big-time! And this continued for the next few years.

Pat

I thought the music of T. Rex was okay. I was more impressed by his style and the way he commanded an audience. I mean, Marc Bolan had so much charisma you couldn't believe it. He

JESUS IS JUST ALRIGHT • 113

totally knew how to work an audience every night. We were so basic at that point when it came to playing music. Just went out, plugged in, and played. Watching him and his band every night was influential, I think, for all of us in the Doobie Brothers. He was taking things to another level when it came to production, costumes, and everything else. It was a real education. I think what we learned watching him was that if you really wanted to endear yourself to an audience, then you had to be a little bigger than life. You had to dress the part and you had to act the part. Watching him, I started thinking to myself, wow, I need to change the way I dress. I needed to have a more rock and roll attitude. And I think everybody in our band was thinking along similar lines. John Hartman for sure was into it. John was always very influenced by the Who, so he liked big theatrics and explosions and things, and I think watching T. Rex got him thinking. Pretty soon, he would start having ideas for our stage show.

With Marc, it was kind of like Elvis. I mean, when they were done playing it was like, "Elvis has left the building!" He was definitely the star. We were all starting to drink a lot on the road and do a few other things. But the members of T. Rex hit things hard. Near the end of the tour, Bill Legend, the drummer, pulled me aside and said, "I really need help. I'm just drinking way too much." He and I became friends, and I started to see that if you weren't careful on the road, it could get the best of you. I'm happy to say, Bill is still around today. A talented musician and artist. He was probably the guy I got to know best, and I'm so glad he is doing well.

That tour was the next level up for us as far as being on the road. We played a lot of legendary venues like the Warehouse in New Orleans and the Auditorium Theatre in Chicago, the Santa Monica Civic Auditorium and the Winterland Arena in San Francisco, which was basically a hometown gig for us and a very exciting one. There's nothing like going back home as part of a real tour like that. We saw a lot of the country on that tour, and it really was the next step in getting our road chops honed and ready for the rest of our lives.

I'll never forget the last day of the tour. We had been all over the country and finished up at the Hollywood Palladium, which was a really big deal. Mick Jagger and Keith Richards were hanging out backstage. They were in town working on their album *Exile on Main St.* right across the way from the Palladium at Sunset Sound studios. There were lots of musicians there that night, and one of the best crowds we have ever played for. After the show, to celebrate the end of the tour, Marc and his crew held a big party at the famous Hyatt House on Sunset Strip, which of course was nicknamed the "Riot House." It was, as usual for us, a night of revelry, especially because it was the end of the tour. The next morning before we checked out of the hotel, Marc invited us to his room, where he had a couple of bottles of champagne on ice. After we each were handed a glass, Bolan raised his to us and gave us a generous toast. He was such a kind spirit. And I think watching him affected all of us in the Doobie Brothers. It taught us how to treat bands that are playing under you on the bill. I mean, he made it very easy for us, and it wasn't always that way.

Sometimes you hear real horror stories about what it's like on the road for an opening band, but he was the exact opposite. At the end of it all, I realized that what he was doing out there was just a beautifully honed act. He had a wife and child. I'm sure he was just a family guy at home. But out there onstage, he was a force to be reckoned with, and it definitely played a part in what we did next. (Kind of ironic that, eventually, the Doobie Brothers and T. Rex would be inducted into the Rock & Roll Hall of Fame in the same year, 2020.)

I know that Marc Bolan really influenced my own personal style. I mean, I always kind of loved rock and roll style. When I was young, I would try to emulate my teenage sister's boyfriends by wearing Levis, engineer boots, and things like that. When I was done embracing that style, it became more about Mick Jagger and Keith Richards. Then I would just be like a hippie. Whatever style I would come with at the moment, I tried to dress the part. Part of it was definitely a reaction to how conservative my parents were. They always wanted me to wear what I considered to be "square" clothes: oxfords, penny loafers, things like that. I would actually stash clothes outside of my house so that when I went to school, I could change into clothes that looked cool. Marc Bolan really inspired me to take things to another level. He was so flashy, and you could tell his fans reacted to it. There was a girl who lived across the way from me who made clothes. I started talking to her about things I wanted to wear, and she actually began making me some stage clothes. Really cool stuff. One of the suits she made back in the early '70s I still have today; this amazing brocaded outfit that's like silver/pink. True rock star threads. But then there was this brown velvet shirt, laced up the front, that became my favorite thing that she made for me. What made it unique was that the sleeves were taken from an old dress. That's what she would often do, find antique clothes, rip them apart, cut them up, and create new clothes with the remnants. Well, the sleeves that she used from this one dress were made out of metal. They kind of flared out at my wrists, and the whole thing hung over me, very form-fitted. It was incredibly heavy to wear but also very cool onstage. And the sleeves were actually made of metal mesh. Over time, they rusted and eventually dissolved from all of the sweating that I did onstage. But there was one really funny thing that happened with that shirt. In 1974, we were playing at the Rainbow in London. It was a really big show for us; in fact, we even had this show videotaped, because we knew it was going to be a big night for us. We wanted it for posterity. This was during the time in London when we met Stevie Wonder, and he was using what today is called a talk box onstage. But this was before Peter Frampton used it or Joe Walsh used it on "Rocky Mountain Way." This was early, and as usual Stevie Wonder was totally out ahead of the game. It was a very primitive rig, basically, a tube came out of the box and the box was held in his bag. The contraption was connected to a driver, and you would play through it and make strange sounds by regulating how much air came out of the tube in your mouth. I would play my solos through it sometimes onstage, and it always went over really well. So I wanted it onstage at the Rainbow. So we were playing "Eyes of Silver,"

Pat, three years old, in Aberdeen, WA.
(Courtesy of Pat Simmons)

Tom, 1965, playing a Kent electric in his parents'
living room. *(Courtesy of Tom Johnston)*

Pat, about age thirteen, during a talent show with
Harmony acoustic. *(Courtesy of Pat Simmons)*

Tom in the Mt. Whitney
High School marching
band, Visalia, CA.
(Courtesy of Tom Johnston)

Pat playing an Epiphone at
a friend's place in Half Moon
Bay, CA, 1969.
(Courtesy of Belinda Balaski)

In the backyard on
Twelfth Street, 1970.
The first album lineup.
(Courtesy of Tom Johnston)

The house on Twelfth Street.
Birthplace of the Doobie Brothers.
(Courtesy of Doobie Brothers Archives)

The original lineup, on the porch at the Twelfth Street house.
(© Jim Marshall Photography LLC)

Playing at the Chateau Liberté.
(Courtesy of Doobie Brothers Archives)

An outtake from
The Captain and Me
album cover.
(Courtesy of Magic Studio)

During the Warner Bros. tour in 1975, some
rock royalty visited us backstage; Keith
Richards, Rod Stewart, and Mick Jagger.
(Courtesy of Doobie Brothers Archives)

John Hartman, 1973.
*(Photograph © 2020 by Dan
Fong)*

Tom, 1973. (*Photograph © 2020 Dan Fong*)

Promo shot at the remains of the Sutro Baths near San Francisco, circa 1973.
(Courtesy of Doobie Brothers Archives)

An alternate shot at the Sutro Baths near San Francisco.
(Courtesy of Doobie Brothers Archives)

The night Elton John got up to play with the Doobie Brothers in 1975 during the Warner Bros. European tour. *(Courtesy of Doobie Brothers Archives)*

Rocking out, 1973. (*Photograph by Gijsbert Hanekroot / Getty Images*)

In Zermatt, Switzerland, 1974, when the band posed inside a four-hundred-year-old hay barns for horses used in town.
(Photograph by Michael Ochs Archives / Getty Images)

Bassist Tiran Porter, lost in a groove.

Photograph by Ian Dickson / Getty Images

Tom playing at the Rainbow in London, 1975.

Photograph by Ian Dickson / Getty Images

Near the Cloisters in New York City, 1973.

Photograph by David Gahr / Getty Images

Tom and Pat, rocking hard together in the mind-1970s.
(Courtesy of Doobie Brothers Archives)

At the Record Plant in Sausalito, Jeff "Skunk" Baxter in the middle. Check out the boots!
(Photograph © 2020 by Dan Fong)

Tom with Marlon Brando at the SNACK Benefit Concert put on by Bill Graham (out of frame at right) in San Francisco, 1975.
(Courtesy of Doobie Brothers Archives)

Playing poker on the Doobie Liner. *(Photograph © 2021 by Dan Fong)*

Keith Knudsen on the right and at left Mike "Mazdo" Barbieri, one of the crew guys who did lights on stage every night. *(Photograph © 2021 by Dan Fong)*

Passing time on the
Doobie Liner.
*(Photograph © 2020
by Dan Fong)*

Playing MORE poker
on the Doobie Liner.
*(Photograph © 2021
by Dan Fong)*

Everyone in front of the Doobie Liner, band and crew included.
(Photograph © 2020 by Dan Fong)

An outtake from the *What Were Once Vices Are Now Habits* album cover.

Backstage at
Winterland, 1974.
*(Courtesy of Warner
Records)*

The full band, 1976.
(Courtesy of Warner Records)

Appearing on the *Dinah
Shore Show*, 1976.
Michael McDonald, far
right, had joined the
band by now.
*(Courtesy of Doobie Brothers
Archives)*

A promo shot from about 1980 taken on a back lot at Warner Bros. *(Courtesy of Warner Records)*

With the cast of the TV show *What's Happening!!* in 1978 after taping the now-famous two-part episode, "Doobie or Not Doobie." *(Courtesy of Doobie Brothers Archives)*

The one and only Cornelius Bumpus.
(Photograph © 2020 by Dan Fong)

Bobby LaKind on the Doobie Liner.
(Photograph © 2020 by Dan Fong)

Producer Ted Templeman, and Doobie drummer Keith Knudsen.
(Courtesy of Doobie Brothers Archives)

and that metal sleeve all of a sudden touched the metal part of the bag; the amperage kicked up, and I started getting the shocks whenever I used the effect. It was so funny. It's like that shirt could've killed me if it started running enough current through it.

Anyway, early in my life, I had been affected by rock and roll style after watching the Beatles, Rolling Stones, and other British and San Francisco psychedelic bands playing live, in film, and on TV. I liked the new styles coming from England, and the bands that wore them, and now here I was again being influenced by another British rock star, Marc Bolan.

I would shop in women's clothing stores, and if I saw something I liked, I bought it. I think this was still my kind of lashing out at my parents' conservatism. Wearing clothes that were outrageous was my way of hitting back at conservative attitudes and the strict religious principles that I grew up around. It was also fun going out onstage wearing wild outfits.

And then, of course, we went from clothing to theatrics. Again, I give John a lot of credit for pushing this, but we decided to incorporate explosives that would go off during the last couple of songs and megaclouds generated with dry ice, dissolved in barrels of water. I mean, we weren't Alice Cooper or Kiss or anything, but these effects were pretty big.

Tom

We wanted to start looking the part, especially after being around Marc Bolan, so the two places that I started going to get flashier clothes were called Granny Takes a Trip, which was located in Los Angeles, and the aforementioned Jumpin' Jack Flash in New York City. Those two places had amazing clothes, and I would always go splurge whenever we were in town. Once we started making a few bucks, clothes were definitely something that I was investing in. And rock and roll was getting more theatrical around that time. We were never going to be like David Bowie or T. Rex or Slade or any of those bands. But an upgrade seemed like a good idea. For us, a little bit of style went a long way, and each member of the band started developing his own look, which I thought was really cool.

10

ROCKIN' DOWN THE HIGHWAY

1973–74:

Tom Johnston / Patrick Simmons / John Hartman /
Tiran Porter / Keith Knudsen

Pat

John Hartman loved Keith Moon. I mean, he loved the Who, but he really loved Keith—not just the power of his drumming, but his theatricality. The explosions and all the craziness onstage. That was something John felt we needed to start incorporating. So when we began getting ready for one of our first headline tours, John Hartman came to us and said, "I have an idea. We need to make our show more interesting. So let's start using a lot of smoke and explosions." That was it. The rest of us in the band listened to John, and it made sense. Why not make a bigger show? We played with Alice Cooper and saw what his show was like. I mean, our music was a lot different, but it made sense that you give fans more than they paid for. And I personally always liked watching those big shows. It was just entertaining. So we hired a guy named Marty Wolf, a promoter who worked with a big production outfit in Colorado. Marty told us he could get it together using cups full of flash powder, running positive and negative electrodes through them to generate a spark, and running it all off the batteries—and then BOOM. Marty would send a charge to the wires that was kind of like the explosive pop and ensuing smoke of antique cameras. The idea was to just use the explosions at the back end of the show. Usually, we closed the main set with one of our best rockers, "Without You." And then the encore was "China Grove." So for those two songs, we would set up the explosions and let 'er rip. Once we took that on the road, we realized right away that John had been exactly right. Our fans went crazy over it. It was a little bit weird each night waiting for those things to go off, because we knew basically when they would explode, and sometimes we'd cover our ears. It was always a little bit nerve-racking. But it did help us take our game up to another level.

Tom

Before we got to the "Boom Boom" era and after the T. Rex tour we were playing with many different acts, like Edgar Winter,

Loggins and Messina, Ronnie Montrose, Rare Earth, Redbone, Bob Seger, Jim Croce, Chicago, and Billy Preston. And we did TV shows like *Don Kirshner's Rock Concert* and *Midnight Special* with quite a few different artists and bands. We also did TV shows in London (*Old Grey Whistle Test*); Bremen, West Germany (*Musikladen*), with Stevie Wonder and the Pointer Sisters; and Amsterdam, at a time when pirate radio stations operated on ships off the coast of the Netherlands and several other countries in Europe. It was an exciting time.

One time in '74, we had a day off in London and I'd been invited over to the Who's studio in London to watch the Baker Gurvitz Army. I already knew Paul and Adrian from touring with Three Man Army, so I gladly went to see what it sounded like with Ginger Baker as the drummer. The place was in a funky part of town where the cab wouldn't even drive down the street, and I had to get out and walk a couple of blocks in my high-heeled boots and rock clothes. I stuck out in that neighborhood! Anyway, I got to the studio, which looked like every other building around and had only a small doorbell. So after ringing it, I ended up standing there for about fifteen minutes because they were jamming and couldn't hear the bell, I guess. Paul finally let me in and took me back to the studio, and I had a small reunion with him and Adrian and then I met Ginger Baker. Man, I was a huge fan of this guy, and had loved Cream! His drumming was iconic! Ginger, however, was a bit reclusive and just kept asking me for a cigarette, which he called a "fag" in a thick cockney accent I could barely understand. At first, I thought he was calling me a fag, which didn't go over very well, but Paul jumped in and said he meant a cigarette. Then we just sat and talked after they finished playing. They sounded really good, by the way, and Ginger hadn't lost a step. After a couple of attempts to engage him in conversation, I gave up because he wasn't very talkative and I couldn't understand most of what he said. Adrian then took him to pick up his five-year-old (in a Corvette!), leaving just me and Paul. So he gave me a ride back to the hotel, and that was the end of that story. But at least I had met *the* Ginger Baker.

I can remember that after John brought up the idea of having explosions and what became dry ice "smoke" onstage, our show became a lot more dynamic! And LOUD! Marty Wolf's guys, Walter Finger and Michael Barbieri, took care of the new visual effects, and the result was, shall we say, "explosive." It fit perfectly with the songs we played during the effects: "China Grove" and "Without You," both closer tunes and heavy rockers. I recall that during one show in Europe (Germany, I think), we played at some beautiful place that had frescoes on the walls. Well, when Walter set off the explosions, it cracked a lot of the paintings, and the guy who was overseeing the place came out screaming about what we'd done to his frescoes, and he was looking for some scalps! We used the explosions extensively in the United States on tours for *The Captain and Me* and *What Were Once Vices Are Now Habits,* and the crowds went nuts! They absolutely loved that stuff. It was a powerful boost to the show, and I think we all felt it, even if we were deaf after every show. John Hartman was a happy camper, and his stage outfits became more outrageous to go along with our shows. He dyed his hair platinum blond and wore human-hair wigs on his shoulders, tights painted yellow and green with veins painted on them, and a leather codpiece to complete the ensemble! I loved it!

During those years, this all became part of touring, which we did for long periods of time in the United States and Europe. The venues were bigger, as were the crowds, and we had kind of arrived with big record sales. It was an unexpected and pleasant surprise when we saw how much people in Europe liked us. We never imagined our music would stretch across oceans like that. In our minds, we were just another rock and roll band trying to make it. But when you travel to places like Europe and you see people singing along out in the crowd, then you start to understand what's going on. You start to grasp the idea of just how universal music is and the power it has when it connects with people.

Tiran

Right away, I knew the Doobie Brothers were going to be putting in a lot of miles. That's just what the band was about: existing on the road. So much of that band came together out on the road. We started off in vans and then ultimately went to the Winnebago mobile home. I remember Tom was driving one night and ran the thing into a telephone pole. Pat and I got really close on the road. I would eventually room with him, but I started rooming with Michael Hossack. That was always kind of crazy. I remember one night somewhere in the Midwest when people brought a couple of women back to the hotel room. I looked over at his bed, and he was pulling out a Jesus Christ dildo, so I knew I had to get out of his room. That's when I started rooming with Pat. I surrounded myself with women on the road. That was my vice. I mean, I ended up doing a fair amount of cocaine and other things, but women were really my crutch. I just couldn't get enough of them. I think that's what helped insulate me from a lot of the other craziness on the road. But come on, think about it. You go from being unknown and then all of a sudden all of these gorgeous women are just waiting for you. It's a temptation that I doubt anyone would be able to resist. Me? I always figured, you never know how long this is going to go on, so enjoy it while you can.

11

THE CAPTAIN AND ME

THE CAPTAIN AND ME

On *The Captain and Me,* the follow-up to *Toulouse Street,* the Doobies proved that creating anthemic hit singles was not a onetime deal. Tom Johnston handled lead vocals on seven *The Captain and Me* tracks, including soon-to-be classics "Long Train Runnin'" and "China Grove." Juxta-posing the rough-and-tumble Johnston hits are a pair of country rock ballads crafted by Simmons that quickly and quietly became fan favorites. "Clear as the Driven Snow" and "South City Midnight Lady" perfectly represent the subtle nuance Simmons brought to the band. The balance between Simmons and Johnston on this album is nothing short of majestic.

Pat

Ted brought such great ideas into the studio. I mean, at first none of us were really sure about the guy. He had been in Harpers Bizarre, but we thought we had all of the answers in the studio. As it turned out, he was the one that had most of the answers. He just understood how to get records made. Plus, he played drums, was a really great percussionist, played keyboards, and could sing. You want your producer to be able to do all of those things, because they can relate to what you are trying to do. So Ted just brought so much. When I brought the song "South City Midnight Lady" into the sessions, I had the basic song, the chord structure, and all of the changes and everything. I had this vision of it being kind of longer than it wound up being: lots of sections and departures, this long jazz thing in the middle, and overall kind of countrified. I thought I knew exactly what it needed. Ted heard the song and then decided it needed a string arrangement, which at first I wasn't too sure about. In fact, I didn't like the idea. But then he put it together, and in my opinion it wound up making this song what it is. He just had a great ear for things like that. Jeff Baxter from Steely Dan also played pedal steel guitar on the song, and little did I know that within a couple of years he would actually become a member of the Doobie Brothers. But there was one thing that I think Tommy and I mostly came up with.

Tom

While touring in England, we heard the new Stevie Wonder album *Talking Book*, the first album to have a lot of synthesizer on it. And we loved it. We met him over there while we were on the road, and he was a cool guy—and what a genius at layering keyboard parts as well as vocal lines and harmonies. And God what a voice! Pat and I both agreed that the synthesizer sound was something really special that we wanted on our next record, which was going to be *The Captain and Me*. So we talked to Ted about it, and he tracked down these two guys, Malcolm Cecil and Robert Margouleff. They had worked with Stevie Wonder on the *Talking Book* album, which had really gotten our attention. They came to California from New York to work with us. I have to say that Ted was our secret weapon in the studio. Both on *Toulouse Street* and now on *The Captain and Me*. Whatever ideas you had or wanted to try, Ted would facilitate it and had so many great ideas of his own. Plus, he was fun to work with and could pull the best performances out of everybody in the band. He'd really come into his own as a respected producer both at Warner Bros. and in the business at large.

Pat

Malcolm and Robert were very impressive and a bit eccentric. They had formed something called TONTO's Expanding Head Band, a project based on a unique combination of synthesizers.

It's hard to believe how arcane all of this stuff was back then, but this was really the beginning of this kind of production. They brought out this giant cabinet with quarter-inch plugs and banks of oscillators; each oscillator had a different waveform. There was a rolling waveform and a spike waveform—these guys would combine them and then control the sound with a keyboard. They could get just one note at a time. It was really slow and really tedious but totally worth it once you heard what they were doing. I think you hear the sound best on Tommy's great tune called "Natural Thing."

Tom

The beginning of the song "Natural Thing" features these really interesting and different Roman horn–sounding synthesized chords and notes, which gave the song a very unique feel. Playing the parts was something new for me, and we did harmony tracking with some of the lines we used. There were quarter-inch cables all over the place to get the keyboard to talk to the banks of synthesizers. It was pretty wild at the time, and both Malcolm and Robert were characters in their own right! I think having them in the studio added a cool atmosphere. And Ted was there overseeing the whole session and coming up with ideas. And "Natural Thing" was a departure from any style we had recorded before. Not a lot of American bands were experimenting like this. I'm not sure we ever got much credit for it. People think of us as a kind of straight-ahead rock and roll band. But we were always interested in and incorporating what was happening in the recording world and trying to stay ahead of the curve, using the regular stuff like wah-wah pedals, Echoplex parts, and both phasing and flanging guitar pedals to spice up guitar parts on recording and live stuff. And I remember Pat using the talk box / bag device onstage, which got a cool sound. We also used horn sections on a few of our recordings, working with the White Trash horn section (led by Jerry Jumonville) from Edgar Winter's group (on *Toulouse Street*) and later the Memphis Horns (on *What Were Once Vices Are Now Habits*).

Pat

On "South City Midnight Lady" they played a sound that reminded me of a woman's voice, and I just loved that. I really wanted that on there. The whole process was so crazy to watch. All of these multiple waveforms playing together, triggered by the keyboard. Somehow they got everything to line up and be exact. It was really exciting being on the cusp of new technology like that, but looking back, it seems so primitive.

Ted

"Long Train Runnin'" was originally called "Osborn." I have no fucking idea why, but I always loved it. I loved the riff and I loved the driving nature of it, but it didn't have a framework. I had heard them play it live a bunch of times, and it was just kind of like a jam. So I said to Tommy, "We need to focus and make this about something." And he said, "What should it be about?" And I said, "What the fuck? How about a train?" And that was it. Tommy went off and wrote the lyrics in about a half hour, right there in Amigo. There was another song idea kicking around for a while, which the great piano player Billy Payne added a bridge on, and it sounded Chinese to me. I used to surf at a place called China Ladder, and so I was thinking about the word "China" and "Chinese," and then I see Tommy sitting down with an atlas looking through it alphabetically, and he finds a place in Texas called China Grove. And he said, "I think I got it."

Bill Payne

I always loved playing with those guys. It was an exciting time for both of our bands at that point. Little Feat was busy as well, but I loved the Doobies. What I learned playing in sessions with them is that they were totally open to whatever you wanted to do. There were no rules. The only basic rule was play what you feel, and let's hear how it sounds. In sessions with other bands, there were sometimes egos involved that didn't allow for that kind of environment. It was basically: play this. But with the Doobies, it was the exact opposite. And Ted Templeman definitely had a lot to do with that open and giving spirit. He didn't care where a good idea came from. He just wanted the good ideas. I remember when I played that little bridge on what would become "China Grove," and Ted just freaked out. He loved it. He kept saying that it sounded "Chinese" to him, and I wasn't sure what he meant. Looking back on it, I kind of get it. But at the moment, I had no clue. I just liked that he liked it. And the fact that it sounded Chinese to him actually wound up being pretty important in the development of the song. I got to play on a number of classics during those sessions, including "South City Midnight Lady," "Ukiah," "Without You," and "Dark Eyed Cajun Woman." I had already played with them on the previous album, on the songs "Jesus Is Just Alright," "Rockin' Down the Highway," "Cotton Mouth," and "Don't Start Me to Talkin'." I was totally comfortable and familiar with the guys at this point. And you could tell they had really developed since the last album. I thought *Toulouse Street* was a fine album, and I still do. With *The Captain and Me,* they took everything up a couple of notches. The songwriting was just incredible, and production-wise they were continuing to push the envelope. The fact that I'm playing with the Doobie Brothers today is something I could not be more proud of. And not a night goes by onstage when I don't look over at Tom and Pat and think back to those days so many years ago when we were just starting out and the world was young. They are two of the hardest-working guys I've ever worked with, and two of the most talented as well.

Tom

There was a lot of good stuff emerging on that record. "China Grove" started in my little room on Twelfth Street. I wasn't quite sure what it was. I just had the chords and little else, but

I really liked the chords. That epitomized the rock guitar style, only a heavier version of what we had done up till that point. I remember that after getting the original feel on acoustic in my room, I went and grabbed Hartman and said, "Let's take this song down to the basement and go electric with it." I knew it had to be distorted, so I cranked the amp. We started blasting while I would try some different passing chords, and John would try various drum ideas. We both liked where it was headed, and that's how it stayed till we actually cut the track at Amigo. Either Donn Landee or Ted had the idea of using an echo on the opening chords, an idea I liked a lot! It drove the point home. But I didn't have the lyrics yet, and the thing that really got it going for me was when Billy Payne came up with that Chinese-sounding piano part in the bridge. That sparked my idea for the lyrics, and so I ran with it. Rarely when I sat down to write would I be very specific about things. It would just be what I was feeling at that moment, making up a story on the spot. And then you never know what will get stuck in your brain from being on the road. In this case, it was a leftover from driving toward San Antonio on a tour in '72. There was a road sign that said "China Grove city limits." I completely forgot about that until Billy played that piano line. And even then I didn't remember the road sign, but that's where the idea for the sheriff and the samurai sword came from. The rest I just filled in with lyrics about this make-believe town and its inhabitants. As an aside, I remember catching a cab not long after "China Grove" started getting played on the radio. I was in Houston, Texas, and the driver said to me, "Why did you write a song about that little town?" And I said to him, "What little town are you talking about?" I had not even remembered the road sign and had thought I had made it up. Well . . . I guess not! For me, I'm usually just writing about a general feeling that I had. Like Ukiah. I was always a big fan of fresh air and camping. That's what that song is about. When it came time to actually record "China Grove," I was hanging out with a couple of the guys in Three Dog Night's crew up in Laurel Canyon. It got a little crazy, and I came back to the studio pretty stoned. I'm really thankful for the patience everybody had in the studio with me that day. They had to come get me up at the house in Laurel Canyon.

Pat

I know that for a lot of Doobie Brothers fans, *The Captain and Me* is the definitive album. It's one of my favorites, too. I love "Dark Eyed Cajun Woman" because I think on that one Tom really got in touch with his blues side, which is a big part of his musical style. I mean, that sounded like an authentic blues song because Tom is just such an authentic player.

Tom

We finally turned "Long Train Runnin'" into a finished song after playing it live for years with no lyrics other than the phrase "without love." Ted had the idea of writing about a train, and that was the spark that got me to finish the lyrics "Miss Lucy down along the track" and so on. It was a cool rhythm song that lent itself to great drums and percussion. After recording it with lyrics, it was performed live as a more defined jam song than it had been previously. I played a harp solo on it, and Pat came up with a great picking part that worked perfectly with the rhythm I was playing, which really brought the song to another level. It helped define the song. Then Pat and Tiran and I put the harmonies on the chorus after I had laid down the lead vocal, and it was done.

The song "The Captain and Me" was sort of a leftover from the early *Toulouse Street* days. I spent the time to make it a more lyrical song by weaving together whatever floated through my mind. It featured picking parts at the front, which were like Crosby, Stills & Nash; semi-rock parts in the B sections, with harmony lines we all sang; and at the end a driving rhythm, strumming, and percussion behind some cool harmony lines that morphed into a sung "do, do, do" rhythm part.

Another song that was special for me was "Dark Eyed Cajun Woman." Having come from a blues background, I finally got to write and record an actual pure blues tune. It felt so good! It was a tip of the hat to B.B. King in style, its lyrics featuring a story about a girl down in New Orleans. And I loved playing a solo that was an actual purist blues solo to cap it off.

Pat's tune "Clear as the Driven Snow" is one of my favorite tunes he had written to that point, and was a great song for this album. And it was strong! It incorporated his unique picking style, cool chord changes and lyrics, plus a big, dynamic, rocking solo section. Just a great song all around.

I've said that we never wrote songs as a complement to other songs already written, that we just wrote, and whatever worked best is what got used. But I thought this song fit the other tunes on the album like a glove.

Pat's song "Evil Woman" had the opposite effect: it was one of the harder rock songs we ever cut. It added an element that we hadn't tried, which was to rock but over a complex guitar line. So, again, we were stretching ourselves.

"South City Midnight Lady," besides being a fan favorite live and very pretty song, sort of brings in that Moby Grape influence a little bit.

"Without You" was a complete ode to the Who. We had fooled around with the idea at rehearsals, but it really came together in the studio and was one of the few tracks we ever cut "live in the studio." Everyone had a part in this song as far as the writing went, and it still kicks ass live to this day!

"Ukiah" was really a story about hanging around and camping in Northern California towns like Mendocino, Fort Bragg, and Ukiah in the early '70s, as I used to do during and after college. Brings back great memories of being out in nature and by the ocean camping. When we play it live, it's preceded by "Busted Down Around O'Connelly Corners," which is a cool little picking thing Pat did on that album.

As far as the album cover goes, it's definitely a special album cover for us. And the artwork set the tone. After kicking a bunch of ideas around in the office of Ted Templeman's assistant, Benita Brazier, the shoot date was set, and the art department at Warner Bros. had this idea to get us out on

Interstate 5 right by where it crosses California State Route 14 near Sylmar. Just on the edge of the San Fernando Valley and right after the earthquake in '71 had happened, leaving the overpass half there after part of it collapsed in the quake. And then they went to the costume department on the Warner Bros. studio lot and came out with top hats, coats, and tails reminiscent of nineteenth-century England. They also brought a carriage (like a stagecoach) and a team of horses, complete with handlers. There was a big old table for us to sit around, which ended up on the centerfold. They even brought some old-style coffins for one of the vampire ideas that got floated. I can remember looking over the edge of the freeway, where it had collapsed a few times. It was a long way down from up there! It was a really crazy shoot, but fans love it to this day. Michael and Jill Maggid, a talented husband-wife photography and design team we'd worked with before, did the photography again. By this time, they really had a good idea just what our albums should look and feel like. It definitely stands the test of time. It also introduced two songs to the world that helped define the early Doobie Brothers sound. I love that "Long Train Runnin'" and "China Grove" still get played on the radio a lot. It always takes me back to that little bedroom on Twelfth Street in San Jose. Some of the music I wrote there changed our lives and helped make the band successful. A major tour was booked for pretty much the rest of the year, and so there was no turning back.

Pat

Ted Templeman's assistant Benita Brazier put the photo shoot together. As I recall, John Hartman was the one who got the idea going. We all sat around brainstorming, and as the concept began to take shape, we all started throwing in ideas: coach, horses, top hats, vampires, gothic, banquet table, creepy stuff. The freeway ramp we are standing on had collapsed during the Sylmar earthquake in 1971 and had yet to be rebuilt. It was a complete surprise to me when I got there. All the costumes and props, the coach and horses, and the wranglers to handle the animals and harness them to the coach came from the Warner Bros. movie studios in Burbank. Somebody from the record label pulled some strings and helped us make it happen. Arguably our most interesting album cover, it was certainly the most complicated production in my estimation.

12

CLEAR AS THE DRIVEN SNOW

Pat
___

So in 1973 we got our own plane. Nothing fancy, an old Martin 404. We dubbed it the Doobie Liner. The Doobie Liner had our eagle logo on it. And eventually we had a plane for the crew called the Crewbie Liner, which had a buzzard. It was so funny that we had a plane just for the crew. But honestly, we needed it. We were always on the move, always on the road, and so while it might've seemed a bit frivolous, in the end I think it saved us a lot of money and certainly a lot of headaches. We could create our own little universe on the plane and not worry about crowded airports, flight delays, or anything like that. The Martin was piloted by Sam Stewart. He was our guy. He got us through thick and thin.

Tom

When we became headliners in about 1973, we decided to lease our own plane, the Doobie Liner, which was painted accordingly with the logo. By that time there were a variety of rock and roll jets, including the infamous Starship, that bands could lease while they were on the road, so we thought it made more sense financially given the amount of touring. We had started to make more money, but we weren't the Rolling Stones or Led Zeppelin, so we opted for something more modest. The Doobie Liner was a Martin 404, which was an old twin-engine mid-range prop plane that had formerly been an airliner. That plane made it possible for us to tour the way we did, since we no longer had to race through airports trying to catch commercial flights. We could sleep a little bit more, because we knew that plane was waiting for us.

A funny incident regarding sleeping in is that our drummer Keith Knudsen, who had definitely slept in one day, missed the plane call. So everyone was kind of worried about him and the gig that night, but as Sam was taxiing the plane, low and behold there was Keith with his thumb out and his suitcase sitting there on the runway. Fucking hilarious! So we stopped, picked him up, and away we went. You could fly direct to places. You could leave clothes and other things on board and not worry about it. It was kind of like having a flying hotel room. You could sleep, play cards, shoot the shit, or work on music. Whatever you wanted to do. Obviously, a plane could also get you in a little bit of trouble. Let's say a girl got on board and then flew to the next city with you and maybe her family didn't know about it. That was also part of rock and roll back then. Whether it was a band member or a crew member or whoever, occasionally stuff like that went on. But for the most part, the Doobie Liner was a practical and functional part of our band that allowed us to be the road dogs that we were becoming. We had very aggressive tour schedules that could easily result in a couple of hundred shows a year, and the routing sometimes made it impossible to go by bus or commercial flight. So with Sam Stewart, our trusty pilot, and our trusty stewardess, Faye (and with Sam's wife, Donna, occasionally filling that role), we had our very own coach in the sky. We also eventually had a second plane called the Crewbie Liner to make sure that our crew, who often had a different schedule from ours, could also get where they needed to be on time. I think it's worth pointing out that these planes were not some luxury jet like we see bands use today; it was more about convenience. The Doobie Liner just made life easier. No more commercial hassles. It gave us a lot of freedom, but we didn't realize there were inherent dangers that came with using the plane. It was old, and although Sam was on top of the maintenance of the plane, there were some unexpected repair issues, mostly engine-related. We lost an engine coming into Detroit once, when it was really windy in the middle of a big thunderstorm. I looked out the window and saw the prop feathered, and there was smoke coming out of it, and the plane rolled a little to that side. Sam said calmly over the radio, "Everyone strap in; we just lost an engine, and we will be making an emergency landing." It was stuff like this that was portrayed in *Almost Famous* that, whether it was meant to or not, was eerily accurate.

I recall a trip inside Canada to play a show. Going in was fine, and the customs folks were chill. Coming back into the United States, however, was another story. Our road manager at the time went around to everyone on the plane and told us to get rid of any drugs, usually weed or hash, because the U.S. customs folks had a reputation for being over the top. That turned out to be accurate, and they went through the plane with a vengeance. Had a dog that ran up and down inside the plane, checked out the chemical toilet, took the band members into their headquarters and did a "pat down," and in some cases a strip search, which was ridiculous after going through everyone's luggage.

The worst part about the whole thing is that although none of the band members had anything illegal, our road manager, Jack, who had a legal bottle of Librium, had forgotten to remove a small amount of hash he'd stashed in the bottle. Well, that was all it took for the customs agents who found it. This probably preceded the pat and search we'd all gone through. And what made it worse is they came after Sam and started taking the cowling off the engines, or at least that's what I heard. We relied on Sam; he was a solid pilot and person and was a sweetheart most of the time, but this put his license to operate as a pilot in jeopardy, and that really pissed him off, which I believe he explained in pretty graphic terms to Jack!

It all subsided with Warner Bros. interceding on our behalf, and afterward we were allowed to leave, but it was a sore spot for a while with Sam and Jack.

13

ROAD ANGEL

Tom

I finally moved out of the place on Twelfth Street in 1973 and bought a house in Fairfax, a little town in Marin County. It was a great neighborhood; Elvin Bishop and Van Morrison lived in Fairfax as well. I ran into them at Nave's, a club down on Bolinas in Fairfax, and we ended up back at my place jamming for a couple of hours. Of course, I wasn't home that much because we were basically on the road all the time, but I do remember one night when Freddie King was playing a place nearby in San Anselmo called the Lion's Share. I had to go see him; he was one of my guitar heroes! He was onstage doing his set, and about halfway through his amp blew up. I heard him yell to someone in the crew, which was pretty small, and even though he had no clue who I was, I walked up and said, "Hey man, I live nearby and I've got a Fender Twin. I'll be right back." I ran home and brought him back the amp so he could finish the show. He was a good guy and grateful for the assist. We talked for a little while before they took off. I have often wondered why he didn't have a guitar tech with a spare amp, but that's the way it happened. The next time I saw Freddie was at the show in Knebworth, England. He just showed up in a Rolls-Royce to watch the show with the Allman Brothers. A lot of what went on back then became a blur because of all the travel, bookings, and time in the studio, since we were doing an album a year. I am amazed that we found the time to write all the songs, but we did.

I also ditched my brown Volkswagen bug and got a red 1973 Audi sedan, my VW bug dying as I drove it onto the Audi lot. We were moving up in the world a little, but I still never thought of us as "rock stars." We were still basically semi-anonymous musicians that toured endlessly. But that would all change.

Pat

By the time we were doing *The Captain and Me* tour, there was money coming in, and so I got rid of my MG and bought a pickup truck along with a home in the Santa Cruz Mountains: about five acres that I paid, I think, $50,000 for. I had this dream of living in the country. As a kid, I grew up in suburbia, but on my mother's side we had cattle ranchers, and I really loved the idea of that lifestyle. So I bought chickens and goats, and that was how I dealt with having some money coming in. But we were gone so much of the year, I didn't even have that much time at the house. But I loved where it was, because there was a small commuter airport nearby, and now that we were recording in Los Angeles, I could fly down for about thirteen dollars each way. Flights were like every hour. The round-trip ticket was cheaper than staying in a hotel. So I commuted a lot. We would typically start working at around noon. We would go for about six hours, because that's about what your ears could take. Your ears literally get tired after about six hours, fatigued from all the listening and volume. You need a break. It's taxing on your audio-nervous system. So I flew back and forth all the time, and it was really easy. And, that way, I could really enjoy my new home and property given that we were on the road for the rest of the year.

Tiran

The Doobie Liner was a hell of a way to travel. All of a sudden, we weren't slaves to any sort of timetable, which is what happens when all you do is fly commercial. But it wasn't a luxury jet or anything. It was a pretty basic plane, but it was still a plane, and it was ours. It was like our home away from home. Just like a tour bus but with wings. For the most part, I felt safe. But I do remember a time—I think it was Thanksgiving—flying to Detroit, and the left engine went out. Our pilot, Sam, got on the intercom and told us to buckle down. I thought it was the end. We were surrounded by a crazy electrical storm and experienced the roughest landing I've ever had in my life. After we landed, Sam came over the intercom and said to the flight attendant, "Get me a double right away and a change of underwear, please."

Tom

On Labor Day weekend 1974, we were playing a show in Norfolk, Virginia. During our set, some cops came and spoke to a manager and alerted him that our plane was on fire. We went out there to check out the wreckage after the show, and it was pretty complete. So we had to get a new plane, which took a couple of days. For a while, part of the old plane's nose was salvaged and ended up stuck on the wall at a restaurant in San Francisco called the Caribbean Zone.

By the end of 1973, we were booked to play on the very first *Don Kirshner's Rock Concert* at Madison Square Garden. Led Zeppelin had performed a regular show that night, and we came in after the show was over to tape our segment of *Rock Concert*. Edgar Winter's band, which had Ronnie Montrose on guitar and Dan Hartman on bass and vocals, was also on that show. By the time they'd flipped the house after Zeppelin and we began filming the show, it was the early morning. I spent some time jamming with Ronnie Montrose in the dressing room backstage. The premiere episode was also going to include performances by the Rolling Stones, which was cool for us. We started doing a lot of television at that point, shows like

In Concert and *Midnight Special* being the big ones for us. The shows featured a lot of big names who were popular and pushing songs at the time, and the viewing audience was huge, so it was a great way to extend our reach and be introduced to a lot of people who had maybe never seen us live.

Pat

As I recall, the first show we did was with Earth, Wind & Fire and Edgar Winter. We came in around 4:00 AM, after playing a gig in town somewhere, since that was the time Kirshner was able to get to the venue for the shoot. The next one we did was months later. This was with the Stones. They lip-synched their new single, "Angie." That was all they did, lucky for us. I love the Stones, but it was kind of a corny video. We, on the other hand, played live for like four or five songs, rocking pretty hard. We might've even used our special effects as well. It was a major coup for us. Everybody was tuning in to see the Rolling Stones, but we were able to better connect with the viewing audience. This was early-era music TV, the first network program to present longer-form, multisong special music events. We were so fortunate to get the shot. Another gift from our record label.

The 1973 tour to support *The Captain and Me* was major. We played with a lot of different bands. We did a bunch of shows with Steely Dan. Then we did a run with Steve Miller and Dr. Hook & the Medicine Show. There were also shows with Frank Zappa, Rare Earth, Mike Bloomfield, Chicago, the

Beach Boys, Loggins and Messina, Jim Croce, Foghat, It's a Beautiful Day, and others. We even did a few gigs with Hot Tuna and Quicksilver Messenger Service, which was always nice because we loved to play with Bay Area bands that we grew up with. We did some tapings for the *Midnight Special* and ABC's *In Concert* in early 1973 to help promote "Jesus Is Just Alright," "Listen to the Music," and "Natural Thing." And then pretty soon we had a new addition to our band, not a musician, but somebody who really became invaluable.

Tom

Dan Fong was one of the guys who, even though he was not a musician, became like part of the band. He fed us, photographed us, and handled most of our media stuff. In short, he did the job of three people nowadays. And his photography and videos kept a visual record of the band that has been used extensively in documentaries about the various stages of the band and was used quite a bit in the Rock & Roll Hall of Fame presentation. So he is a valuable guy who was with the band for quite a while.

Pat

Dan was definitely a key part of our team for a number of years. It was unique to have a guy like him on the road, because he wore many important hats, starting with the food, ha ha.

Dan

I guess I was probably born to be in rock and roll. I got to know the legendary promoter Barry Fey while I was living in Colorado. I started catering for lots of the bands he was working with, and in 1972 I catered what I think is still a fairly legendary luau feast when the Rolling Stones came through town. I worked with a lot of different bands, catering, photographing, and just basically doing what they needed when they were in town. And so when the Doobie Brothers hired me to go on the road, I was really excited. But I was nervous as well.

It's one thing to be doing everything in your own backyard. You know all the players and you've made all of your important connections to make sure bands got whatever they needed. But going on the road was going to be something entirely different. And I was handed out a lot of different responsibilities. I can't even imagine today anybody going on the road with a major band and doing all that I was doing. It was just a different world. They nicknamed me General Fong. My official title was "media coordinator," but there was a lot that came under that heading. When they were hitting the road in 1973, I packed my bags and never looked back. Everything would start up in San Francisco, where the Doobie Liner, their private prop plane, would pick up the band and whoever else lived in the area. Then it came to Denver to pick up me and the guys on the lighting crew who were also based there. For my very first trip, my folks came and saw me off at the airport. I think they were a little concerned when what looked like an Indiana Jones plane pulled up, and I made my way to climb up the staircase at the back of the plane. My dad was a military guy, and I think he wanted that for me as well, to go into the military. But it just wasn't in the cards. Most of my friends had been drafted and had to go to Vietnam, but my draft number was 330, so they never got to me, thank goodness. And on that first day the big adventure began, when I turned around and said goodbye to my folks, I didn't have any idea what lay ahead for me. We stopped in Illinois to refuel after leaving Denver and then made our way toward LaGuardia Airport in New York, where the tour was going to begin. Well, there was wind and rain that was so bad that we couldn't even land there. I thought to myself, this is what a rock and roll tour is like? The plane was being pushed all over the sky. Even the band members, who I'm sure were used to things like this, were looking very concerned. There were maybe thirty of us on board, and you could hear a pin drop inside the plane. The pilot, Sam Stewart, came over the radio and said, "Everybody, I need everybody to buckle up at once. This is going to be a motherfucker." Do you have any idea what it's like when the pilot is telling you that it's going to be a motherfucker? I was already beginning to regret my decision. But Sam flies down to Newark Airport, where they think they can get us in. And it's crazy outside. The wind and the thunder and lightning and the rain are heavy and relentless. We do a couple of passes over the airport, and then he comes over again and says, "Okay, we're going to give this a shot." A shot? What the fuck? Well, Sam, brilliant pilot that he is, lands this plane, and it's almost sideways as we get to the ground because of the wind. I'm in the tail, all the way back, sitting at the rear of the plane. I can feel the tail swinging out right, and I know we're not landing straight. But it didn't matter, because we were landing. The second that plane came to a stop, everybody on board began whistling and cheering because we knew how close it had been. And then Sam comes back over the radio and says to everyone in the cabin, summoning the stewardess, who I think was his wife, "Babe, can you bring me some new underwear?" His usual line during rough landings. And we all laughed our asses off. There were several other times when things got dicey in the skies, but Sam always got the job done.

My primary responsibility on the road was going to be feeding the band. I planned out every meal, and I always wanted things to be special to keep the guys happy. So, for instance, whenever we would land in Boston, I would head straight to the wharf and buy forty or so of the best Maine lobsters they had. Or I would go visit the freshest markets to get vegetables for my famous Chinese stir-fry. I would call promoters to find out what the best restaurants were and who could stay open late for us or cater meals if we needed them at the drop of a hat. Before the internet, it was a lot more time-consuming, but I really enjoyed it. Each day, I would get a thousand dollars in cash from management, and that would pay for everything for that day and night. Lunches and dinners for both the crew and the band, booze, after-show parties—whatever we needed. I had to make that money work each day. I was working from about 9 AM each day to 3 AM the next morning. That's just how it was. The Doobie Brothers maintained one of the most grueling schedules that I think any band in history ever had. The basic working theory from the record company seemed to be this: work six days a week and then get Mondays off. Oftentimes, they'd be in six different cities in six days. I remember hearing somebody from the label once say, "Play to one million kids, and you sell one million records." So there were very few breaks in the action. We were always on the road. In addition to my responsibilities as a chef, I also became the band's official photographer. That was really what I enjoyed most. I had been shooting for years and to have that kind of access to the Doobie Brothers was special.

When we weren't on the road, I was commuting every week to the San Francisco area. I think the band wanted me to move out there, but I didn't want to do that. It seemed that everybody out there got hooked on booze or addicted to drugs or divorced. It just didn't seem like the healthiest living environment for me, so I decided to commute. I'd spend a whole week there, flying home on Friday evenings. Instead of keeping a permanent home there, I decided that I would rather stay in John Hartman's spider-infested garage studio apartment or, more favorably, the wonderful Miata Hotel in San Francisco. We would have meetings all week, looking at different album cover designs, discussing media strategies, going through photographs, and more. A lot of the responsibility for building the band's image fell on me, and I loved how much responsibility the Doobie Brothers gave me. The band, and the entire organization, was like a brotherhood—an extended family. It reminded me a lot of what I heard the Grateful Dead was all about.

I always loved it when the band was rehearsing at SIR Studios in San Francisco, because it seemed like every time I went over there to visit all of the other local bands, from Santana to Journey to Tower of Power, were also rehearsing there. There was this big common area with a pool table where everybody hung out, and it was just amazing being there with so many talented musicians. I shot tons of photos of everybody there during that time. One of the perks of the job was meeting lots of interesting people, and SIR never disappointed.

We had many memorable experiences on the road. But I have to say that an airplane with the words DOOBIE BROTHERS stenciled on the side of it became a target for law enforcement. I don't think we were doing anything that different than most other bands on the road. There was a lot of alcohol, a fair amount of drugs, and lots of women. You could not be a big touring act in the mid-1970s and not have at least some of that going on all around you.

But the name the Doobie Brothers really attracted the law, simply because of the fact that it felt like such an easy target. Many cops figured that, because of the name, we were just doing more than any other band, which really was not true. I mean, we were hitting it pretty hard, but everybody was back then.

I remember that one time in 1974, we did a show in Toronto and then flew back to the United States to do a show in Buffalo.

We landed at a private airport, and I got out and took a car to the main airport to organize the rental cars so we could get from the plane to the gig. By the time I got back to the plane, there were customs guards and drug-sniffing dogs surrounding the plane. It was crazy. I forget what happened exactly, but they wound up arresting the tour manager for having a little bit of hash and they also found a joint in the toilet and, I think, a couple of seeds in between the seats. They were going to impound the plane and throw the tour manager in jail. It was crazy. Warner Bros. took care of everything: bailed the tour manager out and got the plane released so we could continue the tour that night. But you just never knew when that was going to happen.

14

BLACK WATER

1974–75:

**Tom Johnston / Patrick Simmons / John Hartman /
Tiran Porter / Keith Knudsen / Jeff "Skunk" Baxter**

Pat

This being the Doobie Brothers, there was, of course, another personnel change by the time we got to the next album. While we started working on *Vices,* Michael Hossack left the band and joined another outfit called Bonaroo. We all knew a guy named Keith Knudsen who around then was drumming with Lee Michaels. We had met Keith during those original demo sessions in San Mateo before we got signed to Warner Bros. He was in one of the other bands that was vying for a record-label attention and didn't get it. Keith was a great player and a great singer and pretty quickly established himself as one of the Doobie Brothers.

When we went in to record *What Were Once Vices Are Now Habits* in 1974, we got the Memphis Horns—in terms of horns, we had already used Jerry Jumonville and his horn section from White Trash on *Toulouse Street,* and also the incredible keyboardist Bill Payne of Little Feat came in to play with us again. We brought in the fabled New Orleans piano man James Booker; percussionist Milt Holland on tabla, marimba, and pandeiro; Eddie Guzman on conga and timbales; Arlo Guthrie on autoharp; and, most important of all, Steely Dan guitarist Jeff "Skunk" Baxter on pedal steel, who had first appeared as a sideman on *The Captain and Me.* For us, the band was like an extended family of musicians, which is what I think made us different. Everything was focused on what will make the band sound better. We didn't make it about our own individual personalities. I also had a riff for a song that I played for Ted at a recording session, just fooling around the studio doing overdubs, and Ted said, "What is that?" I said, "It's just a riff I've been fooling around with." And Ted said, "It's really catchy; you should write a song around that."

Tom

It seems to happen that after a few big hits, the expectations continue to rise. By now we were on the road most of the year, only taking a break to go into the studio with Ted (who by now was essentially part of the band, helping to guide, shape, and mold everything we did in the studio). So when we started *Vices,* we had a few song ideas and the rest got fleshed out as we continued to record.

I already had "Another Park, Another Sunday" written on acoustic as an idea left over from my Twelfth Street days about an old girlfriend from that period, so I just continued to work on the lyric. Pat came up with great guitar parts and a solo that was a perfect fit for the feel of the song. Tiran developed a great bass part that was kind of a departure for him—it worked great and helped drive the song. And on this song Tiran also contributed a really cool guitar part he played through a Leslie that added such a nice feel to the track and was a great fit with Milt Holland's vibes. We came up with the harmony ideas with some direction from Ted, and the song fell into place.

I had the idea for the "Eyes of Silver" guitar line and rhythm started and was fleshing it out with the drummers and Tiran. Bill Payne added his magic on organ, and Ted had the idea to bring in the Memphis Horns, which added such a spark! I loved their work on so many great Stax and Atlantic records from musicians like Otis Redding, Aretha Franklin, Eddie Floyd, Al Green, and others. It ended up being kind of a Doobie Brothers soul tune, and the horns also played on "Song to See You Through," which was a labor of love for me. It was my tribute to Otis Redding and the Stax rhythm section. It also had Bill Payne on organ. It was a departure for me to play guitar on the intro and harmony lines along with the rhythm, as well as to sing the vocal. Mike

Hossack played a drum style right out of Memphis. It sounded like Al Jackson, and that merged with Tiran's bass part. Pat had a cool picking part in the breakdown that made it a Doobie Brothers song, and our harmonies were distinctly the Doobies. Then you add the Memphis Horns playing something right off an Otis Redding–type recording, and it became a really cool Doobies soul tune. One of my favorites off that album.

Pat wrote a song that featured some distinctive guitar lines on "You Just Can't Stop It" that were different from our previous albums. Eddie Guzman (from Rare Earth) played congas. And it was also kind of R&B but different. Bill Payne played clavinet, Tiran played some funky bass lines, and I ended up singing the vocal, but we built vocal lines around it that would start in unison and split into harmony at the end of the line. I think Pat's guitar parts/lines are what make this song different. And the horns played a non-Memphis kind of horn line. It all fit together, with Ted driving the direction.

Breaking the rest of the songs down, "Spirit" was a totally different song from most of the other tracks except "Black Water," just for its acoustic-only guitar sound. Picking at the front and the body of the verse rhythm was the "chunka" style. Pat played a complementary picking part, and the two really carried the song. Bass and drums were different as well in that this song had almost a hoedown kind of feel on the intros and the outro. I think this song might have gotten its start on Twelfth Street as well. The harmony singing parts were all Doobie Brothers, and the overall feel was an early Doobies kind of feel. Great song live.

"Tell Me What You Want" reminds me of something from the earlier Doobies as well. Pat's vocal style, guitar rhythms, and harmony lines, Jeff Baxter's steel guitar. It has a lilting rhythm, almost an island feel. Tiran's bass and Mike's drum pattern and Milt Holland's tabla part in the breakdown just carry it along. Lots of different rhythms and a pretty melody with Doobies harmonies. Great song and distinctively Pat.

"Down in the Track" is a blues shuffle with edge. It's got a driving guitar part to start that continues through the song and blues-style fills. The bass is a blues shuffle with Tiran's style touches, and the drums drive it home. The standout drum and bass intro are really cool. Ted, Mike, and Tiran came up with that intro, and it's an original. The breakdown features a piano legend out of New Orleans named James Booker that Ted magically located after he supposedly just got out of prison. He played the coolest blues piano lines in the breakdown. After I got the vocal done, we added three-part harmonies on the chorus, and it became a driving and edgy Doobies blues tune.

"Pursuit on 53rd Street" and "Road Angel" are out-and-out rockers.

"Pursuit" is a dance hall rocker on which Bill Payne plays rock and roll piano. Everything is solid, but I have to say that, even with the harmonies, it's just not a standout track. The lyrics I came up with weren't anything special. It's a party song.

"Road Angel" is, to me, the quintessential Doobie Brothers rock song. It has a taste of Hendrix at the top, chunka-chunka rhythm, harmony vocals, and guitar lines. Great dynamics in the breakdown that build to an isolated, wailing rhythm guitar that has distorted guitar accents from Pat. The drums and bass are kicking, and Mike put in some fancy footwork on the kick pattern in the breakdown. You add in Eddie Guzman's congas and it's all about rhythm.

The lyrics are simple but really speak to being on the open road and feeling free to cut loose. Tip of the hat to riding motorcycles. Both Pat and I take solos, and it's just an all-hands-on-deck rocker written by everybody. Great live tune!

"Daughters of the Sea" is a great song, and it's underappreciated in my opinion. It's got great lyrics, good chord changes, a driving bass line in the verses, and a good half-time B-section breakdown. Pat is playing some great guitar lines, and it has great harmonies. The percussion on this tune is perfect, with Eddie Guzman on timbales and congas, which really drives it, along with Milt Holland playing marimba during the lead section. This would be a good live tune as well.

"Flying Cloud" was written by Tiran and features him playing guitar and bass. It also has some synth lines in it, and to be honest it hits me as a perfect stoner song. It's pleasant to listen to and different from anything else on the album.

"Black Water" was the first number one hit the band ever had! It was Pat's ode to New Orleans and his experiences there. From what I've heard from Pat, he had this lick, which is the intro and body of the song. Ted kept saying you ought to develop that into a song and kind of gave him some direction when Pat would come up with ideas. It's such an infectious tune and melody that sticks in your head, which is always a good sign. The viola part that Novi Novog played on it is a signature line in itself. Arlo Guthrie played autoharp on the intros, and Milt played vibraphone. I think one of the hookiest parts of this song is the breakdown and call-and-response vocals. It's an instant crowd-pleaser, and they love to sing along with it at shows! Just a great song that made its own way onto radio after "Another Park" was pulled. Being the flipside tune, I guess the guys in Roanoke, Virginia, decided to give it a shot, and it really took off! Which was mirrored in Minneapolis, as I recall. Pretty soon it was everywhere. What a great story!

I look at this album as marking growth for the band after *Captain and Me,* since it went in different directions and tried out new things musically.

Ted

I mean, to be honest with you, I never really knew what the hit records were going to be. I was usually wrong. "Black Water" I put on the B side just to get Pat some songwriter royalties. I figured the A side would do well: "Another Park, Another Sunday." But in the end that single didn't do that well. Beautiful song, but you just never know how it's going to happen. Jumping ahead a few years, it was the same thing when we finished recording "What a Fool Believes." I heard nothing in that song. To me, it was a mess. Never really got it—to me it just went all over the place looking for some kind of direction but never found it. When I played it for the rest of the staff of Warner Bros., everybody said to me, are you out of your fucking mind? Maybe I was. To be honest, I still don't hear it today. Even though it went on to win a Grammy, I don't hear it. To me, it's a good record but not a great record. But I did enjoy recording "Black Water." It had a lot of interesting parts, and the thing I always loved about both Pat and Tommy was how open they were to my ideas. We never really sat there thinking, okay, let's make a hit record. It was all about just making sure the records sounded good and had personality. "Black Water" had so many different moving parts and sounds and vocals that it was just a blast for everybody. But a hit record? Give me a break. How on earth could that wind up being a number one record? You just never know. As crazy as the music business is and as brutal as it can be sometimes, it also can surprise you. The fact that that record blew up the way it did was one of those great surprises. That's the kind of moment that really gives you faith in things.

Pat

We were playing some shows down around the Carolinas, Georgia, Florida, and Louisiana. We were in New Orleans and had some days off, so we stayed there. It was like our hub for that part of the tour. One morning, I was on the streetcar that goes up to Saint Charles through the Garden District where all the beautiful mansions and Tulane University are. I was taking the streetcar up there to do my laundry, and I was feeling great. It was raining outside, but the sun was constantly shining, just like it does in the south. It was a very evocative moment, hot and sticky with the rain to cool things down a little bit. It was just so beautiful. I was carrying a pad of paper in my pocket and started writing lyrics down on the streetcar, thinking of that riff Ted had liked so much . . . "If it rains I don't care don't make no difference to me I'll take the streetcar that's going uptown . . ." I was just scribbling ideas down as I did my laundry, and then a song started to take shape. I was thinking of the Mississippi River and tried to paint a little bit of Mark Twain, "Well I built me a raft, and it's ready for floatin'." I was feeling that Tom Sawyer vibe. I would go out at night and listen to Dixieland, and at that time there were good clubs in the French Quarter where you could hear lots of jazz. They had real traditional bands—clarinets, drums, trombones, trumpet, banjo, tubas—and it was just amazing. That was part of my experience there at that time—"I wanna hear some funky Dixieland." It was such a great time in my life. Just strolling through the French Quarter was such a great experience. Like a tourist, I wanted to reflect it. The French market where I'd enjoy my gumbo and chicory coffee—the whole mood there was affecting this new song. It's very multicultural in New Orleans, a real melting pot, and I loved that. So this song was born that way.

The next time we were back in the studio, I showed everyone what I had and we started building upon it. I had thought about actually bringing in some Dixieland musicians, but Ted thought it might be better to do something a cappella. All of a sudden, we were playing yet another classic American music form, street-corner doo-wop. In my head, it was a cool night and we were a bunch of guys standing around a garbage can on fire.

I loved how the sessions went. One day, Ted called me and said, "Hey, Arlo Guthrie is down here today. Would you mind if we put a little autoharp at the beginning of "Black Water"? I thought that was a great idea. And then there was the viola playing alongside as well. For me, this song was a labor of love. I never thought for a moment that it had any real commercial potential, but that was okay. That's not why we made music. As kind of a favor, Ted suggested we put it on the B side of Tom's great single "Another Park, Another Sunday." That way, I could get some publishing dollars out of it, which I appreciated. And then that was it. We finished the album and hit the road as usual. At some point when we were in Europe, we got the strangest message. Something was going on back home with "Black Water." It seemed there was this little radio station down in Roanoke, Virginia. Not far from the station was an actual river called Black Water River. Because of that, the station started playing the B side, and the local folks loved it—so much so that word got out about this quirky little B side, and then somehow it caught fire. We had our first number one record.

That time period was when we had started using dry-ice "smoke" onstage, usually toward the end of the show, and it was pretty thick when used. We enhanced it with explosions (which were getting pretty LOUD) for the start of "China Grove" and sometimes at the end as well. We may have used it on another song as well, but that's the one I remember. Traveling in the Doobie Liner and always on the road, this shot really captures that era.

Dan

The first album cover I was going to work on would wind up being *What Were Once Vices Are Now Habits*. My idea for it involved taking a photograph looking straight down on the band from the ceiling of the venue, which that particular night was going to be in Kentucky. It was December 4, 1973, and the band was playing at Western Kentucky University in Bowling Green. It was going to be a very complicated photo to take, so I got to the venue early and climbed up the scaffolding with a spot meter so I could check what the lighting was going to be like up there. In those days of shooting film, you have to plan out what you were going to need. That night, when the band was in the middle of their epic show closing, which usually featured the songs "Without You" and "China Grove," with all kinds of smoking explosions going off, I got the shots that I thought would work. I soon presented them to management, and everybody flipped out. They just loved them, and I felt really good about that.

Tom

Absolutely one of my favorite album covers of ours. Just a totally unique design that captured our stage show perfectly at that time. The photo was shot by Danny, and it was an amazing cover shot taken from above the band on the building's catwalk. The cover also used that interesting font that John Hartman discovered in his old high school newspaper. With the Doobie Brothers, you never knew where an idea was going to come from. And it didn't matter: if it was good, you used it. The album came with a poster that had several live shots of guys in the band in an oval around two live shots with a picture of the Doobie Liner in the middle shot. Great poster!

Another thing about Danny is that he would work for hours getting our backstage catering together every night, and he was good at it! But one night at the end of a tour around the time we did that album cover, he outdid himself. On this same night, the crew decided to have a blowout. They bought cans filled with chocolate pudding that were pressurized somewhere, like whipped cream. And after the encore, they came onstage and let everyone have it! That shit was everywhere! We were covered in it! And walking on that slippery mess was a real challenge! Danny's hard work in catering was used for a gigantic food fight and was everywhere on the stage. The coup de grâce was Keith (on his first tour with us, I think) deciding that he wanted to drop-kick his drum kit into the audience. Just a little crazy! That was followed by a change of heart, and he wanted the drums back, so a couple of crew guys and Keith and I went out into the audience and retrieved the drums, which they didn't want to give up. And Dan was sitting backstage, just beside himself that his food had been weaponized for the blowout. I felt bad, but that was the road, and the end of a long tour was always a reason to blow off steam and party!

This was after Keith had taken Mike Hossack's place when

Mike decided he wanted a change of scene and joined a band called Bonaroo, which was headed up by Bob Winkelman and Jerry Weems on guitar and vocals, Bill Cuomo on keyboards and vocals, and Bobby Lichtig from Seals & Crofts on bass. The band was from Marin (I think Larkspur was home base). As it turned out, Keith Knudsen was playing drums with Lee Michaels, and he and Mike worked out a transition for the two bands. Hossack had played drums along with Hartman on *What Were Once Vices Are Now Habits,* so Keith just took over playing all his drum parts, but he also did some vocals. The icing on the cake was that we all knew Keith—I knew him from living in Marin and hanging around with him and some other musicians in San Anselmo. So he fit right in, and that was the start of a long friendship for Keith and me, right up until he passed away in 2005.

15

DOWN IN THE TRACK

Tom

In 1974, after the record came out, we took on another new band member. Jeff "Skunk" Baxter had actually recorded with us on a number of occasions. He was a founding member of Steely Dan and played some really memorable guitar on their first few albums. We got to know him because we played shows with Steely Dan a number of times when they were taking off, and Jeff occasionally joined us onstage as well. Steely Dan was retiring from touring, and Jeff needed a gig and we thought, what the hell—he's a great guitar and pedal steel player and a fun showman, so why not? He definitely added a lot to our sound as an excellent guitarist playing electric, pullstring, and pedal steel. He was also a wild man on the road and loved partaking in all of the rock and roll excess.

I will say that I enjoyed his playing with us early on, and he was fun to have onstage with us. He really added some energy that fit what we were doing, but as time passed and the road became our home, he started developing a separate performance style, like playing while seated on a stool, almost jazz style. That didn't fit with what the rest of us were doing onstage We were a rock and roll band; that was something I never understood and something he didn't do for at least a year on the road, but something changed for him, I guess. If you wanted the crowd to get involved, it always seemed a better idea to stay active onstage.

But Jeff did contribute some great stuff in the studio on songs like "South City Midnight Lady," "Neal's Fandango," "Texas Lullaby," and a great solo on "Take Me in Your Arms."

Pat

Jeff would start showing up, and I could tell he was angling for something, but I mean we liked him because he was a killer guitar player and a good guy, so his attention meant a lot to us. It was good for all of us. I didn't think too much about it when he would sit in originally, and then it got bigger and bigger. We played around California a lot, and so Jeff would show up for many of our gigs. Then one day he said, "I'm getting kicked out of Steely Dan because they don't like touring anymore." Tiran said, "Hey, let's bring him in. Then we have three guitar players up front like Moby Grape." That concept made a lot of sense to us, and so once again the band personnel changed. Jeff immediately established himself as a primary member of the band. He was very entertaining and had amazing chops. But he had a big personality that was sometimes over the top and could eventually start getting to people. But we definitely liked having him in the band, and fans responded favorably to him.

Of course, there was a massive U.S. tour set up to help promote the *Vices* album. But it also got us over to Europe to play for the first time. The Allman Brothers were headlining what would become the very first Knebworth festival in England. Sixty thousand people showed up to see the Allman Brothers, Mahavishnu Orchestra, Van Morrison, the Alex Harvey Band, Tim Buckley, and us. A few days before, we played a couple of warm-up shows in Amsterdam.

Playing with the Allman Brothers was something I was personally thrilled about. I played their album *Brothers and Sisters* nonstop and was truly a fan. I thought there was really nothing like them at that time. When we got to Amsterdam and I got my room keys at the hotel, I noticed in the hallway that Dickey Betts had a room right by mine. I was thrilled. I walked over to him with my bag and said, "I can't tell you what a pleasure it is to be over here playing with you. I love, love your band; I love the new album"—and with that, he gave me a look that basically said fuck off and slammed his room door in my face. Oh well! Sometimes it's better not to meet your heroes, I guess.

Tom

We were on the road so much that letting off steam could sometimes get pretty crazy. I don't think anybody spent time dwelling on the fact that we were working and traveling our asses off, and it took a toll on everyone. There was nothing like the mid-1970s. I remember one time when Jeff kind of ran off with the road manager's girl, and it didn't help that she was okay with it. This caused a rift (fairly heavy) and Phil (road manager) wanted to dole out some payback in a big way. So because we used quarter-inch sticks of dynamite onstage every night, Phil decided he wanted to basically blow Jeff and the girl up in Jeff's room. So one night Phil figured out what room Jeff was in with the girl and he had some roadies wire that door with a couple of these explosives, and then BOOM! The deal being that none of the crew would have anything to do with setting it off. That was on Phil. I don't think we ever saw her again. And, of course, there were the TVs being tossed out the windows, all the women, mostly one-night stands just out to hang with the band. Some were stewardesses we met when flying commercial; others would just show up at gigs and get backstage somehow. I don't think any band had anything on us when it came to wild behavior on the road but in the '70s, anything went. And not just for us. We learned a great deal about "crazy" from other bands we toured with early on. Our crew was very inventive as well. They would sabotage hotel rooms so the rooms were basically upside down when you walked in. Or rewire the buttons on the hotel elevators so you couldn't get where you wanted to go. We had rental-car races and door wars while driving. Some of those rental cars got wired differently and on and on. Everybody in the band and crew had their wild times, but it was really just a way to release the pressure of constant touring. And let's face it, touring and the music business, in general, isn't a nine-to-five type of life-style! And we all had our personal pressure valves. Be it the bar, certain chemicals, women, or combinations of the three. And sometimes, when the opportunity presented itself, a couple of us would sit in with the band at the hotel bar or a club in town where somebody knew the band. That happened in Europe and the States. A great example of this is the time we were in Amsterdam after playing Hilversum in July 1974, and every-body was down at the Melkweg, or Milky Way Club, a famous and crowded hangout for pretty much all bands that were in town as well as the locals. The Doobies were doing a couple of shows with the Allman Brothers, Van Morrison, and John Mc-Laughlin's Mahavishnu Orchestra, which would include a stop at the first Knebworth show (called the Bucolic Frolic) outside London, with sixty thousand people there. Anyway, after the show at Hilversum I ended up down at the Milky Way, as did Tiran, and there was already a jam going on, which was pretty much Gregg Allman, Butch Trucks, and Dickey Betts from the Allmans. So Tiran and I jumped in and played a few tunes, with Gregg leading the direction. It was a fun thing to do, and I was an Allman Brothers fan, so it was a cool way to spend some off time in Amsterdam.

16

EYES OF SILVER

1975–77:
Patrick Simmons / Tom Johnston / Michael McDonald /
Jeff "Skunk" Baxter / Tiran Porter / Keith Knudsen /
John Hartman

Tom

In the early winter of 1975, Warner Bros. booked a package tour to Europe with a bunch of its artists, including us, Little Feat, Tower of Power, Montrose, Graham Central Station (featuring Larry Graham from Sly and the Family Stone), and a band called Bonaroo was also playing on that tour, featuring our former drummer, Mike Hossack. On the tour, we would alternate in combinations of three—like Bonaroo, Little Feat, Doobies and the other three would be Montrose, Tower of

Power, and Graham Central Station. Then we would change that around for the next show, and we would take turns as headliners. Warner Bros. wanted to give everyone a chance because it was a showcase for Warner's acts to build up audiences overseas. And I would like to state for the record that following someone like Tower of Power was not an enviable position! They were as tight as a Swiss watch, funky as hell, and really took it to the crowd! I can remember one night in Germany being so tired from watching their set and dancing that when it came time for us to play, I was exhausted! I love those guys to this day! One night in Paris, we followed Little Feat, who were huge at that time. This too was a tough position to be in. They played an incredible set that left the crowd standing screaming for more encores. So you had to follow that, knowing it was going to be very hard, if not impossible, to top their performance, no matter how well you played! That crowd was there to see Little Feat. Our following in Paris was a little smaller, so you had to deal with the cards you were dealt.

But the part of this tour that I really enjoyed was hanging around and getting to know some of the bands that I didn't already know. We traveled by train quite a bit, which I loved. You'd get a chance to hang with all kinds of other musicians and road managers and techs. When we flew commercial, that wasn't usually the case. The airports were crazy and not real enthused about dealing with this traveling onslaught of musicians and their entourage. The trains didn't care. The hotels we stayed at were usually a big hangout scene. One day/night

I'd hang out with the guys from Graham Central Station and maybe Tower. Others, I'd be hanging with guys from Bonaroo. And I'd always see the guys from Little Feat at either breakfast or dinner.

There were special events that Warner would set up in advance, like meeting celebs in the city we were in. For example, in London/Manchester Mick Jagger, Keith Richards, Rod Stewart, and Elton John (all on Warner Bros. or an affiliate) would show up at both the show and at an event during the day at some government-sponsored thing. Elton got up and sat in with us in Manchester on "Listen to the Music," our last song. Afterward, Elton gave Jeff Baxter and me a ride back to London in his limo. Another event that stands out was the dinner thrown for everyone in Hamburg, Germany, in some huge, lavish place that had a swimming pool in the middle of it. There were big tables of food and drinks set up for everyone. A humorous aside: when we got there the burgomaster greeted everyone as we came in the door. It turns out that he had been a German soldier in World War II and had lost an arm in battle, so he had an electric arm with a hook on the end. Well, this presented a problem, because you didn't know what to grab when "shaking hands." And then in came Bobby Winkelman (Bonaroo), who thought this guy was the designated coat-check person and threw his coat over the outstretched "arm" of this guy and just kept walking. Probably not funny now, but it was then! There was also a stunt being discussed by a couple people in the Tower group (not musicians) and a couple of guys from the Little Feat camp that involved tossing the burgomaster in the pool to short him out. I know that sounds pretty bad, but I don't think anyone would have really done it. It was mostly the alcohol talking. You have to remember: this was all music with a buzz on, all the other band members and the crew guys were there, and it was a crazy night just getting revved up!

One of the other memorable things was being involved with writing the song "It Ain't Nothin' but a Warner Brothers Party." It was a song Larry Graham wrote most of, with him on bass and vocals; Butch, his organ player, on keyboards; me on guitar; some of Tower's horns; and Mike Hossack, Keith Knudsen, and John Hartman, along with Lenny Williams, the vocalist for Tower. A bunch of road guys were all just hanging out in a big hotel room in Germany. Anyway, Graham Central rehearsed it, got it stage ready, and using Tower's horn section, along with their guitar player (David) and me playing guitar and singing a line, played it at an outdoor show in Amsterdam. As a kicker, Warner Bros. execs Joe Smith and Mo Ostin got up and sang on the chorus. What a trip. That song was on the next Graham Central Station album, *Ain't No 'Bout-A-Doubt It*. Killer tune!

People turned out, and the reaction was incredible. Everybody got a chance to do their thing, and everyone got a chance to shine. I loved grooving on the music and watching all these great players every night. It was as much fun for me as for the crowd. Traveling on trains was an enjoyable way to travel and see the countryside. And at times, it was kind of crazy. At any given time, there were almost a hundred people traveling together. It was like an oversized gypsy caravan. And we did fly commercial a few times, which was insane with all the people and gear—a real carnival atmosphere. But musically it was a resounding success, and socially we just had a ball. Something for everyone to remember for years to come.

There was lots of hash. Everybody was smoking hash. Everybody had it. Going from city to city, we actually had to eat it to get across the border.

Pat

We really had to ditch the hash or else. I had eaten pot brownies before, so I thought I knew what I was doing. On the bus heading to the airport, I had a gram of hash that I didn't want to waste, so I ate it. I figured I would just get high, and that would be okay. But then someone else said to me, "I don't know what to do with this gram of hash, I don't wanna throw it away," so I went ahead and ate that one as well. I really wasn't thinking. Once I got on the plane, I got so high that I literally passed out. I mean, I was out of it. My heart was doing that slow-motion beat . . . beat . . . beat . . . that you get when you ingest a lot of THC, but this was different. THUMP . . . THUMP . . . THUMP . . . I was really out of it. I was fading big-time. When we landed in Berlin, I couldn't even walk, so the PR person from Warner Bros., Russ, a really good guy, got a wheelchair for me. They wheeled me off the plane, and I guess they took me through customs, but then I went directly into this really nice Mercedes taxicab that was waiting out in front of the airport. Someone had grabbed my luggage, and so me and the PR guy got settled in this cab. It was a really nice ride. Belgian-lace headrests and everything. But I was still really hurting. This was not going to end well, so I started messing with the power windows. I knew what was next. None of my cars or trucks back home had power windows, so I was fumbling. Too late. I couldn't get the window open in time, and I blew my cook-ies all over that beautiful interior! The driver was completely freaking out, but the PR guy was great; he took out some cash to make sure this guy would be able to get a really nice car wash afterward. I heard later that over in Europe they rolled hash in camel dung to keep it compact. Was that true? I have no idea, but I know that's probably the most out of it I ever was when it came to taking anything. Despite that crazy episode, the tour really was amazing. As excessive as it was, the music was truly inspired, and we played our asses off, just like all the other bands. I think everybody really rose to the occasion.

There was one incident on that tour that made me really wonder if any of us would make it home, especially me. I had done an interview with this newspaper in Amsterdam. We were talking about motorcycles and biker culture, and the reporter said to me, "You know we have Hells Angels over here in our country, too." I was aware of that, and I made a comment that I thought it was interesting that in Amsterdam the Angels were riding Hondas and some other bikes. I added that in America, Angels would never ride a foreign bike; it had to be a Harley or nothing. That was the gist of my comment. No big deal. Well, when the article came out, the writer misinterpreted what I said and made it sound as if I was putting down the local Angels for being less macho or something than their American counterparts. We were playing a big gig at The Hague. All of the bands were on hand: Montrose, Little Feat, Graham Central Station, Tower of Power, Bonaroo—everybody and their crews. And when I got there, at the back of the arena in the backstage area, I noticed four of the local Hells Angels coming toward us. Big guys wearing the colors. And they were pissed off, carrying chains—real outlaw bikers. What the fuck? I finally figured out what was going on when one of them said to me, "So you think we are pussies?" They'd read the article. "No, no, no," I said to them. "I didn't say that at all." They were not hearing it. "Oh really, well we're going to fucking kill you!" the leader barked. Well, we had some pretty tough guys on our side too, heavy-duty crew guys that didn't take any shit from anybody. They all started grabbing microphone stands and came up behind me to go toe-to-toe with these Angels. Also, this was The Hague. It would've been like Hells Angels busting into Carnegie Hall, so the local cops were pissed off, and they got into it as well. It was chaos. Thankfully, the Angels knew they were hopelessly outnumbered and hauled ass out of there. But that was a close one.

Tom

After we came back from Europe and a month or so later, we played a huge Bay Area show. March 23, 1975, we played what is still one of the most memorable concerts in Doobie Brothers and San Francisco history. At least for me. It was called the SNACK concert, and it was organized by Bill Graham. SNACK stood for San Francisco Students Need Athletics, Culture, and Kicks. Public schools were about to lose lots of money due to fiscal cutbacks, and so Bill Graham stepped in to raise money by booking the sixty-thousand-seat Kezar Stadium in San Francisco. It turned out to be the biggest rock benefit concert ever at that time. Even bigger than George Harrison's Bangladesh concert. Kezar Stadium was packed, and it was wild to see people on top of buildings surrounding the stadium. I had literally just driven over from my house in Mill Valley. It was interesting: I just parked and walked in. Not like today, where you would have all the special handling. Pretty laid back for an event that big. I just went to the backstage door and gave them my name, which I guess was on a list. But man, once I got in there, what a scene there was backstage. All the musicians and VIPs. For only five dollars, the crowd got to see the Doobie Brothers, the Grateful Dead, Jefferson Starship, Santana, Tower of Power, Eddie Palmieri, Joan Baez, and Graham Central Station, plus Neil Young with two members of the Band (Levon Helm and Rick Danko are who I remember), plus appearances by Marlon Brando and Bob Dylan, who also played with Neil Young and the guys from the Band. Bill Graham introduced me to Brando backstage, which was surreal. He was there with Sacheen Littlefeather, the Native American woman who stood in for him at the Oscar ceremony a couple of years earlier. The concert was a once-in-a-lifetime kind of event. And I remember Graham said he'd never, ever throw something like that again! I'll bet it was a logistical nightmare! But what a great show and experience hanging backstage. And after I was done hanging out, I just jumped in my car and drove home. That pretty much never happens!

17

TAKE ME IN YOUR ARMS

Pat

I really enjoyed making the *Stampede* album. Jeff Baxter brought a lot of cool ideas. I think that album is less pop and more roots for us. Ry Cooder played some great guitar on "Rainy Day Crossroad Blues," and Jeff's soloing on "Neal's Fandango," something that I wrote, was really amazing. For the first time, we also played around with backward guitar sounds. "Take Me in Your Arms (Rock Me a Little While)" was an old Motown song that Tommy had wanted us to cover, and he just killed it on the vocals. That song had a lot of good stuff going on. Jeff played a great solo, but I think what really elevated the track was that Ted brought in the Motown musical arranger Paul Riser to work out the string arrangements. We also had Sherlie Matthews and Venetta Fields come in to do backing vocals. They worked together as a group called the Blackberries and had sung background vocals on a ton of great records, including *Exile on Main St.* by the Rolling Stones, and they also toured with Humble Pie.

Tom

My health was becoming a problem on and off, starting with the latter days of touring on *The Captain and Me.* I had an ulcer that was pretty bad. Sometimes it would mellow out for a while, but the constant touring and the wild lifestyle that went with it eventually caused the ulcer attacks to become more frequent, which caused problems on the road. I remember going into Cook County Hospital in Chicago for a week right in the middle of a tour, causing all the dates to be moved back a week while I got my gut straightened out. I started to fly back and forth more often from my home in Marin to Burbank to record. So by the time we started *Stampede,* it was an ongoing situation. But the album got done without a hitch and on time. I'd love to break it down for you song by song.

"Sweet Maxine"

This song has a genuine Doobie Brothers feel. Really upbeat, with Little Feat influences provided by Bill Payne on piano. It's a rocker that Pat wrote a great music track for, and Ted asked me to write the lyrics. This was a first for Pat and me, but it worked out great. I sang the vocal, and we all sang the harmonies. It was the first official album with Keith Knudsen, playing drums and singing background, as a full-time member of the band. I still love playing it live. Just a great-feeling song with some really cool half-time sections and great chord changes that Pat came up with. And Paul Riser's horn parts really fit the track. It was the next single after "Take Me in Your Arms."

"Neal's Fandango"

This track always reminds me of the Santa Cruz Mountains. Pat wrote this about Neal Cassady and living up in Loma Prieta. It's another Moby Grape–influenced Doobies song. Pat's vocal was rapid-fire and really worked in the track. It was Jeff Baxter's first album as a member of the band, and he played some sizzling solos on this. A fun track to do in the studio, and even more fun to play live.

"Texas Lullaby"

This song was a departure for me in writing style. It is kind of a country song describing life in the open Texas countryside and the lifestyle of the people who live there. I played a basic electric picking part with tremolo and some rhythm strumming, Jeff is on pedal steel, Nick DeCaro wrote the strings, and we all sang the choruses, which were rhythmic in style, over an R&B-style lead vocal throughout. Jeff also played a Marty Robbins–style acoustic guitar solo, which really fit the feeling of the track. The bass and drums rounded out the track feel. It was both laid back in the verses and a little more driving in the choruses.

"Music Man"

This started out as a kind of rock and soul tune. It had a driving bass part over a straight-ahead drum part and a slightly distorted rhythm guitar part for a basic track. B3 by Bill Payne, an R&B-style vocal with everyone singing harmony background parts on the chorus. At this point, Ted took himself and the track to visit Curtis Mayfield in Chicago and let him do his "Superfly" magic on it. Curtis added strings and horns, wah-wah guitar, and some female background singers. It sounded amazing. And to this day, I don't really know how that all came about. But I'm glad it did. Ted had so many great ideas on all our albums, and this is a great example of that. After Ted got back, I got to try something I'd always wanted to do. Play a backward guitar solo (à la Jimi Hendrix). When that part of the solo was done, I added two regular solos over the top of the continuing backward solo. Watching Donn Landee (engineer) put all this together was jaw-dropping! Pieces of two-inch tape everywhere, splicing the tape. I don't know how he kept track of it all, but man he nailed it.

"Slack Key Soquel Rag"

This is another example of Pat's incredible facility as a finger-picker. And he played it beautifully. For him to sit down and write something like this is amazing. It's his signature element and style.

"Take Me in Your Arms"

For about a year, I had been pushing the band to cover one of my favorite Motown tracks, Kim Weston's "Take Me in Your Arms." It's not that the guys didn't like the song. I think they thought it would be better to do something of our own and we didn't need it, but we ended up doing it anyway. Thanks to Ted for that! And, man, I'm glad we did! That became one of my favorite tracks—a feel-good, upbeat, rockin' arrangement. The band played the hell out of it after we figured out the arrangement. Bill Payne played piano, Bobby Hall Porter played congas, and Paul Riser charted and directed the strings and the horns on it. We had Sherlie Matthews, Venetta Fields, and Jessica Smith sing background vocals, which really took it up a notch. It was the first single off *Stampede* and is still one of my favorite vocals I've ever done.

"I Cheat the Hangman"

Pat wrote this, and I wasn't involved in the cutting of this track and wasn't at the studio when they cut it. This wasn't uncommon by this time. Whoever wrote the song generally cut the basic with drums and bass, and whoever wasn't involved in that part of the song would do other stuff or sometimes hang out to watch. On this track, I don't think I played at all and, at most, might have done some background vocals. It was a big arrangement track that had two distinct sections. The first part was all picking with lead vocal and background singing parts and clean electric accents by Jeff. The second section had a distorted guitar part that set up the chord changes that drove the whole thing; strings and percussion and a wild ending that kept building. It was a different kind of track for the band and added to the depth of what the band was capable of. And I'm sure Ted came up with a lot of ideas for percussion and had Conte and Pete Candoli play the trumpet parts.

"Précis"

Jeff wrote and played this on a classical acoustic, and it's kind of somber, but it's a nice segue between "Cheat the Hangman" and "Rainy Day Crossroad Blues."

"Rainy Day Crossroad Blues"

This song was written mostly on the road and was an acoustic-based rhythmic blues tune. It started with a chunka-style strumming acoustic guitar with a complementary picking part, a walking bass, and a simple drum part played on the snare with brushes and kick drum. And it had no background vocals, just the lead vocal, which was unusual for us. It had two sections as well and had a great slide solo by Ry Cooder between the first and second verse. The second section was instrumental and basically a half-time version of the first section but more laid back with strings and some pedal steel. The lyrics were based on being down and out in the South around Mobile, Alabama, and dealing with an inner fight between the "lord above and the devil below." Yeah, I think it kind of encapsulated the touring life, but it sang well!

"I Been Workin' on You"

Having this song on the album was kind of a fluke. It was recorded in Nashville on what started out as just a jam out on Murfreesboro Road at Buzz Cason's studio (later called Creative Workshop) between the summer of '73 and early '74. It was just a fun night and something to do. I didn't really expect it to go on an album, even though I really liked the groove of the track. It was just a jam. The way it came about was that Karl Himmel, the drummer for Mother Earth from our first tour, called and came over to the hotel where we were staying in Nashville. He just wanted to hang out, and at some point he came up with the idea of going out to Buzz Cason's place to play around in his studio. Tiran went with us, and we took our guitars and started fooling around. I came up with this guitar lick, and we just kind of built on it till we had a basic track with guitar, bass, and drums. I added another rhythm guitar track, Tiran came up with a bass part, Karl played congas on it, and then we put a work vocal on it with no real lyrics. And that's the vocal that is on the album. I played a guitar solo on it, and that was it. I actually don't remember how it got resurrected for this album. I must have played it for Ted at some point. He liked the feel. I think it was his idea to put it on the album and add the three singers we had used on "Take Me in Your Arms."

"Double Dealin' Four Flusher"

Pat wrote this southern rock–style shuffle with an Allman Brothers kind of feel to it. The breakdown after the B section has Bill Payne playing some nice electric piano riffs. It's also the first and maybe the only song with three different guys singing lead parts on it. The first parts were sung in harmony, and then Pat, Keith, and I sang solo lines followed by three-part harmony lines. This song rocked pretty hard and was fun to do live.

The cover was also really great—once again, the work of talented photographer Michael Maggid, whom we worked with many times. The concept for the album title and cover sort of evolved from collective discussions with the band while we were recording. Michael set up to shoot the principal photos in Marin County, since most of us lived near there. So on the day of the album shoot, it was arranged that we'd all have an early-morning meetup at the bus station in downtown Mill Valley. Band members, various wives and girlfriends, several Warner production and art folks, horse wranglers—a big group. We all caravanned to Mount Tamalpais, where we had arranged to have permission to shoot on a little dirt road. We had costumes and gun belts from the Warner prop department. All set up, we go up the dirt road and charge on our horses, as best as we can, toward the camera.

Pat

We finished the shoot, and the folks who supplied the horses were generous enough to allow us to hang on to them for a while longer and to take them for a little ride if we wished to. I rode around the property for a while and made my way back to the stable, where I dropped off the horse a little while later. This was out near Muir Woods.

18

I CHEAT THE HANGMAN

Pat

April 9, Assembly Center, Baton Rouge, Louisiana. We were just about five shows into the 1975 tour in support of *Stampede*. The day of the gig, at the venue, our road manager came backstage and said to me, "Tommy's been rushed back to L.A. It's serious." I knew he had not been doing great lately. We were all drinking a lot and doing some other things, and evidently Tommy had an old stomach issue that was aggravated by all that. We all had been living hard, and it obviously took him down. And in the middle of all the crazy success, it happened. "What do you mean?" I asked. *He's leaving?* Tommy had seemed okay earlier that day. I mean, we were all indulging, we all had our moments, but this sounded serious. "He's bleeding internally. The doctor is sending him back to L.A. Major emergency." That was it. He was gone. Just like that. But we still had a show to do.

Tom

To be honest, I don't even remember exactly what happened. I had been hitting things pretty hard and then had also been throwing up blood a few times. So I knew something was going on. But I've actually had to rely on the memories of others when it comes to the details of flying to L.A. It sidelined me pretty hard.

All of a sudden, you find yourself bleeding out on a table and you know things have to change. We were just one or two dates into the 1975 tour for the album *Stampede*. We were flying high: the album was taking off, and we had some really big hits, including "Long Train Runnin'," "China Grove," "Listen to the Music," and "Black Water" under our belts and were touring like there was no tomorrow. And all I could think was, *Man, I feel bad. This could really mess things up for us!* I'd been getting sick for over a year on and off leading up to that night in early 1975. But back then, we were all young and indestructible (or so we thought). We had been burning the candle at both ends before anyone ever knew we existed. By now we were also playing a couple of hundred shows a year, on average, and basically lived out on the road. When I started getting the stomach pains, I had no idea what it was. But there was no time to slow down and check it out. When I started throwing up before shows, even onstage a few times, I still had no idea what was going on. Little did I know that my hard-living life-style had aggravated an old stomach ulcer I had developed as a teenager. I also didn't know that it could kill me if I didn't do something about it. So I just ignored it as much as possible and kept on pushing through any pain because there really wasn't any alternative while on tour. Not fun, but there weren't any other options. Next thing I knew, I was being rushed from Baton Rouge onto a plane headed for L.A.

Pat

Was this really happening? Was he going to be okay? I had no idea. It was serious; we knew that. And my first thought after thinking about my musical brother was, maybe it was just over. We really couldn't complain. Just five years in, and we had accomplished more than most bands ever will in their entire career. Big hit records, millions of fans around the world that adored our music, bandmates that you appreciated and trusted, and the craziest rock and roll lifestyle this side of paradise. No complaints. We had achieved everything beyond all of our wildest imaginations, and so if this was how it was going to end, maybe we just had to accept that. It was very confusing, but I remember that was what I thought. Just accept the end, be thankful, and move on. I mean, what else can you do when the guy who, for all intents and purposes, is your front man goes down for the count? Because Tommy sang most of our hits, and up until that point he defined a large part of our sound, at least to the fans. The Doobie Brothers was always a very democratic band in terms of how we played, but the fans always saw Tommy up front. So my first thought was, without Tommy, it's going to be hard to keep going. People may not accept us.

Tom

I was really sick. Flying from Louisiana to a Los Angeles hospital was a blur. Everybody was living pretty hard; it had just caught up to me first. What were they going to do? I felt really bad for having to leave the tour and leaving the band in a terrible position at the beginning of a tour, and I knew I was going to beat myself up over this. This wasn't supposed to happen! But it did. I never knew how serious my ulcer actually was, or maybe I would've taken it a little easier on the partying. When you're achieving the kind of success that we were, it's easy to get out of control. First things first. I needed to wake up the next day. I had never felt anything like this before, and some of the "attacks" I'd had on the road were pretty painful. I was just twenty-seven years old, but I hadn't been living a Jack LaLanne lifestyle. Good thing I wasn't thinking about how twenty-seven was the "magic age" for losing rock musicians: Jimi Hendrix, Janis Joplin, Jim Morrison . . . I got to the hospital and came close to dying on the table. They lost me there for a few. No heartbeat. I remember having what they call "astral projections" while I was on that table. It was really weird. Like I floated up to the ceiling and was looking down on everyone in the room. A few days later, I'd recognize people that had been in there while I was totally unconscious. Or at least that's what I thought.

Pat

Being in a band, especially a band like ours, it's very much like a family. You love each other deeply, but there's always a conflict around every corner. And then you need to deal with things as a family. Together you have to figure out what the next move is. I was scared for Tommy when he had to leave us so suddenly at the beginning of the tour. My initial feeling was that maybe this train had reached its final stop. But then I took a step back and thought about how hard we had worked to get where we were. And I also started thinking about other bands that have had to deal with this kind of loss. How did they survive? Maybe there was a way we could manage to keep things going. Eventually, my musical brother made it. Our band made it. But it wasn't always easy, and a lot happened.

Tiran

The night when Tommy went to the hospital was really tense. I went out onstage and started to announce that we weren't going to play because we weren't all there that night. Just as I was going to start speaking, Pat ran out to the microphone and said, "Wait a minute." He addressed the crowd calmly and said, "Look, Tommy isn't here tonight, and we are not sure what to do. We want to play for you, but only if you want us." And they went crazy, and then we went on and played maybe one of our best shows ever. Tommy's parts and everything. We pulled it off. But after the show, I still think we were a little bit stunned and confused. There was no real plan in place. That's when Jeff called Mike McDonald. We brought him down to New Orleans and rehearsed for a couple of days to get him up to speed. I wasn't sure what to expect, but it wasn't much. But I will tell you, the second I heard him open up his mouth, I said holy shit. My mind was blown right there. I immediately thought, this is going to be great; he is so soulful and unique that it's going to give us a real chance to grow. The way we adapted always reminded me of the way that Genesis adapted after Peter Gabriel left. You just do what you have to do. You figure out how to get it done. And then once in a while, you can be even stronger than you were before.

Pat

At the hotel the next day, we got constant updates about Tom. It sounded bad. I started thinking, maybe we are just done. But then I thought, wait, other bands have been through this. How did they cope? We will just make it up as we go along. So that's what we did. We started playing shows, and I took over most of the lead vocals. We were treading water, but the tour was booked, the album was out, and we decided that until our brother came back, we would do the best that we could. And we gained a fighting spirit and learned a lot about ourselves. We had to keep going on. We hit the road without Tom, and the first thing the fans wanted to know was, where is he? We were honest. I would get up there and address the audience and let them know they could have their money back if they wanted it. But nobody would take us up on it. They gave us a chance. But we still needed to think of something quickly.

Jeff Baxter pulled me aside backstage one night in the middle of the smoke and general chaos. "Hey man, remember that guy we had singing background in Steely Dan?" We had toured a bunch with Steely Dan when Jeff was still playing with them, and I had a vague recollection of a young background singer they had taken on the road. "He's good," Jeff said, speaking low enough so that only I could hear him. "I mean, he's young, like twenty-two, but he's good. Plays keyboards, too . . . who knows?"

I wasn't sure what to think, but Jeff was adamant. "We need to do something, man. Let me buy him a plane ticket. I know he's no replacement for Tommy, but he's talented and shit—we have to do *something*." "Go for it," I told him. I thought that was kind of cool given that Bill Payne played so many identifiable piano parts on our records. Now we could have that sound onstage. Would this new guy be up for it?

A few days later, a shaggy-haired, bearded background singer arrived from L.A. Jeff brought him to the hotel and said, "Pat, Michael McDonald is here." "Good to have you here," I told him. "My pleasure," he said sheepishly. "I've been playing some of your tunes in a little cover band out at a bar in the San Fernando Valley. I can't believe that now I'm here with the real guys."

We started rehearsing right there and then on our day off. It was obvious right away the shy, soft-spoken McDonald was more than just a "background singer." This was a guy who could easily trade off lead vocals with me and add keyboards to our live sound.

His voice was much different than Tom's. It wasn't raw and bluesy, but rather gospel-inflected and soulful, like a young Ray Charles or Joe Cocker. It was different. But it worked. We got through the tour.

Michael McDonald

It's just so funny how some things work out. I was a big fan of Steely Dan, and I already thought I had had the gig of a lifetime playing with them. I mean, that was a dream job. We went to Europe and did an amazing tour, then came back to the States and did another great tour, and then, bam, the band broke up. And then I was back in the club scene doing cover songs. That was when I first realized just how fast things can come and go in the music business. It's a jagged line. But I learned a lot from Donald and Walter while I was in Steely Dan. They were so professional and so tight when it came to the music. Every night onstage was like a clinic with those guys. I felt my singing getting so much better, and then that was it. I think the last show in Santa Monica, I thought, maybe that was it. Maybe that was my moment. I had my shot, and it was simply over far too fast. Then I got a call one day from Jeff Baxter, who had also been in the band with me. But he had left earlier to join the Doobie Brothers. We'd played with those guys a number of times, and Jeff would occasionally sit in with them. I think he was a great fit for the Doobies. It always kind of amazed me they brought in a third guitar player, because they really had everything covered. But as I would learn later, that's just the Doobies. They do what's right for the band. Nobody gets too personal or protective of anything. If it makes the band better, you do it. So that's why Jeff was in there. So then he called me this day and explained what was happening down there, that they were in the middle of this big tour and they needed some backup. Did I think I was the guy to take the place of someone like Tom Johnston? No way. He had such a one-of-a-kind voice and was such an amazing musician. What could I possibly add to the Doobie Brothers? But Jeff was adamant, so I flew down to New Orleans, and it was pretty fast-paced when I got there. We hit the ground running, and there was no time to waste. I literally had just two days to learn the entire set. We took over an old club down there called the Warehouse and just basically worked around the clock. I just turned up down there, me and my Wurlitzer piano, and it was off to the races. It was one of the most challenging things I think I've ever done in my life. You have to remember: the Doobie Brothers play a lot of different kinds of music. It wasn't like so many other bands back then that maybe played just blues or hard rock. Stylistically, they covered a lot of ground. I was never that great a keyboard player. I thought my strengths were more as a vocalist, singing the background and higher parts, and so that's what I focused on with the Doobies. I honestly think that if they had more time to think about it, they would have found somebody more seasoned. I mean, it's not like there weren't a ton of great players around. So I think the urgency worked in my favor. I had to just be a fly on the fly, and I really thank God for Jeff Baxter suggesting they bring me in to just fill in a few of the holes. I mean, that call obviously is a game changer in my life.

And so after a couple of days, we headed over to Shreveport, and I played my first gig with the band. I was really nervous at first. I mean, Tom's voice is so recognizable and so unique. He essentially was the trademark of the band. There was no way I could replace that. I could just do my best. So I did the full tour. Dozens of shows in sold-out arenas all over the country. It was an amazing opportunity for a guy like me, a guy from nowhere.

Pat

Once we had all gotten back home to California and things started to settle down, we still didn't know Tom's status. In the meantime, we had scheduled studio time in L.A. to record some songs of mine I had written for the upcoming album. I asked Ted if it was okay to bring Mike McDonald and Bobby LaKind in to play on the tracks. He said whatever I wanted to try was fine with him. We cut "Wheels of Fortune" the first day. We were all set up waiting for Keith Knudsen to arrive. Richie Hayward from Little Feat had come by to say hi and hang out for a while. I forget what happened, but for some reason Keith couldn't make the session that day. I suggested to Ted that maybe we could try cutting the song with Richie. Again, Ted said fine. We ran the tune down with John and Richie on drums, Bobby on congas, Mike on Fender Rhodes, Jeff on guitar, and Tiran on bass. We recorded the song in one take, all live solos. This was the first song ever recorded by what would become the new incarnation of the Doobie Brothers, except for Keith, who would be there to work on all the other tracks on *Takin' It to the Streets*. I wanted Michael to sing for Ted Templeman. Ted was a huge part of our success, almost like a band member himself, and his opinion mattered. Michael had a song he was working on that I thought was really strong, but Ted was skeptical. "Pat, seriously? I know he's a strong singer, but a writer? Really?" Michael came in, quiet as ever, sat down at the acoustic piano, and started playing his song. After a brief intro, he started singing, "You don't know me but I'm your brother . . ." Over Michael's shoulder, so he could not see, Ted looked at me and mouthed the words "Oh my God." The song was "Takin' It to the Streets." Little did we know that another Doobie Brothers era was beginning right before our eyes, and it's a story unto itself. It would include an entirely new level of success but also a new series of conflicts, inner struggles, and ultimately what seemed to be the end of the band. But, you know, never say never.

Michael

One thing about the Doobie Brothers is that they're very generous when it comes to everyone in the band. Whatever you can contribute—fine, they are open to anything. We would always talk about Moby Grape. They were all about diversity and taking chances. The Doobie Brothers always embraced that ethos, and I mean on any given night we could go from full-on rock to R&B to jazzy to soulful—that really gets to the heart of what Moby Grape was about. Never holding back and never failing to explore or follow your instincts. I was having dinner one night at Tiran's house, and he said to me, "Hey, come check out my little four-track recording studio. Maybe we can lay something down tonight." So we went to a different part of his house where he'd set it up, and it was really cool. "Let's do something," he said. So we recorded something I was working on called "Losin' End." I had not written much by then. It was just kind of a little one-off I had done. Well, lo and behold, our producer, Ted Templeman, heard it and really liked it. Then there was this other song I had been kicking around . . . "Takin' It to the Streets."

Dan

When Tommy had to leave the band, it was a very big deal. He was having a lot of problems at that point, and I knew his stomach had gotten really bad, just because of all of the excess on the road. We were all involved, but I guess he had this condition that evidently really flared up and almost cost him his life. Nobody knew if the band was even going to be able to go on after that. I mean, how do you lose your primary front guy? I was very scared for Tommy, and of course we were concerned for everybody's future after that. I remember when I first met Michael McDonald, who Jeff Baxter suggested could step in and help out for a little while. He was just the nicest guy you would ever want to meet, and he's the exact same way today. Just incredibly humble. I remember watching those first few shows that he was part of, and I thought to myself, wow, they may have a chance to keep going. This guy seems pretty good; I wonder what else he can do? Well, obviously, as it turned out, he could do a lot. I remember shooting the very first promotional shots of Michael. We did a bunch of them in his house with these mountains in the background and then went off to some local gun show and got some images there. He was always really easy to work with. It was a different band without Tommy. I'm not saying what's better or worse; it was just different. The energy of the shows changed, because Tommy was just so rock and roll and so hard driving. Michael was a lot softer and laid back, but they would still cover Tommy's songs, which I thought was smart. You just couldn't erase that portion of their career. Those early songs were just too good. It was definitely different. I liked it when they did shows with everybody once Tommy came back for a little bit. I loved that sound, because it just had everything.

19

TAKIN' IT TO THE STREETS

Tom

This was a transitional time for me and for the band. They had started working on the new album, and I knew little about what had transpired musically in the studio, which was a weird feeling, but one I'd get used to. I'd go over to the studio and visit from the hospital after they got back from the road, and as things progressed I even cut a track called "Turn It Loose." That and singing a verse on "Wheels of Fortune" would be my only contributions to the album, to the best of my recollection, but everybody had made me feel welcome and pitched in to make "Turn It Loose" as good as it could be. The guys were all supportive, and Ted was welcoming as well. And while it felt very different working in the new band environment after all that they'd been through since I'd had to leave, I was grateful for the chance to just be a part of it. So the band finished the album, and the first single was "Takin' It to the Streets," which I had heard on one of my visits to the studio. As different as it was from the material I was used to hearing, it was still a really great song, and Michael's voice was one of a kind. It was soulful, hooky, and it made sense to go with it. After meeting Michael, I realized he was not only really talented but a great guy as well. Laid back and easy to get along with. I got to hear pretty much all the songs by the time they finished the album. And by that time, my health was way better. The ulcer had healed up and I'd gained weight. So, as a result, we were going to go out on a spring tour to push *Takin' It to the Streets,* the new album and single. All of us! We were also taking the Memphis Horns out with us, which was a phenomenal idea and a great sound addition! It was a natural fit, and they really were fun to have around for the whole band. Killer players, total characters, and they had so many great stories about having played with some of the biggest R&B artists ever on so many hit records! Aretha, Otis Redding, Sam and Dave, Al Green, as well as a few rockers! All artists I loved!

I went home to get everything in order, and before long we started rehearsing for the spring tour to push *Takin' It to the Streets.* We did stuff from both past albums and also from the new one. And when the tour started, I found myself adjusting to the new style we had onstage as well as to an entourage that was a pretty good size when you include the Memphis Horns, whom I became good friends with. And it was fun to be out touring again. The crowds were great, and the shows were tight and energetic. We tried some different amp configurations that took some getting used to, but it was a great experience for me. Touring was still as I had remembered it, with a few new faces and styles, but I didn't let it get in the way of a great experience. I worked hard to contribute and enjoy being around the guys again. I loved having the horns on board! The band had moved on, much to their credit. My departure had thrown a wrench in things on the *Stampede* tour, but they had not only persevered, they had come up with a new style, with both Mike and Pat writing the material, which proved very successful! I think because we had packed so much into the previous five years, it felt more like fifteen, so I was adjusting to a new musical entourage and style. We were lucky to have Mike, and I spent some time hanging with him after shows occasionally—even sitting in together one night with a club band in some town on the tour playing songs like "Barefootin'" just for fun.

The 1976 tour is interesting because it really represented both styles of the band. The crowd loved it because they got everything. We played a lot of the songs from before mixed in with the new tracks, but it did not feel like the Doobie Brothers I was accustomed to anymore, but rather what the Doobie Brothers had become. Michael's music was such a different direction for the band, but just as valid as anything we had done previously, and with this configuration the band had moved on. They had a future, and as much as I respected where they were headed, I felt a little out of place. Now, in defense of them, they never said that. On the contrary, I think they did their best to make me feel part of things. But I knew that my having to leave in '75 had put them in an awkward position, and that was hard to forget. It left a hole they hadn't planned on. But they had gained Michael McDonald, which proved to be a big win for the band; it changed everything. On the road, I hung out with the Memphis Horns and a few people like John Hartman and Keith. The Horns were great to have around, and I enjoyed their company. Up onstage, everything was fine. We played really good shows, and the crowd ate it up. Michael was absolutely the right guy at the right time for them. Mike's so talented and unique, and his impact was pretty much immediate. His influences were definitely helping shape the new sound of the band, and I felt out of place. I had put a lot of heart, soul, and sweat into the Doobie Brothers, and I didn't see how the two diverging styles would fit going forward. But I never had any bad feelings about that. They had all been great, fun to play with, including Michael, and I respected that. It was a lot to deal with at that time. And to be honest, I decided not to and just moved on. I would occasionally drop by one of their shows if we were in the same town, and they always made me feel welcome. I even went to their Grammy party after playing a solo album gig in Bakersfield the night they won. I was happy for them, and it was great to see everybody, including Ted and some of the Warner Bros. folks. But I needed some time off from the Doobies, and after about a year and a half I was back at it again doing my solo albums and touring. And that proved to be liberating for me.

Pat

I was walking on the beach in Santa Cruz when I ran into Tommy. We both did double takes. I looked at him and said, "Hey, man, I really love your new album!" And I did. I thought he did a fantastic job on it. We stood there chatting for a few minutes, and I was happy for him. It's not easy to come out of a band like the Doobie Brothers and have people pay attention to what you're doing, but his record was great, and it was getting a great response. I thought Ted had done a great job producing it, and I was happy they were working together again. I thought it was also cool there were other familiar faces and voices on there, like Michael McDonald, Keith, Billy Payne, and some other folks—even the Tower of Power horn section and the Memphis Horns. And "Savannah Nights" got a lot of airplay. It was great for Tommy. Even though Tommy wasn't in the band anymore, the fact that he had all those contributors was a testament to just how strong, tight, and extended the Doobie Brothers family was. Just because you weren't in the band didn't mean you were not going to play with everybody. I think that speaks to the power of the relationships of the band. We've all been through a lot of shit with each other. But most of the relationships survived and even got stronger over the years. It's the brotherhood of being in a band, I guess.

Tom

I remember walking on the beach in Santa Cruz in '79, and out of the blue I bumped into Pat. "Hey, man, I heard your record and I loved it," he told me. Which was really good to hear, and I appreciated the support. It was cool catching up with Pat. He had played on that album and would play and sing on the next solo album as well. And it was kind of like old times, having been through so much together in the band. Now I was extended family, and that was a good feeling because a few guys who had played or were playing in the band had been on that album. And as I've said, Pat and I would occasionally get together just to hang out. Usually while he was living up in the Santa Cruz Mountains. We went riding with Bill Craddock once, and I took my wife, Diane, up there once, too. This would have been in the '80s. I would also contribute a little on Pat's solo album in that era. I also played with him and his band in Oakland at a club one night. This was post–Doobie Brothers, in the early '80s.

Dan

The next album cover that became a big project for me was *Takin' It to the Streets*.

So my "big idea" for this was going to be a hologram on the cover. Hologram technology in 1976 was basically unheard of, at least in this country. Alice Cooper had attempted something like that a year or two earlier, but it never worked out. So I thought we could include a four-by-five holographic sticker on the album cover, which would really captivate buyers. Everybody loved it, everything except the cost. It was going to add about 40 cents to each unit, which may not seem like a lot, but when you multiply that over numbers like one million, it adds up pretty quickly. Well, for about nine months I worked on this thing and then it turned out either the band or somebody at the label didn't want to do it; I believe because of the costs. I think that's finally what killed it. So I wound up designing another cover that was originally all black but that I really liked, but that Pat evidently didn't like. We had shot the band portrait up in Chinatown on the streets of San Francisco that wound up on the back cover; on the front cover was a very tight image of Pat wearing his sunglasses. In fact, the record label made some really cool promotional sunglasses to help promote the album. I think one of my most vivid memories of this album coming out was how nervous Michael McDonald was about it. He kept telling me over and over, "I don't think anybody's going to like it and I think my contributions may even end up hurting the band." That's how humble and modest he was, to a fault. I said, "Umm, I think it's going to be okay. The music is very good, and I think it will do great." But he was bordering on depression before it came out. Well, I think it sold three hundred thousand units on its first day, which I think made Michael very happy. And that became the birth of the next era of the band.

Pat

I wasn't at all sure about the cover of *Takin' It to the Streets*. I thought the photo on the back would have been better. Just us posing on the streets of San Francisco up in Chinatown; I thought that looked like a really cool shot for the cover. But what do I know? As it turned out, that cover became one of our most iconic. That's actually me that you see on there with my sunglasses. I guess the reason I was so skeptical was because of all of the pressure on that record. I was nervous about the band. I knew how great Mike was and how good the music was, but it was still a real transitional phase for us. You never know what's going to happen. People knew us as one thing, and now all of a sudden we were shifting gears. I had no idea whether or not fans would go along with us. I love what Michael brought to the band, but it was a pretty big departure. Well, I guess I was wrong about that as well. Obviously, that album did great, we all did great, and with Michael in place we were ready to go to a new level.

After the *Takin' It to the Streets* album and the tour that followed, we put our heads together and tried to figure out when we might be able to find the time to continue working on some new material. I think we were all hoping that Tom would want to get back in with us and record some songs. Unfortunately, that just wasn't meant to be. He made it clear that he wanted to work on a solo project, and so we plowed ahead. I knew this record, which became *Livin' on the Fault Line,* was going to be different. Our boundaries had shifted, and so, for me anyway, I kind of let go of more traditional forms and tried to write songs that were a little more experimental. I felt like Jeff and Mike might be able to help me with the crazy ideas that had worked their way into my consciousness. The two craziest being "Fault Line" and "Chinatown." I was always infatuated with San Francisco, its history and culture, so the lyrical content in those two songs is linked directly to the city. There are bunches of 1906 earthquake references in "Fault Line," and I wanted to try something outside the pocket. Listening to the track even today, it's definitely outside! It's like five or six movements in one, and more jazz-fusion than rock. Bless Ted for letting me do something like this. On the other hand, "Chinatown" is one of my favorite tunes that I have ever been involved in writing. A lot of credit goes to Mike for his input on these songs. It's obvious from the vocal arrangements how much he did to bring the vocals to life and help me find the cadence to the lyrics I had written. But the intricate arrangement, vocals, and solos of "Chinatown" are, to me, some of the coolest playing ever. Keith's drum part and Tiran's parts are inspired. Ted did some outstanding percussion that makes the whole track groove and percolate. This is Jeff's introduction of the guitar synthesizer, and it's otherworldly. I had written the chords and my parts for the song, and it's my recollection that I was still developing my picking parts during the quieter passages, and it was a bit of a jam as we proceeded to the guitar/synth solo. I still don't know how it came together so perfectly. I remember at the time thinking, is this what telepathy feels like? We hadn't really played the song together much, but we all hit the accents exactly together, all the way to the end. We entered all the different sections precisely together, and the subtlety and intensity of attack on the instruments is incredibly tight. I knew when we'd hit the last note that this was the take, and as complicated as it was, I was amazed that I had been able to make it through the song without any major clams.

"There's a Light" is still one of my all-time favorite songs from Mike. Great lyrics, melody, performance, and Norton Buffalo's harmonica playing is superb! I always feel good after listening to this tune. "Made That Way" is another great song from this record. I have wonderful memories from the making of this album. It was probably the least commercial of all the records we had done up to this point, but one of the most rewarding for me musically. As usual, Ted asked me to come up with a little acoustic guitar ditty, as he called them, to stick on the album somewhere, so I threw all my ragtime riffs together and came up with "Larry the Logger." Thinking about my old friend Larry, who had departed this life as I laid it down, it was the last track we recorded for the project. All the songs on this record were fun, and once again an amazing gift and memory to carry with me.

Tom

That tour was followed by moving rehearsals to Montara down by Half Moon Bay. I was living in Novato by then, and it was a helluva long drive to and from every day. We rehearsed and worked up songs for the *Livin' on the Fault Line* album. And I was feeling like I was in the wrong place musically. They had established a new direction, and it wasn't one I was comfortable with. So I made a decision to take whatever songs I had and basically get out of the way so they could continue with the new style. In other words, I left the band. It was a big step, but it was definitely time to move on. And, truthfully, it was kind of a relief.

I felt removed watching the kind of success they were having. Michael is a great songwriter and obviously a great singer and keyboard player. It was just a different band than the one I had been in. I felt good about their success, but I had made the right decision by leaving the band.

I took a year off doing little musically, moved back to Mill Valley, and ended up playing softball for a bit and gaining weight while occasionally jamming with some local guys. By '78 I was getting the itch to do something musically and started writing and got in touch with Ted Templeman. He came by the house a couple of times when he was in the Bay Area. Before long, we had decided to do a solo album on Warner Bros., which was probably the most fun I'd had in a studio since the early seventies. It was the perfect tonic at that time. I could do whatever style and try any musical idea I had, and we had great studio musicians to cut the tracks with, and the same for any overdubbing. Both Tower's horns and the Memphis Horns played on some of the tracks; Bill Payne, Mark Jordan, David Paich, and Michael McDonald played keyboards; and Jim Keltner, Rick Shlosser, David Garabaldi, and Keith Knudsen played drums. We used Bob Glaub, Paul Stallworth, and Rick Chudacoff on bass. Paul Barrere played some guitar, and Nicolette Larson, Ted, Steve Perry, and I did the background vocals. I had such a great time doing that album—it was cathartic for me to have all that freedom. Revisiting Heider's in San Francisco and doing the rest at Amigo in Burbank was like going home. Ted and I both had a great time being in the studio together again. Warner released "Savannah Nights" as a single, and it did pretty well. The album sold okay, too. Doing my solo record was a new direction I really enjoyed. And the pressure was a lot different. I could focus a lot more on my writing and my playing and call all the shots. I was really proud of the record. It was called *Everything You've Heard Is True,* which seemed appropriate, and it was an important step for me because I was in transition from being in the Doobies to being on my own. I still had a way to go, but that really represented me getting my shit together and taking things more seriously. I had been drifting a bit after the *Livin' on the Fault Line* sessions with the Doobies, and I really wanted this record to be good. The familiarity of working with Ted really helped make the project feel comfortable, just like old times. And I took a great band, with people I knew from the Doobies (John Hartman) and from the Bay Area, plus a three-piece version of the Memphis Horns, on the road to support the album. Another thing that tied it together was having David Gest doing my PR to help promote the release. I had come to know him while still playing with the Doobies around '76, and he brought some great people/celebrities around as well as press/radio and TV to help work the album. I did two shows with Dick Clark in L.A. and did a show on *Soundstage* in Chicago. I also did a couple of shows like Mike Douglas and Merv Griffin that seemed a little strange for what I was doing musically. But Stevie Wonder had done them already, and if it was good enough for Stevie Wonder, it was definitely good enough for me. Some years later, some of the guys in the Doobies and myself played shows that David and Michael Bolton put on to raise money for charities both in L.A. and New York, and the entire Doobie Brothers band itself would go on to do these "extravaganzas" that David would put together. They featured people like Chaka Khan, Whitney Houston, and Dionne Warwick—with a huge backing band and even a gospel choir at the show in L.A. That was an amazing show! Other shows like the one in Hawaii at the old HIC Arena in Honolulu had artists like Isaac Hayes, Martha Reeves, and Chaka Khan, and some of the others featured big-name movie and TV stars, mostly from the past. Crazy combinations of people. The last one of these was in Memphis with a lot of R&B artists from the '60s and '70s. After that, David Gest relocated to London, where he eventually passed away. But I think his wedding to Liza Minnelli in New York in 2002 was the topper of all his shows. That was insane! Even crazier than the Michael Jackson thirtieth-anniversary show in Madison Square Garden in 2001 (a night of stars both old and new), and that's saying something! David had a knack for getting all these celebrities to show up for anything he did. I don't know how he did it, but it worked. And he was in his element!

When it came time to do the follow-up album, Ted wasn't

available. So I did the album with Michael Omartian. I hadn't met Michael before that album, but I knew his work from the Christopher Cross albums he'd done, which I really liked.

Like the first solo album, I had written most of the songs, so I had an idea where I wanted to go musically. Michael worked differently from Ted but had great ideas and was a keyboard player himself. This album was approached differently in that we had basically the same players on every song. And besides me on guitar, we had Mike Baird on drums, Greg Douglass on guitar, Phil Aaberg on keyboards, and Dennis Belfield on bass. That was the band on every track. Pat Simmons played and sang on a couple of songs, Bobby LaKind played congas and percussion, Novi Novog played viola on a track, and Red Rhodes played pedal steel. We used three guys to sing backgrounds, and they were incredible together: Tommy Funderburk, Joe Chemay, and Jim Haas. I felt good about this album, and the songs were a different direction from *Everything You've Heard Is True*, except for "Wastin' Time," which sounded like a Doobies tune. And that was the single. But, unfortunately, the album didn't do as well. I toured a little, mostly in California. And that was that.

Michael

One of the first things that jumped out at me about the band was that they loved being on the road. They were the ultimate road warriors. That was so different from being in Steely Dan. Those guys hated being on the road. But for the Doobies, it was just a way of life. I mean, that plane, the Doobie Liner. I had always flown commercial with Steely Dan. But with a plane for the band, everything changes. No more rushing to catch a flight. It doesn't leave until you show up. And they toured so much that you might be home for just a couple of weeks, with just enough time to do your laundry and then head back out again. I had always admired the Doobie Brothers. I mean, in my cover band we used to play some of their songs.

Pat

When we hit L.A. on our tour before *Streets* came out, we played, and had a nice response from the audience, and were feeling good about the performance that evening. The record label had arranged a reception, dinner, and drinks for after the concert. Gregg Allman and Cher, who were the new power couple at that time, were invited, and there were several other notables, as well as family and friends, there. At some point during the evening, the head of promotions for the record company pulled me aside and said, "What do you think you're doing?" "I beg your pardon?" "You're never gonna make it with this band!" Holy shit! The guy who is in charge of the branch of Warner Bros. who's supposed to promote our records is dissing me and the band. I couldn't believe what I was hearing. I told him that this was not the time or the place to be saying these things to me, and that anyway it was inappropriate coming from someone whose job it was to help the label's artists, since it is we who provide the income that he enjoys. What an asshole. I turned my back and walked away. I have never seen him again. Before the year was out, he was gone from the label. Not through anything I said. Obviously, I wasn't the only one he was insulting. He must have pissed somebody else off. We were doing everything we could to survive as a band. All we were focused on was keeping things together. I started thinking about all the bands that had come through heavy personnel changes. Fleetwood Mac came to mind. I wasn't sure what was going to happen with Michael, but I knew he was really good, and I knew that we had to keep going. We had only been a band for five years at that point. I know it seems like we had been around a long time, but we really hadn't been. We were still a new group in my head. We had done a lot, but I thought we had a lot more to do. I wasn't going to let someone's comment like that get in our way. We were going to give it a shot. And I was feeling really hopeful about it.

Michael

For a long time, people have said to me, "You changed the Doobie Brothers. They adopted your sound." But that's not true at all. It may be my voice on some of the songs, but it was the band that adapted everything, not just me. That's what's so great about the Doobies. It's a total band situation. Their sound evolved as a whole unit, not just because of me. They all wanted to try new things, and they did. Maybe my being there created some sort of opportunity to do things differently. But it was hardly me doing all the work. That was always a band of very talented musicians that always rose to the occasion, and in Tom's absence they absolutely grew. I know Warner Bros. was really scared about not having Tom's voice on there. Tom then went off and did a solo album that I thought was brilliant. Really important record for him to show what else he could do. I was so happy for him and proud of him. And, of course, Warner Bros. eventually came around to not being so scared once *Takin' It to the Streets* started doing pretty well. As for Pat, well, I'm not sure how to put into words how much his friendship, loyalty, and band leadership has meant to me over the years.

I never thought that they would need any of my songs. They had so many classics already when I came aboard. I mean, really iconic songs that are still timeless today. When I look back on it, as a solo artist, to have enough material to do a real show, I'm not sure I ever really had enough. But when I do Doobie Brothers songs, then I am all set.

Pat

Michael McDonald definitely brought us a different kind of sound. Personally, I just loved it. I know it represents a different chapter in the band's history, and there are always going to be people that prefer the way things have been before. But I just looked at it as a growth process. Quite honestly, if he hadn't shown up when he did, it would've been very hard for us to maintain exactly what we were doing. Our sound definitely got more sophisticated with him, and I think that's a good thing. I was proud of the audience's reaction. I was proud of winning Grammys. It was just different than before. Not necessarily better or worse, just different.

Michael

One of the things I really liked about working with Ted Templeman is that he would always enlist other artists that he was working with to appear on each other's records. Whether it was Carly Simon or Little Feat or whomever, you ended up playing on each other's albums, and it was a very collaborative concept. In that respect, he was helping really change the face of music by creating this amazing melting pot. Everybody he was working with brought something different to the party. By allowing us to collaborate and mix it up, he encouraged the creation of new forms of music. I don't think Ted gets enough credit for that, but he really did make a big difference. This was back when certain producers worked very closely with certain artists and almost became a member of the band. That was Ted with the Doobie Brothers. He and the band had grown together because of the great work they had done together. So they really were kind of inextricably linked. They had so much trust built. But Ted just always seemed to have a million ideas, and most of them were pretty good. It's amazing to me that everything functioned the way it did, because honestly there was a lot of excess during that time as well. Lots of drinking and lots of drugs. But somehow the music always turned out okay. It's like, no matter what, no matter how things might have seemed as if they were getting out of control, you knew it had to come back to the music. That's why you were there.

Pat

Around 1976, I was hanging out with my wife's brother, Bill Craddock, one day, shooting the breeze. "If you could do anything in your life, what would it be?" I asked him. He told me he had always dreamed of starting a little shop catering to old motorcycles, early Harleys, Indians, that kind of a thing. By that time, I knew I would be getting a Harley, but this concept Bill mentioned began to intrigue me. I immediately started looking around to see what was out there in the marketplace. I was certainly a novice, but I had some experience as a mechanic, having worked in a garage as a teenager and fooling around with my old BSA motorcycle. I bought every motorcycle magazine I could find, subscribed to *Hemmings Motor News*, sent away for every motorcycle-parts catalog listed, and visited shops around the Bay Area that I thought might give me a clue as to what Bill might have in mind. In San Jose, there was this guy with his shop, Antique and Modern. He literally had a city block's worth of motorcycle parts underneath an old tin-shed roof. In Oakland was Stan's Cycle Shop, another antique and vintage guy. Also, Arlen Ness over in San Leandro. There was another place called The Shop in Ventura.

I began to understand what was possible and started to get excited about the prospect. I went to Bill and told him I was willing to put up the capital for a shop if he would help me manage the business and take over when I had to be away working. He enthusiastically agreed, and we began to brainstorm our way toward what would become Classic Motorcycles of Santa Cruz. I discovered there were companies that specialized in obsolete parts for mostly early Harleys and Indians, both original-new old stock and reproduction. After a lot of discussions, I started ordering samples and storing them in my old barn, building our future inventory. After a year or more, we found a location for our shop, did some interior improvements, and transferred our stock. We had nostalgic T-shirts made to sell, bought leather clothes and goods, antique and modern books, and magazines, pins, patches, memorabilia, and parts, parts, parts! When I was on the road with the Doobs, I would comb the local papers for bikes and parts and stash them in our equipment truck, and our driver, Oscar, would bring them up to our shop. I had the idea that having some cool vintage bikes on the floor in the shop might attract customers. I bought four '20s-era Harley JD models for $1,800, and I think that was the beginning of my love affair with really old bikes. I began reading about the history of motorcycling in America and discovered there were hundreds of manufacturers that have come and gone through the years. The more I learned, the more I wanted to know. I read about Steve McQueen's love affair with the old bikes and met Bud Ekins, Steve's stunt double, through a mutual friend. Bud took me under his wing and allowed me to view his collection of mostly pre–World War I bikes, and that was it. I was completely infatuated with motorcycles, old and new. It was about this time that I bought my first new Harley from Sam Arena's shop in San Jose. A Super Glide that I would spend most of my waking hours driving up and down the Coast Highway. I began attending auctions and motorcycle shows, as well as scouring classifieds for old motorcycles. In those days, a lot of old, used bikes were cheap. I acquired and sold quite a few, hanging on to some that I fell in love with. Bud sold me a few of his bikes, and when Steve McQueen passed away, I attended the auction held by his family and bought three of his old bikes. At some point years later, I was introduced to his son, Chad, and daughter, Terry. Both nice kids. They came to a Doobies rehearsal one time, and Chad whips out a big, fat doobie, which we proceeded to smoke, on the spot!

One day, I was at the shop and a few Harley riders walked in and introduced themselves to me. They were all executives from the factory who were in town for the San Jose Mile, a premier national AMA flat-track-oval motorcycle race. We had a great visit, and they invited me to be their guest at the race. That began a relationship with Harley that has lasted for over forty years. I have been fortunate enough to become friends with so many wonderful people associated with the company: Willie G. Davidson, and his wife, Nancy; Willie's daughter, Karen; his sons Bill and Michael. Racers Jay Springsteen, Scott Parker, and Randy Goss. And many others, too many to name.

As the years rolled on, my passion for motorcycling began to rub off on my bandmates. Keith had ridden bikes on and off for years. Now he went full on, and bought a new Harley, as did Chet, Bobby, John, and even Mike. Wow! Many of us eventually participated in Harley events and parades, and the band played many shows, including Harley's hundredth anniversary, which was a huge landmark celebration for the company. I was like a pig in shit. This was my tribe, and I was so proud to be there with the Doobie Brothers.

20

WHEELS OF FORTUNE

Pat
___

The PR guy we hired in late 1975, David Gest, was so interesting. He knew all of these celebrities, so you never knew
who was going to turn up at a rehearsal or show. Michael
Jackson was a good friend of his and evidently was a big Doobie Brothers fan, so we saw Michael all the time. The same
thing went for Angie Dickinson. She was just lovely. David
brought this Hollywood element to our lives that I don't think
we would've had otherwise, and it was fun. We got to know
David through the Memphis Horns. He was their PR manager,
and he did the same thing for Al Green and Willie Mitchell
and Hi Records. David had so many great connections. After
I wrote a song for Al Green, the fact that he was one of David's clients made it easy for me to get it to him. I love soul

music and was a huge fan of his. We went to Chicago to see him. He didn't record my song, but something else happened. David and I were in the club in Chicago where Al was performing, and when he did "Let's Stay Together," he actually called me up onstage. It was crazy. The club was called the Burning Spear. He kept asking the crowd, "Did he testify? Did Pat testify?" The place was going crazy. Honestly, it was one of my most memorable moments as a musician. He passed on the song I wrote for him ("Echoes of Love"), but I sure had fun sitting in with him.

Dan

I worked with the band to hire the publicist David Gest in 1975. The timing was great. With Michael in the band, there was a lot of news to talk about, and we were getting lots of radio play. I put together an event to kick off the second half of the southern tour in late 1975. I called it Moonlight on the Mississippi. David was able to get Al Green and lots of other musicians to come play. It was one of the craziest events we pulled off. In the second half of 1975, I wanted to plan a big event down in Memphis. "Black Water" had really blown up, and the band was doing well on the road with Michael McDonald. The shows were strong, and there was a lot of momentum. I hired a riverboat with little boats to taxi people to and from the shore. It was a really big deal. Elvis Presley was actually supposed to show up at night but couldn't make it. But it was still a great time. It almost didn't happen. The day before, I had flown down to Memphis to make the final arrangements, but the band got stopped in Nashville. Another example of an over-zealous cop that thought he could make a big score with the trophy of a band like the Doobie Brothers.

Pat

David got us some of the most prominent and influential south-ern musicians to play under the stars on this beautiful riverboat. Talk about a lineup: Al Green, Sam and Dave, Carla Thomas, Rufus Thomas, and others. It was amazing. Sitting in and play-ing guitar with Jerry Lee Lewis on "Great Balls of Fire"? I mean, how can you beat that? It was a very memorable night for the Doobie Brothers. David was always good at getting our name in the papers, especially after something happened in Nashville just a day before the show on the riverboat. We were spon-sored by a company at the time that provided us with daily vitamins. I forget what the business arrangement was, but our stewardess would set them out on the counter of the Doobie Liner every day, and we would grab them as we boarded. There were maybe eight or nine pills in the clear bags: vitamin A, vi-tamin C, fish oil, and so on. The idea was that we would down a bag every day to help keep our systems balanced on the road. Well, when we landed in Nashville, cars pulled up on the run-way to pick us up and take us to the gig. Evidently, there was a part-time cop on the driving crew, and he got wind of these packs of vitamins. Suddenly, he called his bosses at the force and claimed that we were smuggling pills across state lines.

There were a ton of Nashville cops there in a matter of minutes, and Sam, to his credit, stood out there and said, "Nobody's getting in my goddamn plane without a search warrant." The cop said, "Why not?" And Sam said, "Because I'm not letting anybody plant anything in here." They went to get a search warrant while we jumped in the plane and started getting rid of everything we knew would get us in trouble, mostly pot and hash, which we then digested or flushed down the toilet on the plane. When the cops finally arrived with their warrant, this part-time cop (who clearly was looking to impress his bosses) led them into the plane, where they saw the packs of vitamins and realized this was all much ado about nothing. The chief of police pulled us aside and was deeply apologetic, and I think that guy got fired for trying to make something out of nothing. David, never to miss an opportunity, made sure the event was in papers all over the country, however. I guess it gave us a little bit of a badass rock and roll edge, even if we were stopped just for vitamins. David knew a news story when he saw one.

Dan

I left around 1976 because of some issues with band management, but I always stayed in touch with the guys. They were my friends; that's the brotherhood I was part of. I think I shot about thirty-five thousand images of the Doobie Brothers, and today I maintain an archive I am very proud of. I also shot a lot of film with them and handled and arranged most of their meeting interviews—I mean, I really got involved with crafting the image that helped them build their brand, which is still so strong today. I think that's what I'm most proud of. For all the great meals and running around and all that, when I see the album covers for *Vices* and *Takin' It to the Streets,* it takes me back to those crazy days of working with them. When they were inducted into the Rock & Roll Hall of Fame, I contributed a lot of the imagery. That forced me to go back through everything and carefully analyze everything we had done together. It actually blew my fucking mind. The number of shows they did in the number of places and the number of miles covered. I honestly don't know how any of us got through it. The experience was one thing for guys like me, working behind the scenes. It was an entirely different thing for those guys onstage. They had no place to hide. They had to get up there every night and deliver. And they did. Every night that those guys hit the stage, even during the wildest, craziest days on the road, they gave the fans exactly what they came for. No matter what, it was always about the show.

Pat

Bobby LaKind had joined the band by this point. Such a great story. He was originally a roadie for the lighting crew. Bobby told us he played the conga drums and asked if he could sit in and play on "Listen to the Music." None of us thought this was a good idea. First of all, we weren't sure of his ability. Plus, we weren't sure how the other crew members would feel about this. And would this start a precedent that might start problems down the line? We put him off for a long time. But Bobby was persistent, and I think at some point we just gave in to get him off our backs. I think Hartman was the one who said, "Let's give him a chance." Well, lo and behold, he was pretty damn good. Then he wanted to play on other tunes. Oh boy, what had we started? Well, finally we let him play on "Long Train Runnin'." Suddenly, the song came alive. From there he worked his way into other songs, and pretty soon it was something that we began looking forward to. Bobby wanted to be a serious musician. He started taking lessons from Afro-Cuban teachers and developed his style and abilities in ways that were very impressive. As far as I was concerned, he was a fantastic player, and one of the best percussionists I've ever played with. Incredibly inventive, committed, and inspiring. He had a tough-guy personality and could be kind of a hard-ass sometimes, but he was a sweet guy underneath it all. We started using him on some sessions in the studio, and before you knew it, he had worked his way into a regular role in the band. So he went from being a roadie to a session guy to a full-time performing member. I'm not sure there were many other bands that ever promoted a roadie to band member, but that was one thing that made the Doobie Brothers special. It didn't matter where you came from.

Tom

In '76, when the band was touring for *Takin' It to the Streets,* we subleased a Conveyor twin-engine turboprop (a more modern aircraft than the Doobie Liner) from Seals & Crofts. Its pilot, Pete Fumagalli, wasn't much of a pilot. He would show up at the gig almost every night kind of drunk with a couple of female "friends." He was kind of a character. A bit of a swinger, who liked to party and drink. He had trouble starting the plane every morning, and he let Baxter land the plane once, which caused Sam, who was flying the crew at that time, to observe that we almost didn't make it. Not a good call, and Dan Fong, our tour photographer and caterer, along with James Mitchell (one of the Memphis Horns, who were touring with us), jumped ship and rode with the crew after that.

Michael

Traveling with the Doobie Brothers was a special experience, but the story that really sticks out to me was flying into Long Beach one night. I mean, I was not and still am not really a comfortable flyer. I've always had a basic fear of it. We were touring with the Memphis Horns at this particular point, and one of those guys, James Mitchell, was just like me, totally scared of flying. So he and I would usually sit together and kind of freak out if the weather was bad or anything. Just misery loving company. So this one night, as we're coming in for a landing, we fly clear past the air traffic control tower. It went by really quickly. That was weird. And then all of a sudden, the runway lights come right up to the plane, and we hit the ground and bounce up about twenty feet, wings flapping and everything going crazy. Evidently, Jeff Baxter had been given the controls of the plane. While trying to land us, he almost killed us. So basically we're in the middle of an aborted landing. The plane had a rocket pack kind of one-shot deal in the tail of the airplane. It wasn't like regulation equipment or anything; they had kind of hot-rodded it on there. So then the pilot takes control of the plane and sets off that rocket pack that keeps us from stalling. We were just hanging on for dear life as we climbed almost straight up. Total silence on the plane. We finally circled and landed properly, and that was an experience that to this day still makes me uncomfortable to think about. Everybody knows how rock and roll has a pretty weird history with airplanes: Buddy Holly, Otis Redding, Lynyrd Skynyrd—lots of really sad stories. When you are on the road in a band, you start to understand how mistakes get made. Rushing around, tight schedules, and other pressures definitely create an environment that is sometimes dangerous. You are just going full tilt all the time.

At least, that's how it used to be. Today, of course, it's a totally different environment. Things have slowed down, and the pacing is different. But in the 1970s, it was freewheeling and often out of control. I think a lot of us look back and breathe a sigh of relief that we are here today to talk about everything.

Pat

Pete said there was a wind-shear problem that blew us off course while we were landing. We were all pretty shook up by the experience. It just so happened that our old pilot, Sam Stewart, was at the airport that day when we arrived. When Fumagalli said "wind shear," Sam said, "bullshit, there was no wind." About a year later, Mike and I were hanging out, and he says, "Hey, remember when Jeff tried to land the plane?" "What the fuck are you talkin' about?" I had no fucking idea! Of course! That's what Sam was intimating; it all made sense. I couldn't figure out who was stupider, Jeff Baxter or Pete Fumagalli. What imbeciles! After we quit leasing the Conveyor, I heard Pete started doing cargo runs in and out of South America— Colombia, Bolivia, who knows where else? My instinct told me, smuggling . . . Anyway, the story I got was that Pete flew off into the Bermuda Triangle and was never seen again. If anyone has any information that might confirm or discredit this story, please let me know. I would hope it turned out better for Pete. Whatever his issues, he was always a nice guy.

Tom

While the band was making *Livin' on the Fault Line,* I was living up in Novato, at the north end of Marin County, which proved to be a mistake. It was very conservative at that time, and they didn't appreciate a "longhair" driving a nice car in their midst. I was practicing in Montara, near Half Moon Bay, where the Doobie Brothers were rehearsing at that point, so I had a long drive each day. I just finally said, "This isn't working for me. I don't belong here. I'm done, and I'm leaving." I felt more and more out of place and had to get away from that lifestyle, so that's when I officially left. I moved back to Mill Valley, played a lot of softball, and played music with people I knew locally.

And I was okay with that. And I was grateful for the time away from the road and everything that went with it. Time to pause and reflect.

Ted came by to see me about making some solo music when he was in the Bay Area, and I give him credit for getting my first solo album going. I visited my sister in Seattle, where I actually sat in one night with the Doobie Brothers. Later the next year, I remember going to L.A. for the band's "Minute by Minute" Grammy party. I was touring on my first solo album and had played a show in nearby Bakersfield the night before. I was happy to see the guys and congratulate them on their success. I was okay with watching them get all of this acclaim. They had earned it! They had created a really successful and popular record that was all over the radio. It was so different from what I had worked on with the band. It was kind of surreal watching them and what they were going through. I felt distant and knew at that point that it would never have worked with me there. I did not belong in the new version of the band. I was happy making my solo music and had made peace with the decision to leave. I felt great for Pat and the whole band.

Pat

I would sometimes hang out with Ted when he was working with other artists. I went with him a couple of times to Van Halen sessions. I just loved them. It was fun to watch Ted work with them and then compare it to how he worked with us. Van Halen sessions were unlike any others. There was probably a little blow going around, David Lee Roth had a fifth of Jack Daniels that he'd offer, and I'd politely accept. He would carry on an endless, funny, brilliant stream of consciousness for our benefit. And then of course there was Eddie Van Halen. I think watching him was my favorite part of the sessions. He was just simply better than anybody, sitting there inventing and reinventing the art of playing guitar. It was really mind-blowing watching a band as great as them.

Keyboard player extraordinaire Billy Payne, from Little Feat, and a part of the Doobie Brothers for many years. (*Photograph © 2020 by Dan Fong*)

Luke Bryan and the guys in 2011 on the Country Music Television show, *Crossroads*. Luke's a big Doobie's fan! (*Photograph by Rick Diamond for CMT / Getty Images*)

Pat's family, left to right: wife, Cris; their daughter, Lindsey; her husband, Nadav; son Pat Jr.; grandson, Malu; with his mom, Darci; son Josh and Pat in the front.
(Courtesy of Nadav Benjamin)

Pat with the gifted John McFee. *(Courtesy of Mark Weiss)*

Pat with his grandsons
Malu, Kukui, and Kolea
at home on Maui.
(Courtesy of Pat Simmons)

A recent shot of Pat with the Epiphone
he bought back in 1967. (*Courtesy of Nadav Benjamin*)

Pat playing one of his favorite Taylor guitars. (*Courtesy of Andrew MacPherson*)

Tom getting the crowd up!
(Courtesy of Mark Weiss)

Pat doing what he
does best.
(Courtesy of Mark Weiss)

Promo shot of Tom from
their first photo shoot
after signing with Full Stop
Management. Shot as the sun
was going down out at
a Disney-owned studio lot.
(Courtesy of Andrew MacPherson)

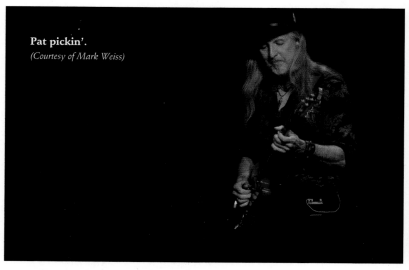

Pat pickin'.
(Courtesy of Mark Weiss)

Pat's wife, Cris, getting ready
for the Motorcycle Cannonball
Endurance Run, in 2014. Pat's
is a 1914 Harley, Cris's is a
1915 (named "Effie").
(Courtesy of Nadav Benjamin)

Tom around 1997 with his kids, Lara and Chris. (*Courtesy of Tom Johnston*)

Tom with his family in the mid-2000s when the band played the Mountain Winery in Saratoga, California. His daughter, Lara, opened that night for the band!
(*Courtesy of Tom Johnston*)

Tom with his wife, Diane.
(*Courtesy of Tom Johnston*)

Tom playing some
acoustic.
(Courtesy of Mark Weiss)

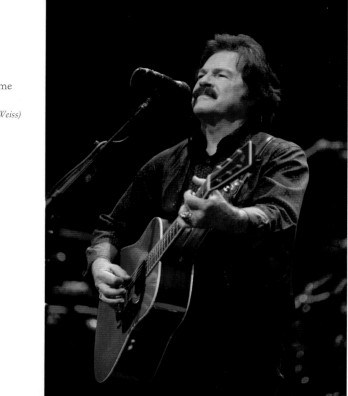

The Johnston family, left to right: Tom's daughter-in-law, Kristen (Chris's wife), holding
grandson, Ash; daughter, Lara; wife, Diane; me and son, Chris, 2020. *(Courtesy of Tom Johnston)*

If it has strings, he can play it. The incomparable John McFee.

Courtesy of Mark Weiss

John McFee. (*Courtesy of Tony Scarlati*)

Pat warms up backstage. (*Courtesy of Tony Scarlati*)

John McFee with Peter Frampton when the Doobies toured with Peter in 2014.
(Courtesy of Tony Scarlati)

John McFee, who brings so much to the band.
(Courtesy of Tony Scarlati)

John McFee, in action.

Photograph © 2020 by Dan Fong

John McFee, the "new guy" since 1979. (*Courtesy of Tony Scarlati*)

A recent, classic shot of Pat. *(Courtesy of Tony Scarlati)*

Playing in the rain! *(Courtesy of Tony Scarlati)*

Rocking hard for more than fifty years, ladies and gentlemen, Tom Johnston. *(Courtesy of Tony Scarlati)*

Pat jamming with
Peter Frampton.
*(Courtesy of Tony
Scarlati)*

Pat's timeless playing has
helped keep the band steady
for more than fifty years.
(Courtesy of Tony Scarlati)

Tom, warming up backstage.
(Courtesy of Tony Scarlati)

Tom, in the spotlight.
(Courtesy of Tony Scarlati)

Still pleasing the fans
after all these years.
(Courtesy of Tony Scarlati)

John, Tom, and Pat.
(Courtesy of Tony Scarlati)

Left to right: Pat, cowriter Chris Epting, and Tom. *(Courtesy of Chris Epting)*

More than 50 years down the road, Tom and Pat, the Doobie Brothers are still rocking. *(Courtesy of Will Hart)*

21

WHAT'S HAPPENING!!

1977–79:
Patrick Simmons / Michael McDonald / Jeff "Skunk" Baxter /
Tiran Porter / Keith Knudsen / John Hartman /
Tom Johnston

Tiran

I just did not want to do the *What's Happening!!* TV show. I was adamant. What bothers me most is that it was supposed to be a show about Black people, but it was written entirely by white people. So I really didn't want to do it. I just thought there was something so wrong in Hollywood that things were allowed to be like this. I felt like they were trivializing the Black experience. So why should I help them do that? There are times in life when you have to take a stand, even if it's not good for your own personal business. I just could not get behind it. I got where the other guys were coming from, but I didn't think they understood where I was coming from. I was the Black guy in the band. Nobody else knew what that was like.

Pat

To this day, one of the things I get asked most about is when we appeared on the television show *What's Happening!!* in January 1978. I don't think we appreciated at the time the effect that that show would have on our career, but that was just the power of television back then. Our publicist, David Gest, was doing a great job for us at the time. He was getting us lots of high-profile interviews, even though he was just in his twenties. He reminded me of a Swifty Lazar in the making. He was just that good at what he did. He was so plugged into the Hollywood scene, and I think that was a big part of his success, at least with us. For instance, at one point he got us to co-host Dinah Shore's TV show for an entire week. I remember playing in a golf tournament around that time with tons of celebrities that I never would have met before. We actually played songs with Dinah at a benefit for the United Way after the golf tournament. We played her songs, and then she sang our songs. There were tons of stars in attendance: the Jackson 5, Mickey Rooney, the entire cast of *Leave It to Beaver,* Scatman Crothers, Will Gear, and the cast from *The Waltons*. I could go on and on! It was really fun. So David came to us one day and said, "Okay guys, I have something here that I think is really special. The ABC sitcom *What's Happening!!* actually wants to build an entire episode around music featuring you guys. You're even going to get to play some songs and read some lines and be actors for a day or two. It's going to be magnificent exposure, and I also think it will be a good time for you guys." I thought it was a fabulous idea. It definitely would expose us to audiences that maybe weren't that familiar with us, and it just sounded like a good time. Michael didn't really care either way. I don't think Hartman wanted to do it. And so I called them both and said, "Come on, you guys, we have to do this. It's a really fun show and also a really well-written show. It will be a good time and it will be good for the band." I was always thinking about what was good for the band. Michael watched it, thought it was great, and agreed with me. A problem arose when it came down to Tiran. He didn't want to do it. In fact, he was adamant about not doing it. He thought it was stereotypical and portrayed Black people in a way that was artificial. I thought the exact opposite. I thought it was refreshingly down-to-earth and honest, but he obviously wasn't feeling it, and I respected that. He is Black and I am not. I tried explaining that our band's shift to an R&B sound was a good reason to do it. He just wasn't hearing it, but I was relieved when he did ultimately say, "I don't want to do it, but I'll do it."

Tiran

To be fair, I know a lot of people watched that show, and to this day people come up to me and tell me much they loved it. I respect that. But at the time I really just did not want to do it. I will say that all of the guys in the band seemed to totally respect my viewpoint. Nobody challenged me or tried to tell me I was wrong. We were doing a lot of other television at that time. One of my favorites was *Dick Clark's New Year's Rockin' Eve,* which we appeared on with the Beach Boys and Chicago. All of us doing Christmas songs. Those harmonies were just amazing. Now, *that* was something I wanted to do. But not *What's Happening!!*

Pat

So we go down to the set the first day and everybody is really happy to see us. In fact, they also told us they didn't have enough time to tell the story in one episode, so they made it a two-part episode. Jeff Baxter was having a really great time on the set. He was a huge stoner back then and smoked more than you can imagine. So when Rerun (played by Fred Berry) ran backstage one day and said, "Hey, the Doobie Brothers! Anybody got a doobie?", we all laughed hard and then fired a few up. I think even Tiran eventually had a good time there.

If you haven't seen it, the two-episode arc features a concert by us, during which Rerun's gigantic portable boom box is exposed, allowing us to explain to him why it's not right to bootleg live music when you're at a concert. Overall, I think it was a great chance for America to see a bunch of middle-class white guys doing a show with a mostly African American cast. And, again, of all of the things we've done, that's the one I probably get asked about the most.

22

DEPENDIN' ON YOU

1979–80:
**Patrick Simmons / Michael McDonald / John McFee /
Tiran Porter / Keith Knudsen / Chet McCracken /
Bobby LaKind / Cornelius Bumpus**

Pat

Jeff and I got really close not long after he joined the band, and we grew even closer after Tom left the band. We hung out a lot and had some really great times, but then he started getting kind of eccentric. All of us were still smoking a lot of weed in those days, and some were into a little heavier shit. I don't know whether that might have figured into some behavior patterns. In the beginning, we all—at least many of us musicians—wanted to be more spiritual in our outlook. We wanted to commune with nature and lean more left. And most of us explored those directions. We smoked a lot of pot to feel good. We dropped acid, and that expanded our view of the world. We did all those things, and most of us survived into the early '70s. But then cocaine started taking over; that was different. Downers and junk were a lot more common back then than most people would be willing to admit. For a lot of people in my world, it went from experimenting to addiction. I saw it with many people in my band. And it always made me uncomfortable.

I'm not sure what was at the heart of Jeff's attitude, but something told me he probably knew exactly what he was do-ing. He's obviously a brilliant guitar player. Nobody could ever challenge that. But he started getting, it seemed, very indulgent. I think he started treating some of the shows like a joke. He'd come out onstage in a bathrobe and slippers and sit down and play seated in a chair like he was in some kind of avant-garde jazz band or something. And when he took his solos, he got into the habit of weaving in lots of disparate pop-culture music references. Maybe it would be the theme from *Bonanza* or *I Love Lucy* or *My Three Sons*. Sometimes, he would just throw as many notes into the space as he could fit, without any thought to context or melody. Atonal cacophony. You just never knew where he was going to go. And if you ever said anything to him about it or challenged it, he would go into a speech about having to express himself to be creative and how jazz guys did all of these kinds of things and on and on. Whenever Jeff went off on one of his musical tangents during solos, Michael would look at us and roll his eyes. Mike didn't like it, but he's such a forgiving and easygoing guy that I didn't think he was going to get too confrontational about it. But Keith and Bobby, on the other hand, had a somewhat shorter fuse. Even in the best circumstances, being on the road involves lots of close quarters. It's normal to get on each other's nerves. Jeff had a gregarious personality that was sometimes fueled by foreign substances, whereas Mike was very low-key, and so sometimes that created problems. When you factor in that Jeff was playing these outlandishly indulgent solos every night, it pushed things over the top. To the other guys in the band, it felt as if Jeff was sabotaging the arrangements of our songs. Again, Michael would thoughtfully think about how to approach it all, whereas Bobby would say, "Fuck that shit we need to do something!" So it became a serious bone of contention. We all knew it was going to come to a head. It was especially hard for me. I respected Jeff so much as a player, and he had such an amazing track record musically. Really a brilliant musician. Also, I cared a great deal for him as a friend. But he was changing, and I could tell he was growing distant from me and, really, from everyone in the band. At this point, he just refused to accept any constructive criticism.

It was getting near the end of the tour, and everybody was extra cranky and crabby. In January 1979, we were heading back from New Zealand and had just been in the Far East. We stopped in Hawaii on the way home, and once we checked into the hotel, Mike, Keith, and Bobby came to my room and let me know that they couldn't take it anymore. Bobby said,

"This has to end and it has to end now." I told them I completely understood where they were coming from and that I wish we could've worked it out. I really did. Our band was at such a high point right then that the last thing anybody wanted was some major shift in personnel, but there was no way around this one. I think most of us realized that Jeff knew what he was doing, knew that he was annoying everybody in the band, but just couldn't help himself. What he was doing kind of bugged me, but what bothered me more was that he was unwilling to compromise. And whenever he was called on it, he just shrugged his shoulders and said, "What?" Like he didn't know anything. So I'm sure I had gotten irritated as well that he was pushing buttons in the band. It really wasn't cool. And so that was the band's decision. I was not in the room when it happened, and if memory serves, management let him know that he was no longer in the Doobie Brothers. And that was basically it.

I think it was the next day, and I was at the bar in the hotel with Michael, just the two of us. I didn't know what was going to happen to the band or if we were even going to continue. Jeff had become a major part of the Doobie Brothers. I said to Michael at the bar, "Would you consider reorganizing something with this band? Or are you thinking about moving on?" He looked me in the eye and said, "Pat, I have to think about it." Well, this was all a bit of a surprise for me. I started playing out the scenario in my head. If Mike left, I guess I could go to Tiran and Keith and the rest of the guys and see if they wanted to do something else. If everybody left, I could've put together a new version of the Doobie Brothers. But that wasn't really what I wanted to do. The whole situation made me unsettled, for obvious reasons, and so I went and booked myself a week in Tahiti, just me. I went to the island of Mooréa, just to get away. I don't think there was a telephone anywhere; there wasn't even electricity, just generators. It was a blissful and relaxing week. Every night I would get up and play with the local band at the bar. I had brought a guitar along with me, and it was cool. The island people were wonderful, and the trip gave me a chance to recharge and think about the future.

As soon as Jeff left, I think Mike felt more relaxed and empowered, which wasn't necessarily a bad thing. He had brought a lot to the band, and so it was good for him to have some directional ownership. The first thing he said was, "I think we need two drummers again." Nothing wrong with that. I always liked having two drummers in the band, and so we did some auditions and found Chet McCracken, a really strong drummer. I suggested we add a horn player, which everybody thought was a good idea.

I knew a sax player, Cornelius Bumpus. I ran into him all the time in Santa Cruz. He would stand out there downtown on Santa Cruz Avenue with his sax case open, just blowing his sweet sounds, and people would be dropping money in the case. I would stand there listening, thinking, holy shit— this guy is great. I had seen him play over the years. He was in a version of Moby Grape for a while, along with several other local bands. He was just a remarkable saxophone player and also a decent keyboard player and singer. Very versatile all around. I first heard about Cornelius from Ted Templeman. Before Ted played in Harpers Bizarre, he had played in a few other bands around Santa Cruz, some with Cornelius. He knew Cornelius from his early days and had been friends with him for years. Ted always talked up Cornelius's talents, and I thought, "Well, if he's good enough for Ted, he's good enough for us." I brought Cornelius in to audition, and everyone just went "holy shit" after he took his saxophone solo on "Takin' It to the Streets." And that he played keyboards and sang totally sealed the deal. He was our guy. He informed us that we should not refer to him as Corny; he was only to be called Cornelius. That was fine with me—I thought he was a monster! Our manager went to hire Cornelius at the squalid rooming house where he lived near San Francisco's Tenderloin District. Our manager wanted to bring him a bunch of albums to listen to so he could get ready to play with us. I'll never forget our manager's description of how Cornelius had to unlock three sets of bolts on the door, like he was barricaded in there. And in his tiny little room, all he had was a bed, a stereo, his horn, and lots of albums. Cornelius told me on a good day he could make maybe thirty or forty bucks playing in the streets. And with us, he would start out making about five thousand dollars a week. A big step up for him, but he certainly deserved it.

When it came to hiring a guitar player, I think we had three guys audition, including Bruce Conte, who had been with Tower of Power until recently. Bruce was great. He could play R&B and pop and of course everything else. Tower of Power was one of our favorite groups, and so Bruce came in and did a good job during the audition. But then Keith brought up a guy named John McFee. I knew who John was. He had been in a great band called Clover, which actually opened for us a couple of times, and then I saw him play with Norton Buffalo. John was a great player. I had remembered meeting him over in England when we played the big Knebworth festival a few years earlier. John came to the audition and did really well. And when we were done playing, he said to me, "You know, I love fingerpicking just like you. And your song 'Slack Key Soquel Rag'—I like that so much that I worked it up. Would you like to play it?" I was impressed. I wrote that song in two parts for our *Stampede* album; John wanted to play the counterpoint that the second part is written for. It's a very complicated yet interesting instrumental piece, and he just nailed it. I knew at the end of that little duet that we had found our guy. And I think everybody else was just as enthusiastic as I was. John can really play anything, from jazz, to fusion, to pop, to rock and roll—he's just one of the most versatile players you will ever meet. Electric, acoustic, pedal steel; he's just incredible. He also had a really cool look and was overall just a great person. He would be the perfect addition to the Doobie Brothers. Many people are not aware of John's remarkable pedigree. He played on records by Van Morrison, Elvis Costello, and many others. As a member of Clover, which also featured Huey Lewis on vocals, John helped lead that band for years, and their catalog is interesting and eclectic. But now he was ours. And we were really excited about the future.

John McFee

I loved the Doobie Brothers. My band Clover had played with them a bunch of times throughout the '70s. I mean, how could you not be a Doobie Brothers fan? So many incredible songs, terrific showmanship; for me, they were the perfect extension of Moby Grape. I was a huge Moby Grape fan, and the Doobie Brothers took the whole Moby Grape concept to another level. The intricate, creative harmonies; the blending of acoustic and electric music—to me, the Doobie Brothers were to be celebrated. I also loved what Ted Templeman had done with them. I worked with Ted on the Van Morrison album *Moondance,* and so I knew how good he was in the studio. In 1979 Ted had also started working with Van Halen, which obviously would result in some terrific records, but it was the Doobie Brothers work that I think really distinguished Ted as an amazing producer. Anyway, my life changed a lot, especially in 1979, because my wife and I now had a son. Things get a lot more serious when you have a kid. My level of responsibility had gone way up, so I was looking for something more reliable in terms of career. Don't get me wrong: I wasn't looking to leave music; I only wanted to find a situation that would allow for more financial stability, because the future was much different for me now. I loved Clover, but the reality was that we were not as commercially viable as many other bands. My wife had been talking with Keith Knudsen's wife; we were all friends. Keith's wife mentioned that the Doobies were looking for someone to take the place of Jeff Baxter. She wondered if I might be interested in the gig. By that point, I had played with a lot of people and turned down a lot of different opportunities. But things were different now. I was very interested in hearing more about the opening with the Doobies. I went to rehearsal and listened to them play for a little bit, and the first thing I thought was, they are fine without me! But then we got to playing, and it felt very comfortable right out of the gate. At one point, I saw an acoustic guitar tuned to "Slack Key Soquel Rag." I was such a fan of that song. Pat and I played it together, and that's when I knew that I'd found my future.

That solidified everything. I felt terrible leaving Clover. I believed and still do believe in that band. But this was the right move. I knew a lot about the Doobie Brothers. I had gotten to know Tommy a little bit from living up in Marin County, and I just loved those earlier records that he played on. But the current edition with Michael McDonald was also a cool band, and I would've been crazy to say no to the gig. Soon after my joining, we were playing at Madison Square Garden as part of the No Nukes benefit, and that was something I still remember very vividly today. Being up there onstage with all of those players, from Jackson Browne to James Taylor and Carly Simon—even Ted Templeman was up there playing with us that night. It was like getting onto a rocket ship when I joined the Doobie Brothers. I had toured for a lot of years, but not on this level. Not with a band like this. It's a bit more than forty years later, and we still joke that I'm the "new guy." But that's what you feel like when you join a band that has already created so much history. I'll always be the new guy.

23

MINUTE BY MINUTE

Pat

Minute by Minute was the first album that felt like the "new" band. Tommy had moved on completely by that point, and Michael's influence was being felt. This will be the very first Doobie Brothers record without Tommy as a member and also the last one to include Jeff Baxter and John Hartman. It came out in the winter of 1979 and soon became the bestselling record in the United States for more than a month. It actually went platinum three times. One of the songs, "What a Fool Believes," which was written by Michael and Kenny Loggins, became the biggest single of our career. There were lots of rumors that Michael Jackson had sung some background vocals on the song, but that's not true. He was definitely hanging around us once in a while, and he seemed to enjoy our music.

I wish I could say he was on there, but he's not. Billy Payne was playing with us again, which was great. In fact, that's him playing synthesizer with Michael on "What a Fool Believes." And it was fun having Ted play drums with Keith on the song as well. "Minute by Minute" was another big single from the album, as was a song that I wrote with Michael called "Dependin' on You." I liked working with Michael. He was a great collaborator and always had lots of good ideas. Easy to work with also, because he's such a nice guy. People would say to me back then, "I can't believe this is the same band that put out "Long Train Runnin'," "China Grove," and "Black Water." I think some fans may have even resented the change of sound. But the Doobie Brothers was always about bringing in lots of different influences. Again, a lot of it goes back to Moby Grape. Think out-of-the-box. Incorporate lots of different styles. Michael definitely brought us many new fans, but I also think a lot of Doobie Brothers fans who had been with us from the beginning were enjoying the ride.

Tiran

Photographing the cover of the *Minute by Minute* album was pretty intense. Our pilot took the plane out to thirty thousand feet and then dropped down at a severe angle so that we could all be floating. If you look at it today, you can barely tell the effect, but it happened. We were floating in that plane for a couple of seconds. I think the only one that got sick was John Hartman.

Pat

The *Minute by Minute* album cover was funny. You can't really see in the picture what is happening. It's not as obvious or dramatic as you would think after going to all that trouble. It was a pretty crazy day. We did a bunch of free falls, where our old pilot, Sam Stewart, would take the plane, the Martin 404, to a high altitude and let the plane fall straight down. After going through about six to eight free falls, we were all starting to feel pretty nauseated. I personally was on the verge of getting the heaves. Well, wouldn't you know it, the photographer, David Alexander, was literally turning a strange shade of green. Uh-oh, he puts two fingers to his pursing lips, as his cheeks began to fill with something . . . Marty Wolf, our stage production guy, was along for the ride, and he quickly grabs a plastic bag that David had been using to stash his rolls of film. He shakes it, and film floats to the ceiling of the plane as we are in the midst of another free fall. Just in time, David puts the bag to his mouth and blows chunks that float around inside the bag pulsating like the Blob. I am ready to follow suit without a bag, oh god! Visions of floating barf! Somehow, I'm able to hold it back. Man, that was a close one. . . .

Ted told me that nobody on the Warner Bros. management side thought that "What a Fool Believes" should be the first single from the new album. I definitely thought it should be. But they just didn't hear it. Ted said they wanted to go with "Minute by Minute" as the lead single. I disagreed, but it was their call. It was 1979 and disco was still pretty big. The Bee Gees were huge, and that obviously wasn't us. We were more about rock, blues, and R&B. But I also thought that "What a Fool Believes" could be a good bridge for an audience that liked to dance. Slightly funky and danceable. There was another song out then by the Captain and Tennille called "Love Will Keep Us Together" that was kind of like that.

So the label changed their mind, and lo and behold it was huge. But, of course, so was "Minute by Minute" when it was released as the next single. There were just so many great songs on that album, even ones that weren't hits, which really increased our live repertoire. That album gave us a better show. And when you have the Memphis Horns out with you, guys who played on all those Stax recordings with Otis Redding and Sam and Dave, not to mention Al Green, Elvis, and all the others, our shows just kept getting better and better.

The Grammy Awards in 1980 became a high-water mark for the band. We were very fortunate to have gotten the award for record of the year with "What a Fool Believes," and best pop vocal by a duo, group, or chorus for "Minute by Minute." We never really cared about awards or anything, but it felt pretty damn good to get nominated. It also felt a little weird. Being at the awards, surrounded by so many notable musicians, was a humbling experience. We were kind of in our own little world up in the Bay Area. I mean, I met Bob Dylan that night! The Grammy Awards that year really gave me pause when I looked at the ten years that the Doobie Brothers had been together. We had released so much music and been through so many things. We squeezed a lot of living into that decade. The Grammys were a really nice recognition and obviously made a statement about Michael McDonald's contribution to the band.

On the night of the Grammys, we got the awards, played on the show, went to after-parties, met and saw lots of stars, and just had a great night. Afterward, I headed back to the Sheraton Universal Hotel, where we always stayed when we were working in L.A. in those days. All the guys in the band were hanging out there that night. For some reason, Jeff Baxter had a room there, even though he lives in L.A. The door to his room was wide open, and he's in there with Jaye P. Morgan, the lady from *The Gong Show,* drinking bourbon and smoking weed. The smoke is wafting down the corridor, and music is blasting from some unknown source. I peek my head in and decide it's getting late and I'm tired, so I bid good night and turn to head to my room. Just then, the hotel security guard rounds the corner, "What the hell's going on here?" I try to head him off, "Oh hey, sorry, man. We just returned from the Grammy Awards, where we won a couple of trophies, and the guys are celebrating. I'll tell 'em to cool it." "I don't give a goddamn what you won—this shit has got to stop!" "Uh . . . it's cool, man, everything is cool." I put my hand on his shoulder, like we were buddies, and BAM! He sucker punches me right in the jaw! I'm down, didn't hurt that much, but WTF!? I'm up, and on my way to the hotel manager's office, where I spend the next hour and a half with the hotel manager, the Doobie Brothers road manager, the security guard, and other friends and interested parties, being talked out of filing a police report by the hotel people. They don't want the bad publicity or a lawsuit, and the security guard is cycling between remorse and aggression (he obviously had issues). I don't want to prosecute anyone, but I'm certainly feeling disappointed at the turn the night has taken. In the end, after making them sweat a bit, I just encouraged the manager and his security personnel to take it a little easier on the guests. I derived that this whole incident was simply a sign that I needed to be reminded that, no matter how cool you think you are, the universe is just waiting to knock you on your ass the minute that you think you've arrived. Whenever I look at those Grammy trophies, I laugh about that night. How the hell did Jeff get hooked up with Jaye P. Morgan?

Michael

That was surreal winning those Grammys. I was so proud of our band that night. I remember there were a couple of people at the show that made comments to me that it was now my band, that it was almost like the Doobie Brothers were my backing band, and I took real offense to that. It wasn't like that at all. The Doobie Brothers allowed me to grow as an artist, and everybody contributed to every record. Just because sometimes it was my voice or just because maybe I wrote something didn't take away from the contributions of everybody. They were a well-oiled machine long before I was there. To this day, I still resent comments like that, like somehow I took over the band and they owed their success to me. That's total nonsense.

When you listen to a Doobie Brothers record, you have to listen to everything that's going on, not just the lead vocal. These are seriously talented players, and in the studio the collaboration was always there. It was hard for some people to understand that when they just heard my voice. But every Doobie Brothers record was a sum of its parts. I knew that. They knew that. And I really didn't like it when anybody suggested otherwise.

WHAT A FOOL BELIEVES

1980–82:
Patrick Simmons / Michael McDonald / John McFee /
Willie Weeks / Keith Knudsen / Chet McCracken /
Bobby LaKind / Cornelius Bumpus

Pat

One Step Closer was a fun album to make and something I have very fond memories of. What was unique is that essentially everybody played on every cut and it was all done live. We had never worked like that before. Guys brought songs in they were working on, or some tunes got worked up right there. But everything was done together and everyone was a part of the creative process. So all of a sudden there were new opportunities for guys that maybe had not had a chance to be as involved before. For instance, Cornelius had a chance to shine more than ever, especially on the title track, which he got to sing with Michael along with playing some incredible sax. Chet and John wrote an instrumental for the album, "South Bay Strut," that was eventually nominated for a Grammy Award in the Best Pop Instrumental Performance category. We were branching out and giving every band member every opportunity that we could to contribute something special. Sonically, I think it was so impressive to have this ensemble of amazing players that sounded big on the one hand but then also had a wonderful intimacy on many of the tracks. Michael co-wrote a song with Patrick Henderson, a friend of his who was a choirmaster who also worked on the album. It was called "Real Love" and it became a pretty decent hit for us (Nicolette Larson is singing background vocals on there). Everybody was playing at such a high level at that point that it was almost intimidating for me! Keith, Chet, Bobby, and Tiran were just so good, and so locked in that we felt we could do anything with them behind us. (Tiran would leave the band soon after the album was released and then we got the incredible Willie Weeks). Once we started touring with that album we would take some of the songs and really stretch them live. I think that album really raised our playing levels, which made for some great melodic departures within the songs and really got us started on the road of getting into those little expansive excursions. The one downside to the whole thing was that right after we had completed the album, literally just after we all left the studio and our engineer Jim Isaacson was getting ready to put the final touches on the record, he had a massive heart attack and died right in the studio. It was shocking because he was such a great guy and was really a big part of the album. Ted was on his way over to work with him when it happened and we were all in disbelief when we heard the news. But we pressed on and hit the road. It was an interesting time for the band. More personnel changes would be happening soon and then things got serious.

Just before Jeff and John Hartman left the band, we would usually rehearse at SIR in San Francisco, and so I was doing a lot of driving. We were also laying out lots of money to rehearse before the albums or tours. And paying a lot for storage. I had an idea, why not buy a house for everything? We could store everything there, save some money, and stop driving so much. I thought it would be more convenient and equitable for everybody, and when I ran it by the rest of the band, they thought it was a good idea. I went to a friend who was a real estate agent, and we started looking around in Pacifica and Half Moon Bay and finally found a house in Montara, a little three-bedroom place on about four acres. It was a really nice old 1940s house with a gorgeous ocean view. You could see all the way to the Farallon Islands through the windows in the living room, where we rehearsed. And it was a bargain: $140,000. I said to the guys, "How about we all go in on this?" and they agreed, so we all went in on that house, and that became the home of the Doobie Brothers. It was great. For a couple of years, that was our home base. I used to ride my motorcycle up the Pacific Coast Highway from Santa Cruz, where I lived.

But then management got all hot on the idea of moving everything to Los Angeles, because that's where they were based. I said, "What about the investment?" And the attitude was, "Screw it, we don't care." Well, that wasn't for me. I didn't want to live in Los Angeles. I also didn't appreciate the lack of respect. Forcing my hand and costing me money to further the career of our manager didn't seem right. Then a big storm up north hit, and I had a lot of work to do at my house; we had no power for more than a week, and there was tons of damage in Santa Cruz. It was time for the band to rehearse, and I couldn't get out. But we did have commitments, so it was hard. Everybody became somewhat uncompromising. They all went down to L.A. to rehearse. I felt disrespected, and I knew this was basically it. I called Mike on the phone and said, "The Doobie Brothers, for me, are not a Southern California band. We are a Northern California band. We're a San Jose band. I think I might be done with all of this." Mike was totally understanding. "I get it," he said. "I think it might be time to move on. Everyone's bringing their own songs, and without you, Pat, I don't think there's a band."

Michael

I was in the hospital kind of sitting vigil for my grandmother, who would soon pass away. Pat had been trying to reach me, so I went and made a pay phone call to him. I could tell by the sound of his voice it was something serious. He said to me, "I haven't been satisfied for a while. I think it's become more of an

L.A. band, which is not what I set out to help create. I think it's time for me to leave." And so with that, Pat Simmons left the Doobie Brothers. The rest of us, Keith, Bobby, Willie Weeks, all of us, got together at SIR Studios to rehearse and just kind of see where things were. But it was obvious we couldn't go on without Pat. He was the last original guy. He'd been through everything. No Pat, no Doobie Brothers. That was obvious. I think we all knew at the same time. This was it. But at least we got to do a farewell tour. I get asked sometimes about specific shows that I've played with the Doobie Brothers that meant a lot to me. It's hard to say because, for one, we just played so much and there were countless memorable moments. But I will have to say that the No Nukes MUSE concerts held in New York in 1979 were really special for me. I think the band would agree. I know it sounds hokey, but just to have that kind of spirit, of all of those artists coming together to try to make the world a better place, was heartwarming. This was before a lot of charity concerts came together, so that was very unique for the time. And there was something very organic about it. This was all being done by the artists. And then to have people like James Taylor, Carly Simon, Jackson Browne, and all those other legends come out with us onstage to sing "Takin' It to the Streets"—I just couldn't believe what was happening. I was looking around and thinking, these are all stars up here, and we are just a working band. There's another show that I remember well. It was 1995, and we were playing at this beautiful gorge up in Oregon. My dad had just died that year, and I was hurting badly. I just missed him so much. We came out on the stage, and as I was looking at the vista over the river and at the gorge, it was just so overwhelming, literally one of the most beautiful things I've ever seen in my life. It was so distracting that I almost forgot to start singing at one point. I just got lost in the beauty that was surrounding us. And then as I started to play, this big beautiful butterfly landed right on my shoulder. And it sat there for almost an entire song. It felt so good. I felt that was my dad coming to watch over me. That's exactly what it felt like. A lot of great musical moments, but the butterfly provided one that really stands out among all of them.

Pat

So we told the guys that this was going to be the end. But we also decided to leave things on a high note. We wanted to do a farewell tour. Ted got involved and helped out with some of the arrangements, and we did this big wonderful tour. For me, the best part of it was saying goodbye at the Greek Theatre in Berkeley. Everybody came out, and having Tommy out there was special. I couldn't believe it. Watching that crowd go crazy at the end, I thought to myself, "This is it. This is really the end of the Doobie Brothers." It was so bittersweet. Part of it was that I don't think we've ever played better. The band was so tight. But things were the way they were. I couldn't forget how disappointed I felt when management decided to move the band down to Los Angeles. And basically ignored my wishes. When Tom came out with us and did "China Grove," the crowd went crazy. I hadn't played with him for a long time, but he looked good and he looked strong. He'd been working out and was really buff. At the end of the set, we all stood together and took a final bow. That Northern California crowd was going crazy. It was one of the greatest moments of my life. But also one of the saddest.

Tom

That was an incredible night. I'm not one to get too nostalgic or anything, but man, I couldn't help but get emotional that night. For one thing, that night was proof the Doobie Brothers had successfully gone on separately and that we would both survive and do well. But they were ending. How could the Doobie Brothers be ending? You never know how it's going to be when you show up at a gig and it's not your show. But that band that night made me feel like I had never left. That's a credit to Pat and the spirit of the rest of the guys. I mean, I was proud watching those guys play that night. They were a hell of a band. I almost forgot I had been part of it. It was like, "Goddamn, look at those guys—what a great band!" And then I got up there and looked around and thought, wow, it's so familiar but different. And then the crowd. We've played for a lot of crowds over the years. That one was special. Everybody knew it was the end. But it wasn't sad; the crowd was supportive and showed appreciation of all that the band had done and what it meant to them. It was joyous for everybody, a celebration! And, of course, it was bittersweet for the band, but when we started playing at the end of the show and that crowd got on its feet, we knew we had done well. We knew all the years had been worth it. They had a good run with me and a good run without me. I realized that the thing we created on Twelfth Street had been the start of a marker in people's lives as well as our own. And through all its changes, the Doobie Brothers and everybody who'd been in it would always be a valid musical statement, no matter which style. Pat, Michael, and I had created songs that would go on for a very long time, and I'm proud to be part of that! When that show was over, I wished we had a few more to play. I enjoyed revisiting the Doobie Brothers, and it was a fun reunion on a personal level with all the guys. Quite a night! I was proud of all the music that had been created and miles that had been logged by both versions of the band. We were all part of a bigger story. An American band!

Pat

The band played shows throughout the summer of 1982 on a tour we called the Doobie Brothers Farewell Tour. As mentioned earlier, we had decided to do one more time around in order to express our appreciation to the fans who had been so supportive of our music through the years. Ted, knowing this might be our last chance to catch a live recording of our show, helped us put a set together that we all felt would not only be a nice representation of our material from different periods but also allow each of us to step into the spotlight and have a chance to express ourselves. This was the only live record we had ever done. We actually recorded three nights, two in L.A., at the Universal Amphitheater, and one, the last show of the tour, at the Greek Theatre in Berkeley. We ended up using the last show as the release. It had the most energy and the best performances, and we were joined by Tom and Tiran at the end of the show for a spirited climax and a fitting end to the tour. The band was at its peak musically, and the recording captured the essence of who we were at that time. We were so tight, with interesting arrangements that challenged us and our audiences. Ted, as usual, did a great job with the mixing and production, and we had a wonderful video of the show to match the audio. This was a full circle. Tom and I started this band, and it made so much sense for us to be together at the end. It felt bittersweet, but it was a great way to go out, and I felt a real sense of relief that I would be able to rest for a while and gain a new sense of where I wanted to go with my life.

I knew I needed to deal with my relationship at home and thought this might be the opportunity to figure things out. Also, I had gotten a recording contract with Elektra Records, and pretty much immediately began to write and come up with a plan to get started. Ted Templeman had agreed to produce, and we assembled a studio ensemble to cut the tracks. Rick Shlosser on drums and Willie Weeks on bass, and it might have been Victor Feldman on keyboards? I'm not quite sure. I think we cut seven tunes that I had written, and then I never heard from Ted again. I couldn't figure out what might have happened. I was feeling good about the tracks, but something had happened, and I was stuck in limbo.

A couple of months went by, and I couldn't reach Ted, nor did he return my calls. I called the record company and spoke to the president, Joe Smith. He told me Ted had taken a leave of absence, that I should probably look around for another producer. About that time, someone played some songs for me from a Santana album. I loved the tracks, particularly a song called "Hold On." I inquired about the producer, and after some research was introduced to John Ryan. John had worked with Styx, Santana, and Pure Prairie League, among others. He agreed to work with me, helped me select the songs, and we went to work at Sound City Studios in L.A.

After working with Ted, my friend Chris Thompson, who had sung with Manfred Mann, led the band Night, and opened for the Doobies, came to visit me at my house in Santa Cruz. We began to write together, and we ended up with five songs that I recorded for *Arcade,* as the album would be called. I had a lot of fun working on the record, especially with Mark Smith, the engineer, who John brought in behind the soundboard. Mark and I ended up doing most of the work on the record, but John had lots of good ideas as well, so it was a team effort. We had a ton of players and singers on the record, but the nucleus was a dream section of Mike Baird on drums, Lee Sklar on bass, and Victor Feldman on keys. Chris joined us for many of the sessions, playing guitar, singing with me, and cheerleading.

After the record was finished, I put a band together of local guys from Santa Cruz: Dale Ockerman, Jimmy Fox, Rex Stemm, and Steve Bennet, along with Chris, and hit the road for the summer and fall. The record did pretty well, with the single "So Wrong" making it onto Top 40 radio. By the time the album came out, my biggest supporter at Elektra, Joe Smith, had moved on to another job, and after that I sort of fell through the cracks, and that was that. Still, I had a ball making the record, touring with the band, and doing something different.

By 1984, I was back in Santa Cruz, playing in local bands, doing the club circuit around the Bay Area, still writing songs, and enjoying a newfound freedom. I rode my motorcycles, worked outdoors growing apples and gardening, hiked, exercised, read, and played my guitar. I felt blessed.

25

IT KEEPS YOU RUNNIN'

1987:
Tom Johnston / Patrick Simmons / Michael McDonald /
John McFee / Jeff "Skunk" Baxter / Tiran Porter /
Michael Hossack / John Hartman / Keith Knudsen /
Chet McCracken / Bobby LaKind / Cornelius Bumpus

Tom

So after my two solo albums and the farewell tour show with the Doobies came the '80s. It was a time of hanging out, riding my motorcycle, playing some softball in pickup leagues around Marin County and over in San Francisco, as well as a little football at Crissy Field in San Francisco with musicians, photographers, and whoever else showed up. I did some playing with various local musicians and eventually got involved with a local group that ended up being called Border Patrol. It consisted of me on vocals and guitar, Charlie Williams on guitar and vocals (Mistress), David Hayes on bass (Van Morrison), Hugh Pitts on guitar (out of Atlanta), and Billy Lee Lewis, a local Marin guy, on drums. We played a lot of clubs around the Bay Area, recorded at the Record Plant in Sausalito, and did a small tour on the East Coast, which ended in a club in Boston. Afterward, our truck, with all the equipment in it, was stolen from the hotel parking lot. Major bummer! David Hayes and I flew home the next day pretty pissed off!

While all this was going on, a good friend of mine named Jimmy Robison, who was also part of the Marin social scene and was the photographer who had done the cover photo for my first solo album, introduced me to Diane (Gardner), my future wife, best friend, and mother of my two children, Christopher and Lara. And we are still together. Diane is the love of my life and is the special someone I needed to share my life journey. I learned to give more than I ever had previously. This was important, as I had always just looked out for myself, and music had always come first in most everything I did. I'm grateful our lives took that direction!

During that time period, Pat and I played at a show in Baton Rouge sponsored by the Department of Defense. Pat had already played a DOD tour, and about a month later I got involved in the next iteration. We rehearsed in San Francisco for a couple of days and then took off for Singapore to start. From there, we got on an aircraft carrier group from the USS *Carl*

Vinson and headed out to sea for "exercises" with a full complement of F-14s and various radar planes and sub hunters. We played on board the carrier we were based on and watched flight ops (launch and recover) on the carrier, which I loved. We played the missile frigates, supply ships, and a destroyer. We were transported by helicopter from ship to ship.

The band consisted of all the guys from Kansas, Steve Morris on guitar, a band called Red Seven out of San Francisco, Leon Medica of LeRoux out of Baton Rouge/New Orleans on bass, David Jenkins from Pablo Cruise, and me. Kansas would play a set of their songs, and Red Seven would play their songs, while Steve Morris usually put on a show by himself with a loop machine—he's an incredible guitarist! Then David Jenkins would do Pablo Cruise songs using various players from the entourage, and I would do the Doobie Brothers section of the show the same way. It worked great, and the sailors and pilots on board loved it. Same for the air bases we played.

After playing on board the ships, we crossed the International Date Line, when something called the Shellback Ceremony took place, which was nuts! The first stop after that was Diego Garcia, a small island base in the Indian Ocean, and for some reason we didn't actually play. The island was shut down for repairs or something. After that, we played Kadena Air Base on Okinawa, then an air force base outside Tokyo, followed by Clark Air Base in the Philippines, as well as a naval base at Subic Bay. These places in the Philippines had clubs off base that were pretty wild and crazy, and that's where the enlisted folks hung out. We then transitioned to the USS *Kennedy* carrier group by being flown out to the carrier and doing a carrier-style landing, complete with tail hook on a COD, which was an all-purpose plane used for mail and package delivery. We then started a tour of the Mediterranean. We also got a "cat shot" off the *Kennedy* before flying to the Azores in an S7 sub-hunter jet, which was so cool! What a rush! Places like Rota, Spain, right by the Rock of Gibraltar; the Azores in Portugal, with a seven-hundred-year-old fortress right off the coast; the isle of Crete in Greece. It was such a mind-expanding trip visiting these places, like going back in time a thousand years, and I really enjoyed the time there! Just beautiful. The last stop was a naval air station in Sigonella, on the eastern side of Sicily. We then flew back to the States in a military transport, landing at a base in New Jersey, flying back to our respective home states via airline out of JFK. This was the fall of '86. It had been a monthlong trip, and one I will never forget! But a month after I got home, my dad passed away. I'm glad I was there to help out before he passed. So it was a bittersweet homecoming.

After reintegrating into the Mill Valley scene, I rode motorcycles a lot with friends and kept playing when and wherever I could. I stayed loosely in touch with Pat and visited him at his house in the Santa Cruz Mountains a couple of times. I also flew to L.A. to sing on his solo album *Arcade* and sat in with his band Skin Suit at a club in Oakland one time. I stayed in touch with Keith Knudsen and John Hartman as well and hung out with both. Keith was living in L.A. at the time.

26

LONG TRAIN RUNNIN'

May 21, 1987

Tom

I had never really been one to get nervous before a show, but this was different. We were in San Diego at the Sports Arena about to take the stage for something I could hardly believe—a big reunion show featuring virtually *everybody* who had ever been in the band. The Doobies had bowed out in 1982, long after I had left them, with a farewell tour. But now here we all were for the first warm-up show. It was surreal. This was a big night, and I was feeling it. It was kind of weird walking around backstage and seeing all of those faces. I mean, everybody. That's when it hit me. That the Doobie Brothers was really an extended, diverse musical family. It had grown a lot in my absence, and I was proud of what Pat had done to help grow the band and keep it together with everyone's help and with Michael's strong musical and commercial appeal. It was a homecoming. It was a revival. You could feel the electricity backstage and sense the warmth and camaraderie of a bunch of guys who had been stuck in the trenches together for years. Being in a band really is like that. No matter what, even on those nights when you are at each other's throats, you are going through it together. You will always have those war stories to share with each other. Backstage in San Diego that night, I got the real sense of just how amazing it was that we could all be together to play some music. In all of our minds, it was just going to be a couple of shows. There wasn't a future here. It was all about the moment. It was a chance to reconnect with some of the best friends I've ever had in my life. And then something unexpected happened. The lights went down, and we heard an eruption like never before in our careers. For about a solid ten minutes it continued. We didn't even dare start to play. We would not have been able to hear ourselves. It was overwhelming. We just took it in and waited for it to subside. That's when I knew. That's when I knew what the Doobie Brothers meant to people. These shows were special benefits we were playing for Vietnam vets and a couple of others, like the children's hospital at Stanford. We had played many benefits for many causes over the years. But that night was just a trial run to tighten up whatever needed it, and then BOOM! What a reception! I can't explain what that did for everyone in the band or what it's like to be on the receiving end of something like that. It is very gratifying and something to be shared by everyone onstage.

Pat

It wasn't like we had been out of touch with each other. We would regularly get together in various configurations for the annual Christmas season performances for the patients and staff at Stanford's children's hospital. Those were very special moments for all of us. And, importantly, those times kept us in touch musically. No matter what had happened in the past, we always tried to be there to play for those kids and staff and to put everything else aside. You felt really good about what you were doing.

Tom and I stayed in touch and had recently worked on some songs together, thinking maybe we'd do a project of some kind. I think probably around this time he met Diane, and I could tell he was really in love, and I felt truly glad for him to have found someone to make him so happy. A couple of the songs we were working on, with a few alterations, would find their way onto the next Doobie Brothers album, which, at the time, we had no idea was coming.

Tom

We realized that night that we had to keep going, that we had a destiny together, the original version of our band. And we've never stopped since. That's another big chapter in the Doobie Brothers story: the new life and reformation of the band. How did that night even happen? In early '87, Keith called everyone who ever played in the Doobie Brothers to see how many guys were interested in getting together for a gig to raise money for the NVF (National Veterans Foundation). The gig was to be at the Hollywood Bowl (which became the second-fastest sellout in Hollywood Bowl history, behind the Beatles shows there). Well, everybody said yeah, and we all ended up in L.A. for rehearsals. The "band" consisted of Pat and me on guitar and vocals; John McFee on guitars, pedal steel, and violin, as well as vocals; Jeff Baxter on guitar; Mike McDonald on keyboards and vocals; Cornelius Bumpus on keyboards, vocals, and sax; Tiran Porter on bass and vocals; Bobby LaKind on percussion; and four drummers: John Hartman, Keith Knudsen, Mike Hossack, and Chet McCracken. So one very large band! And we did songs from all eras of the band, which took some serious rehearsal to work out all the parts and get everything going in the right direction.

Ted Templeman came over to hang out and make suggestions on arrangements. It was like being back home. He liked what we were doing and suggested that the original band get back together to make an album. None of us were doing anything of note, and Mike had his solo career going, so we said sure. Only we didn't do it till '89, and it was on Capitol Records instead of Warner Bros. Also, Ted was locked up with Van Halen, so he did not produce the album.

We were stoked and put on a really good show for the crowd at the Bowl, which was responsive as hell! Keith was both happy and emotional about how well the show and benefit went for vets. This was his baby, and he was justifiably proud of the outcome.

We played at Stanford Stadium for the children's hospital next, and it was as successful as the Hollywood Bowl. One of the patients we'd met at the hospital a couple of years before, Shannon, joined us onstage to sing, which was such a great thing. It was probably our most visited cause, and we would show up there every year with whoever was in town and play for the parents and kids. This always happened around Christmas, so it kind of put us in the Christmas spirit.

Next, we played a benefit for Little Sisters of the Poor in Las Vegas, which was a cause Michael was supporting. After that, we played another ten shows just to pay for rehearsals—all the hotels, expenses, travel, and so on. Everybody had a great time, because it was just for kicks with no pressure.

Pat

Who knew? You can't take the stuff for granted, and we never have. We have always taken a very blue-collar approach to what we do. You work as hard as you can and as much as you can, as long as people are willing to show up and hear you play. The feeling we got onstage in San Diego that night reminded us of what we were. The Doobie Brothers. No matter what else we do in this lifetime, and we all have little solo projects that we love to do and that help keep us sane, in the end we are a band of musical soul mates that has grown into a huge, extended, beautiful family. We are the Doobie Brothers.

Tom

We wound up expanding it into a tour. Nothing too crazy, just an eleven-city tour that allowed us to pay the start-up and rehearsal expenses. But it was really fun and a reminder of the effect the Doobie Brothers had made on the public at large. We played songs from every album, the gigs we did went off great, and the audiences loved the shows, eleven in all. And then it was all over! What a rush to get together and play with everyone. Good times. That reunion obviously sparked lots of conversations about what we could do on an ongoing basis. We decided collectively to go back to the original classic Doobie Brothers. But we weren't finished with the full reunions. In the fall of 1992, we all got together again at the Concord Pavilion, kind of a hometown show to do benefit shows for Bobby LaKind's family. He was terminally ill with cancer at that point but was still able to get up and play percussion on a few songs. He died a couple of months later at the age of forty-seven.

While the gigs were coming to an end, Bill Graham had reached out to management to see if we would be interested in going to the then Soviet Union to play for the Soviet American Peace Walk. Glasnost was breaking out, it seemed. Well, Keith Knudsen and John McFee were in a country band called

Southern Pacific, and they bowed out to finish an album they were working on and to tour. Michael McDonald had his solo career, which was going well, so that left the lineup from '75, with Mike Hossack instead of Keith and Bobby LaKind, and Cornelius Bumpus added in, as well as Pat, Tiran, Jeff Baxter, and John Hartman and Chet McCracken also on drums, so three drummers! We said, hell yes, let's do it. And I'm glad we did. It was such a trip to fly Aeroflot to Moscow after looking at Moscow through the lens of the nightly news for years. To actually get to see it up close and personal was an eye-opener! We all got picked up at the Moscow airport by two Russian buses, and they broke out caviar and vodka for everyone. I remember Bill Graham had a big smile on his face! With us were Carlos Santana and his band, James Taylor, Bonnie Raitt, who shared a backup band plus crew, a couple of reporters that Bill had brought for the trip, and Apple Computer co-founder Steve Wozniak.

A bunch of us American entertainers ended up staying at the Olympic Village outside town, which was in slight disrepair, since it had been built in 1980, the year the United States had boycotted the Olympics in Moscow. I think it was their way of saying, "this is our way of repaying your boycott." Nobody cared. Stains on the walls, tiny Russian TVs with Russian western movies on them! Hilarious.

We would go into town with our KGB escort, which we had to have everywhere we went. But it wasn't a big thing because our group had this young gal who was actually very nice and really tried to help us with any questions or directions and so on. So there we were, standing in Red Square by the GUM department store, close to Lenin's tomb and across from St. Basil's Cathedral. And because, throughout the cold war, we had only seen Moscow depicted as a larger-than-life threat on TV news, it seemed shrunken from what we had imagined. We wandered around and went in the department store, which didn't have much in the way of products, and also visited Lenin's tomb, which was surreal. Everywhere we went, the Russians wanted to trade for anything American: shoes, pants, hats, guitar picks—you name it, they wanted it! It was a big deal to them. I ended up trading some guitar picks to a Russian cop for a Russian badge! I've still got it.

Some of us went to Gorky Park the next day and wandered around. It was summer, and it was hot and humid. But it was a beautiful park with swans in the lake and pedal boats if you wanted to go for a ride. They also had a motordome, inside which guys rode small motorcycles in a circle.

It made me dizzy watching them! I don't know how they were able to do that without crashing.

The gig site was this huge soccer stadium that was kept in very good shape. We did go to a meeting at some government building to talk about the wonders of the Soviet peace walk. We all had little earphones on that would supply an English translation of what was being said in Russian. I remember Carlos gave a lengthy dissertation on peace, which seemed appropriate, and a couple of us said something that didn't amount to much, then another *salut!* And we left.

We did a run-through at the stadium, and I was amazed

at the variety of the acts who were there. They had Russian folk dancers and a Russian jazz band, who were all big fans of Cornelius Bumpus and wanted his autograph. They even had a Russian rock group named Autograph (spelled Autograf), which surprised the hell out of me. They were really good! And then there was the American contingent, which was pretty impressive: James Taylor, Bonnie Raitt, Carlos Santana and his killer band (they closed the regular show) all sounded great, supported by top musicians and singers. And us. We worked out a thing where everybody got up and sang on "Listen to the Music," which was probably Bill's idea and sounded pretty great. At the end of the show, everyone from all groups got up and did "Give Peace a Chance," which truly fit the whole event.

And the whole gig was catered by a Hungarian catering troupe, and the food was really good! The first decent food we'd had since getting to Moscow. One of the cooks had a seizure, and John Hartman jumped on him and got a wooden spoon between his jaws. That was pretty intense! The medics on-site took him and got him straightened out. John got a lot of praise and thank-yous, which he deserved for his quick thinking.

The day of the actual gig was kind of unreal in several respects. There were these Russian special police in what looked like electric-blue Lycra running suits all over the place, and the stadium was surrounded by Russian army troops with rifles up on the top. Fucking weird, but there weren't any problems that I saw, and all the marchers who had walked from Leningrad to Moscow for the event were out in front of the stage. They were both American and Soviet. It was such a trip to be there for that—I mean, a once-in-a-lifetime event! And the mood was as sunny as the day. People of all ages were celebrating this occasion, especially the ones who had done the walk. And some Americans had made Russian friends. It was a huge love fest, which didn't happen in Russia till that point. It was amazing, and on July Fourth! And looking back on it, I don't know how the American walkers/marchers even ended up getting over there to begin with. But I saw footage of the Russian folks who lived along the road opening up their homes to the Americans, and more than a few jam sessions on acoustics popped up. It was so cool to see people speaking through music who couldn't really communicate otherwise, unless they had an interpreter. Both Russian and American. That was magical! And everybody getting along . . . glasnost! Another example of just letting people work things out with music instead of politics!

I watched as many of the acts that day as I could. Both Russian and American. And there might have been some Hungarian acts in there as well. Our bunch acquitted themselves very well, all of us! It was great to watch Bonnie, incredible as always, work her magic on the crowd. Same for James Taylor's set: the crowd ate it up, dancing and singing. We came on and did a couple of our hits ("China Grove" and, I think, "Jesus Is Just Alright"), and the crowd responded by singing and dancing some more. We saved "Listen to the Music" for the very end of the show with everybody. Carlos rocked 'em with his Latin rhythms and singing guitar, and they responded in kind. He had an amazing band with him and closed the regular show. After Carlos's set, everybody from the show (and I do mean EVERYBODY) came up for "Listen to the Music," "You've Got a Friend," and finally "Give Peace a Chance," and the vibe was magical as the show wound down. I may not have the day sequenced exactly right, but it's close. The whole place singing along, in Moscow . . . Damned amazing! Something today's world could take a hint from!

We flew home the next day with Bill and his group on Aeroflot again.

What a memorable experience!

27

ENCORE—1987-2020

Pat

We recorded two albums for Capitol Records. The first album, *Cycles,* did well. It was a little bit of a meandering path getting the album started in 1988, finding a producer, finding the musical direction, studio, etcetera. Originally, we had hoped to do the record at Warner Bros. with Ted Templeman, who had encouraged us to get back together with this original lineup. Because of conflicts with Ted's prior commitments and a solid offer from Capitol, which was now being run by Joe Smith, our former benefactor at Warner Bros., we were forced to move ahead or lose the deal and, I was afraid, the interest from the other band members as well. We spoke to a few other producers: Greg Ladanyi, John Simon, Tom Dowd, and finally Charlie Midnight. Charlie seemed to be the right fit for us at the time. He had started working with songwriter-engineer Eddie Schwartz, who had recently begun experimenting with early digital recording. We were very interested in incorporating this process into our sessions. Michael Hossack had obtained a new Simmons electronic drum kit, which enabled us to introduce MIDI tracks, guaranteeing us tight, editable drum tracks and synthesizer options. Being able to trigger MIDI data that we could edit and repair, if necessary, without physically cutting recording tape was something that we knew would give us more flexibility, freedom, and less pressure in the studio and that might save us time and money. We booked ourselves into the Record Plant in Sausalito, with veteran recording engineer Jim Gaines behind the board. The Plant's new Sony 24-track digital recording machine and fabulous digital console was everything we had hoped for. Things started out well but deteriorated after disagreements, primarily with Eddie Schwartz, whose personality seemed to rub some of the band members the wrong way. We were forced to move on with another producer, Rodney Mills, who had recently worked with 38 Special and Gregg Allman, which gave us hope for a better work environment. This turned out to be the case. Rodney was a talented producer, all around great guy, and computer wiz, and he enabled us to continue on the path we had chosen. We felt good about the resulting album and prepared for a summer tour to introduce the new material.

We decided to call the album *Cycles*. This, of course, represented the changes, or cycles, the band had been through, but the title also sprang from my infatuation with motorcycling, which had reached new levels of passion by this time. We even incorporated a version of a Harley-Davidson logo into the album cover, going so far as to ask Harley for permission to use something like this. Because of my friendship with many of the execs at the company, and their respect for the band, they were happy to be a part of the effort. We continued the close relationship with Harley that began back in the late '70s when I opened my bike shop in Santa Cruz, which was featured in their *Enthusiast* magazine at the time. Tiran has spoken of a song he wrote with the title "Cycles." I cast no aspersions when I say that I was not aware of this tune, nor had I heard the track. I think it more likely that it is simply coincidence. Amazingly, there have been so many of them in my life.

My life was turning a corner at about this time. As happy as I was to be reuniting with the band after almost five years of separation, I was saddened to be ending a relationship with someone I had been with for a long time. Diane Craddock and I had been together for nearly eighteen years. I met her right around the time I began playing with the Doobies. She was very different from me, really. I guess in this case it was the old "opposites attract" kind of thing. She didn't fly, didn't drive, was uncomfortable in large social gatherings, and was not into motorcycles, smoking dope, going out, or traveling far from home. All that being said, we got along well, sharing a love for literature, animals, the outdoors, and gardening, and had a loving relationship for many years. You can imagine, though, how hard it would be to keep it together when I spent half the year on the road and months in the studio recording. Music was my life, and in a sense I was married to it, first and foremost. After ten years of this, I knew our marriage could never survive, but because of my tunnel vision, searching for the next song, the next chord, the next musical direction, I avoided the inevitable. I suppose we had become like many couples who live together but can't really admit that it's time to move on. I tried to make a break several times, but I was just too caught up in my own career, and maybe too lazy to make a change. With the reunion of the band, I could see that the time had come to take the big step. On many levels, we pretty much led separate lives. I began to feel an alienation that was pretty dispiriting. I had always pictured having children, and perhaps visiting other countries, experiencing other cultures, going to bike rallies, visiting friends. That would never happen for us. It just wasn't part of her makeup. She had different priorities. I knew we had reached the end and told her how I was feeling. Diane was not surprised, though it was somewhat contentious. That said, she's a strong woman, we had been together a long time, and breakups are never easy. Now we were both on our own.

By this time, she had learned to drive, and I made it clear that I was not abandoning her and would be around to assist her in any way I could. We also engaged in a mediation process that helped us divide our community property in a civil, equitable manner. In fact, I offered far more than was required of me and wanted her to feel that, indeed, we had had a partnership that was based on mutual respect. It was a difficult series of actions, but we finally got through it. I gave her our old house, farm, and eighty acres of land in Santa Cruz and found a little house in town. I packed up some stuff in boxes and began a new phase of my life.

For the first time, really, since the band began, I was on my own while touring and recording. It came as a huge relief. Less accountability and less guilt about leaving my wife at home. She was in her own home now, and we could be independent. I was able to concentrate all my attention on the music we were creating and enjoy the present, without feeling distracted. Of course, that was about to change in a way I could never have anticipated.

Tom

The '80s were a time of growth and change, both as a solo artist and as a member of the Doobie Brothers: My second solo album, my experiences with the band Border Patrol, sitting in on the last show of the Doobie Brothers Farewell Tour in Berkeley.

Of course, meeting my wife, Diane, with whom I would have two children, in '88 and '90, changed my life considerably, all for the better. Then there was another Doobie Brothers album, *Cycles*.

While cutting *Cycles* in Sausalito at the Record Plant, we used three different producers. Eddie Schwartz and Charlie Midnight produced for the first part. I wrote the song "The Doctor" with them, and it was the first and only successful single off that album, though we released two others and made a video for "Need a Little Taste," an Isley Brothers tune we covered. Eddie and Charlie departed the project about midway through, and we finished the album with Rodney Mills, who had a considerably different producing style. Rodney was out of Atlanta and had a lot of experience with southern rock bands and was great to work with. And the finished album sold about 500,000 copies, which was a good reintroduction into the market—not great, comparatively speaking, to former albums, but strong. The sales kept Capitol Records interested in doing a follow-up album.

We toured for *Cycles* all over the United States and Canada, as well as Japan. We were back on the road full-time. This was followed by *Brotherhood*, which was our second album on Capitol. It was also done at the Plant in Sausalito. It featured a somewhat different musical style from *Cycles,* with both Pat and I writing the songs. I made it a mission to get hooked up with Jerry Williams, whom I'd become aware of from his work on Clapton's *Journeyman* album in '89. I loved Jerry's writing style and got in touch with him to set up some writing sessions at his place outside Tulsa. This was quite an experience, since Jerry had written for quite a few successful artists aside from Clapton, like Bonnie Raitt (he had two songs on the Grammy Award–winning *Nick of Time* album), Stevie Ray Vaughan, and ZZ Top.

I spent about three days at Jerry's house and studio in an old airplane hangar, as he lived on a small landing strip outside Tulsa. Jerry would grab coffee and head out to the studio and just start writing. He'd get an idea down with bass and drums, all done on keyboards; lay down a guitar track; and then start singing melody ideas. It was something to watch, since this was my first time really co-writing songs with someone I didn't know coming in. And while Jerry had a different style than people I would later write with in Nashville and L.A., I learned a lot just being there and watching him. We wrote one song together ("Excited"), my contributions being a guitar line and melody while in Tulsa and lyrics/vocals after getting back to California. We also did two other songs that Jerry wrote on the album ("Our Love" and "Is Love Enough"). I wrote "Showdown" and "Rollin' On" myself. Pat wrote a couple of songs, one with Dale Ockerman, our keyboard player; two with Jim Peterik from Survivor ("Divided Highway" and "Under The Spell"); and another with Alan Gorrie ("Something You Said"). With Rodney Mills producing the whole album, it had a different sound from *Cycles* and a different feel. Pat had written a rocker called "Dangerous" that we did a video for. It had a motorcycle theme and had some great slide work by Steve Canali.

Long story short, the album stalled without a big single, and Capitol didn't re-up with us for another album. At this point, Tiran decided he was done touring and left the band, and John Hartman left the band as well. We picked up John Cowan, who had worked with Pat before, on bass and vocals, and both Keith Knudsen and John McFee rejoined the band. So we had two drummers (Knudsen and Hossack); three guitars with the addition of John McFee; Dale Ockerman on keyboards, who had been on both the previous albums; and Cowan on bass and vocals. We went on the road and toured every year until we did another album in 2000. I should mention that John Cowan left to work with his bluegrass group (New Grass Revival) and was replaced by Skylark in late '94 or early '95, and we switched to Guy Allison on keyboards. Another addition was families. Pat, who had gotten married to Cris Sommer, whom he met in South Dakota at the yearly Sturgis motorcycle rally we were playing. Cris had two kids from a previous marriage, and they had a son together. I had my family out on the road with us from time to time. This changed the atmosphere on the buses, hotels, around gigs, and traveling in general. But it was fun. And both Diane and Cris, as well as the kids, enjoyed being out "on the road" with us.

In 1992 Bobby LaKind was in bad shape from cancer, and while he was still able, we did a couple of shows to fund a trust for his family. He was terminal, and he knew it. I give him credit for getting up and playing percussion on those shows. He passed away not long after.

Pat

The band had already recorded *Cycles*, and we were preparing for our first real tour as the newly reconstituted Doobie Brothers. It was an amazing moment for the band and a welcome escape from my recent distressing experience with Diane. I could feel a certain bitterness that remained, even though there was no doubt that this was better for both of us.

Near the end of the *Cycles* tour, we ended up in Rapid City, South Dakota. We were there to play a benefit concert sponsored by Harley-Davidson for the Muscular Dystrophy Association. I had been appointed by the company as the chairman for the Biker's Fight Against Muscular Dystrophy. The head of marketing for Harley, Clyde Fessler, asked us to do the show. We scheduled a press conference to publicize the event, and I was asked to give a short speech. At the end of the festivities, I met and shook hands with Harley employees, bikers, and members of the press. Clyde made the rounds with me, and near the end of the queue I was introduced to two ladies from Chicago, Jo Giovannoni and Cris Sommer, from a women's biker magazine called *Harley Women*. I thought that was really cool, and told them so. We, the band, were planning on taking our bus from the hotel, where the press conference had been held, over to Sturgis, where the famous motorcycle rally was going on. Our bus driver wasn't exactly sure how to navigate his way to the destination. Cris and Jo told us to follow them, and they would lead the way there on their motorcycles. Wow! I was pretty damn impressed once again! Willie G., Nancy, Karen, and Bill Davidson all joined us on our bus for the ride, and we rolled into Sturgis. My first trip to the legendary town. I kept looking out the front windshield of the bus at our guides with increasing admiration. When we rolled to a stop and got out of the bus, Cris said, "Anybody who needs a guide, I'd be glad to show you around." "Sure, that would be great," I said. My friend Mark Allen was with us as well and came along. Cris knew her way around town, and we visited a few landmarks, including the Broken Spoke Saloon. I bought a couple of T-shirts and trinkets and just generally enjoyed the atmosphere and the company. Cris was so sweet, and a really beautiful girl. One of the first women I had ever met who rode a Harley, an '88 Heritage, so for that era, a big bike for a lady her size. We continued to kick around town, then headed back to the bus for the ride back to Rapid City, where we were staying. I said good night to Cris and said I hoped to see her again tomorrow. I told her I would leave some backstage passes for her and her friends if she could make it to our show. She had press passes anyway, so I thought if it was in the stars, maybe I would see her again.

As it turns out, it was definitely in the stars. We hooked up at the show, and we have been together ever since. Cris had two children, Josh (three at the time) and Lindsey (five), from her first marriage. I was nervous at first about this, since I had never been a father, and I hoped they would like me. We hit it off right away, and I love them dearly. Nine months or so later, we were joined by our son, Patrick Simmons Jr. All of the kids grew up on the bus, traveling with the band together, learning firsthand about this country of ours. We have enjoyed an incredible life together, with a family we cherish. Our love of motorcycling is something we share together to this day, and Cris has embraced antique bikes, as much, if not more, than I have. In 2009 she wrote a landmark book about the history of women in the world of motorcycles, *The American Motorcycle Girls, 1900–1950*. It is a perennial reference to women's accomplishments on two-wheeled motor-driven vehicles in the first half of the twentieth century. It's full of incredible photos and stories of powerful women who broke through the stereotypes that were common in those days. The many early motorcycle manufacturers, riding attire, and personalities are represented in the book, and it's been used again and again by motorcycle historians worldwide. She also wrote a children's book, *Patrick Wants to Ride,* and a biographical book about her experiences riding across the country on her 1915 Harley twin. This is called *The American Motorcycle Girl's Cannonball Diary.* Cris and I have participated several times in the Motorcycle Cannonball Endurance Run, a coast-to-coast ride for early motorcycles started by Lonnie Isam Jr. It's a contest for antique motorcycle enthusiasts, usually lasting sixteen days, riding for eight to ten hours a day through the back roads of America. It's an endurance ride, and the earlier the bike, the better the chance of winning—if you can accomplish the miles without breaking down. While riding, you must be able to service and do repairs yourself. Cris has made it three times on her 1915! I've done it as well, on 1914 and 1928 Harley twins, though I didn't do as well as Cris . . . grrr!

We moved to the Mendocino County coast in 1990, where the kids enrolled in school. During this time, Cris wrote for various magazines, and the band continued to tour and record. Around 1997–98, we moved from California to Maui, Hawaii, where we have lived ever since.

Sometime around 1992, I got a call from an old friend, Rusty Young, the singer and guitar and steel player from Poco. He was living in Nashville and putting a group of people together to record a country album for RCA. He had enlisted Bill Lloyd, from Foster and Lloyd, Randy Meisner from the

Eagles, and Levon Helm from the Band. He was inviting me to be a part of this amazing lineup. It would be produced by Josh Leo, head of Artists and Repertoire at RCA Nashville, who at that time was working with Alabama, Restless Heart, Martina McBride, and others. John Hartman and Tiran had just given us notice that they were leaving, and we were on temporary hiatus. I thought it over quickly and told him I was flattered to be asked and very interested in the project. I flew to Nashville and met with Josh, Rusty, and Bill. Randy had opted out, and they had approached John Cowan from New Grass Revival. Also, Levon couldn't do it, and we would be bringing in studio guys to record with. We all offered up songs to record. Everybody sang and played. We booked studios around Nashville, recorded the album speedily, and all of us were thrilled with the results. It would be the first album from the Sky Kings. I came back home to Mendocino, and not long after got word that a new guy had come into RCA as president, fired Josh, whom he had feuded with at some time in the past, and shelved our album. I was stunned. All our work, such great music, stifled because of some loser's bruised ego. I think he was gone after a year, or less, but the damage was done. Rusty, John, and Bill went on to write more songs and signed to Warner Bros. I decided to move on. The Doobies had booked some shows again, with Keith back on drums and John McFee coming on board as well. I was excited to be working with both of them again. I called John Cowan and asked him if he wanted to play bass with us. After he finished recording with Rusty and Bill, he joined us, and we had a great bunch of players once again. Around 1995,

John Cowan called and told us he wanted to devote time to the career he had begun in Nashville before, and during his time with the Doobies. He had a real following with an audience that now might be called Americana. Uh-oh, here we go again. Luckily, Dale Ockerman, our keyboard player at the time, and I knew a guy who had been playing with some bands around Santa Cruz and the Bay Area. He was a six-foot five-inch tall guy with the single name "Skylark." An incredibly dynamic performer who not only was a great player, but charismatic to the extreme. We asked him if he was interested in working with us, and after a short audition, we all agreed we'd found the perfect guy. He played an Alembic bass, created by Owsley Stanley and Ron Wickersham, of Grateful Dead fame. It had a lit-up fingerboard with red LEDs under the position markers. It was a large instrument, which looked like a toy in the hands of this big guy. He was so soulful, an amazing player, and a great singer as well. He added a wonderful energy to our shows and became a favorite of our fans. He worked with us for many years, touring, recording, collaborating on songs, and arrangements. We grew very close and became good friends. His strongest moments, to me, came during our live shows, and really manifest themselves in the video performances *Live at Wolf Trap* and *The Wildlife Concert.* Anyone watching those can feel the visceral strength that Skylark displays during those shows. He was 100 percent at all times while performing, yet a soft-spoken, humble, low-key person offstage. An incredible musician, and wonderful person, he played with us for almost fifteen years, but unfortunately was forced to retire due to health concerns in 2010. I stay in close contact with him, and we have a friendship that I treasure. We called our good friend, former bandmate John Cowan, back to fill in, and have once again been fortunate to have him stick around. He's still with us thankfully, as I write this. As for the Sky Kings, the album we made was finally released for download recently, without promotion or much fanfare. I think it is a great album, but it will probably always languish in obscurity.

A couple of years later, I got a call from Charlie Midnight, who had a budget to record some tracks for a Japanese company and asked me if I wanted to do something. We recorded an album, *Take Me to the Highway*. A few old Doobie songs, and some new ones Charlie and I wrote. We worked at his studio in Burbank, California. Another fun project, with help from a few of the usual suspects, Billy Payne, guitarist Bernie Chiaravalle, and Norton Buffalo.

Tom

In 1993 we did another tour in Japan, ending up at the Budokan, where we ran into Richie Hayward from Little Feat, who'd been over there playing drums for Clapton, and he sat in for a tune. Unfortunately, when I came offstage after the show, I was pulled aside by our road manager and was told my mom was in bad shape in the hospital in Marin, where'd she'd been visiting Diane and the kids. So after showering backstage, I went straight from the gig (the road manager had gotten my clothes from the hotel and booked a flight to SFO) to the airport and flew home. My mom died about five days later. My brother and sister were there for her passing. A huge shock. Diane and the kids were devastated, as were my sister, brother, and I.

In 1995 we did a full summer tour, with Michael McDonald joining us, sharing the bill with Steve Miller. John McFee had other obligations and was replaced by Bernie Chiaravalle on guitar, who played with Michael. Great guitarist and fun to hang with!

In 1996 we did *Rockin' Down the Highway: The Wildlife Concert* in New York City at Sony Studios. It was a benefit for the Wildlife Conservation Society. We did a couple of shows at venues that had Michael McDonald doing three of his songs, and we had John McFee and Keith Knudsen on the album with us, as well as Cornelius Bumpus on sax and Danny Hull on harmonica. This was also the first time that Guy Allison was involved with the band on keyboards, and both he and Dale Ockerman contributed to the project. Allison replaced Ockerman in the band and stayed with us till 2015, when we brought our old recording buddy and friend Bill Payne into the fray. We continued to tour until 2000, when we took a break to record what became *Sibling Rivalry*. All recording had the touring band, which now included Marc Russo (Yellowjackets, Tower of Power, and a lot of studio work with Narada Michael Walden and others), who had joined us in '97, on sax; Guy Allison on keyboards; Pat and me; John McFee on guitar, violin, and pedal steel; John Cowan on bass and vocals; as well as both Keith Knudsen and Mike Hossack on drums. And this album was produced by us and recorded at John McFee's studio.

The songs were written by a few guys. Pat and I wrote songs, but two of the songs I had on the album were written by me and Bill Champlin. And one song was written by John Cowan and Rusty Young (Poco). Keith and Guy also had songs on the record. Guy wore quite a few hats during this project. He played keyboards, did some of the engineering, helped arrange the song "Jericho" at his home studio with me, and did some of the producing. John McFee was pretty involved with the engineering as well as playing and singing, along with Terry Nelson (our front-of-house soundman), who was considered the head engineer.

While the project was fun to do, it didn't make a lot of noise chartwise, and the single, "People Gotta Love Again," didn't do much either. So we went back to touring, and that was all we did until 2004, when we did *Live at Wolf Trap*, which was a live video of a concert at Wolf Trap, a beautiful outdoor venue in Virginia, close to D.C. That was a great show with a packed house, and the filming and sound were first-rate. Ed Cherney recorded the show in a special truck set up for it and mixed it in L.A. We were happy with the end product! The next year (2005) was a tough one, because Keith was having health problems centered around repeated bouts with pneumonia. While convalescing in Marin County, Keith died suddenly. It really shook everyone up! I had just visited him in the hospital the day before, and he had seemed in good spirits and almost broke my hand with his handshake. The next day I got a call from our manager, who was at the hospital with Keith's wife, Kate, and his daughter, Dayna, who were both pretty distraught. I drove down right away and went in the room. He just looked like he was asleep. It shook me to my core. I tried to help console Kate and Dayna as best I could and eventually just turned around and left the hospital. There was nothing I could do, and I wanted some time alone to try to deal with his passing.

We did a gig at Pebble Beach about a week later, and the crew had set up his drum kit in honor of his passing. It was tough to get through, and we all drove up to Keith and Kate's house the next day for a memorial. Mike McDonald was there, too. Man, that was one of the saddest things I've ever had to go through. Keith and I had been through a lot together and were close friends, and when the band got up and sang "Jesus Is Just Alright," I kind of lost it. There were a lot of Keith and Kate's friends there, as well as the band. People got up and spoke about Keith and their memories of various things that they'd done together, a few of which were funny, but mostly it was just sad. I didn't even attempt to say anything, since I don't think I could have gotten very far without breaking down.

There was another memorial at our manager's ranch in Sonoma, and it was attended by a lot of musicians and close friends. I got up with my acoustic and backed up my daughter, Lara, while she sang "Amazing Grace." Man, it was hard. I also spoke about Keith and had a tough time getting all the words out. Pat got up after I did and gave a small remembrance as well. Both Tracy, Keith's first wife, and Kate were there, along with Dayna, his daughter. So were Huey Lewis and all the guys from his band, the News. Mike Hossack had hired a drum corps to do an honorary drum performance, which was a nice touch. But it was all just unreal to me. So goodbye, Keith.

But he left a present for me, at least that's how I saw it. I started writing a ton of songs at my house. At first, they were sad, but after a bit I ended up just writing and writing. His passing had unlocked that stumbling block all writers get, and the songs just seemed to write themselves. And quite a few songs ended up on our next album project in 2008–10, *World Gone Crazy*. With Keith gone, we auditioned drummers (about four different guys) in L.A. and settled on Ed Toth, who had been with Vertical Horizon. Mike Hossack had brought him in, and he knew the songs cold and played great. And that was that. He's still with us.

We started doing our next album, *World Gone Crazy,* in 2008, and it was really a good album but didn't have a real label backing it. Much like *Sibling Rivalry*. We recorded it primarily at Sunset Sound and the Village Recorders in Santa Monica, doing some stuff at John McFee's studio. We took our time recording it, and Ted Templeman was back in the producer's seat. He was instrumental in choosing the material and making suggestions on the tunes before we started recording, as he always had been, and he had good ideas while we were doing the tracking. We used some session musicians like Bob Glaub on bass, as well as Hutch Hutchinson, Bill Payne on piano and B3, Gregg Bissonette on drums on two tracks, and Joey Waronker on drums on a couple of tracks. Mike Hossack played drums on everything else. Guy Allison did some synth work, as well as a couple of B3 parts. Norton Buffalo played harmonica on a song of Pat's, "Don't Say Goodbye," and Mike McDonald sang on it as well. Willie Nelson sang on "I Know We Won," by Pat. Marc Russo and Mic Gillette played horns on "World Gone Crazy" and "New York Dream." Karl Perazzo (Santana) played congas and percussion/timbales on "A Brighter Day," "Young Man's Game," "Old Juarez," and "New York Dream." We also had an incredible group of singers, who sang on three of my songs. Dorian Holley, Siedah Garrett, Nayanna Holley, and Darryl Phinnessee. Unbelievably good, fun to work with, and fast! All of these were done in Santa Monica at Village Recorders. These sessions were engineered by Ross Hogarth, as were the couple of sessions in Sausalito at Studio D. Other musicians/ singers were Tim Pierce (guitar); Cameron Stone (cello); Amy (Holland) McDonald, Gail Swanson, and Tim James (backing vocals); and Kim Bullard (keyboards). The album debuted at 39 on the Billboard top 200 album chart. The first single was a reworked version of our first single ever, "Nobody." We also released "A Brighter Day" and "Far from Home."

Pat

We released an album called *World Gone Crazy* in 2010. It had probably been ten years since we had recorded a whole album. We were pretty excited, because we felt as if we had written some really compelling songs and were anxious to get them down while we were fired up. At this point, it was Tom,

Johnny Mac, Mike Hossack, and me who formed the nucleus of this effort. Keith had passed away, and Mike had recently recovered from a horrendous motorcycle accident and, after that, a taxi mishap, where the cab he was riding in got T-boned by a reckless driver. He was still limping, but if you listen to the tracks on the record, you would never know it. He played his ass off, as usual. Anyway, I know Tom has talked about this record, but I wanted to highlight something that for me was unique. We had enlisted Ted to come in and help to produce the sessions. It had been thirty-five years since Ted, Tom, and I had worked together on a Doobies album, so in a sense we had come full circle. The coolest part for me was actually composing songs with Ted. We wrote three songs together, and I felt totally fulfilled by the experience. We had written together before, but never from scratch. Usually, I already had an arrangement and part of a song written, and Ted would jump in and make some suggestions, maybe pen a few lyrics. This time, we really started from square one and built the songs together, and I loved the results. I think our song "Far from Home" is, at least for me, one of the better tunes I've ever recorded with the band, and really came from my and Ted's shared experience. The other two, "Chateau" and "Don't Say Goodbye" were equally satisfying. Ross Hogarth did most of the engineering on the album and made it fun and creative. He's a brilliant engineer and a wonderful person. Ted and I have become closer than ever, and being able to work with him again was a really fulfilling experience.

Tom

In 2012 Mike Hossack, who had been having health problems for a few years, passed away from cancer. Replacing Mike was difficult since we had been with him for so many years and he was a studio-quality drummer who had played on a lot of our big songs and albums. He'd been a member of the Doobie Brothers both in the '70s and from '87 till 2012. Replacing him wasn't going to be easy. I made a call to Gregg Bissonette, who was playing with Ringo's All-Starr Band, and he suggested Tony Pia. And instead of trying out a few drummers, we just went with Tony, who had been playing with Brian Setzer and Bobby Caldwell. Around 2016, we decided to use percussion instead of two drummers and got Marc Quiñones, who had been with Gregg Allman and the Allman Brothers before that, and that's where we are today.

From 2010 on, we were out every year playing with Chicago, Steely Dan, Gregg Allman, Peter Frampton, Journey (not in that order), and lastly Santana in 2019. They were all great tours, and the shows were always packed. We toured in Europe, Japan, Australia, and New Zealand more than a couple of times, while keeping up our U.S. touring schedule right up to February 2020.

In 2011 we did a CMT special with Luke Bryan in Nashville, where we did some of his songs and he joined in on some of ours. Luke is a fun guy to hang out with and a talented artist, and the show was a hit! I think this might have started the idea of our doing an album with country artists, and with the help of David Huff, we did *Southbound* in 2014, a concept album of our "hits" with country artists in Nashville. I have to say that was one hell of a lot of fun. The studio musicians were incredibly good, easy to work with, enjoyable to hang out with, and we always got the basic track in no more than two takes. David Huff produced the album, which was on Sony Nashville. We worked in Starstruck and Blackbird studios and with quite a few big country acts at the time, such as Zac Brown, Blake Shelton, Toby Keith, Brad Paisley, Chris Young, Charlie Worsham, Sara Evans, Jerrod Niemann, Casey James, Love and Theft, Tyler Farr, and Amanda Sudano Ramirez. Whoever had written the song would be in the studio to cut the track and then trade singing the verses (not always in person) with the artist who had signed up for that song. So that would be me, Pat, and Mike McDonald. When the album was finished, we played a show on board a riverboat out on the Cumberland River with a lot of Sony artists, and then did an appearance at the Country Music Awards, which was phenomenal. We also did an occasional festival that had a country-based crowd. They always treated us great, and we loved it.

In 2016 Pat, John, and I decided that it was time to find new management, and we left our old manager. I had already made calls to a few prospects we all thought were a good fit, and we landed with Irving Azoff and his management team. Things got better fast, and our career really felt as if we were in a professional atmosphere for the first time since the '70s! What a difference! Probably the best business decision we ever made as a band! I only wish we had done it about fifteen years earlier. We also switched our booking company to CAA, which was another big improvement! Touring was better, everything was more professional, new songs were written and ready to be released, and we did a couple of shows called the "Classics" tucked in our touring schedule in 2017. They featured the Eagles, Steely Dan, Fleetwood Mac, Journey, and Earth, Wind & Fire. One in L.A. at Dodger Stadium and the other at Citi Field in New York! Great shows that were sponsored and created by Azoff's office. Pretty amazing stuff.

Before the 2019 tour with Santana, I did some writing with John Shanks and came up with some great songs. After that, Pat went in with him as well, writing a couple more great songs. All songs were co-written and produced by John. So we now had five viable tunes that we were going to release at the appropriate time. (This has since been expanded by seven songs and as you read this, the album should now be available. John was easy to work with and extremely creative, both as a songwriter and as a producer, and all the work was done at his studio and in a very short amount of time, which I liked! Then we found out about our nomination and subsequent induction into the Rock & Roll Hall of Fame, something we'd all talked about over the years, figuring that if it was meant to happen, it would. So we were all pretty stoked! Being chosen for induction cemented the whole thing, and that seemed like the perfect time to release new music in tandem with our summer of 2020 Fiftieth Anniversary Tour, which would include Mike

McDonald. An all-encompassing major musical tour of all this band has been over the last fifty years!

So we were all feeling good about 2020, with a residency in Las Vegas in February that would be followed by the induction ceremony in May and the tour in June. Except I got sick two shows into the residency. Diane was there with me, and she came down with it, too. So did two of our techs. I believe that we had all gotten COVID-19, but it wasn't a "thing" that we or the public knew about yet. Well, shortly after that, it became known that the United States was at the beginning of a pandemic, and the rest is history. The new music got held up, the Hall of Fame induction was moved to November and would be virtual on HBO, and the tour is still in a holding pattern until the vaccine can make a difference. The whole business ground to a halt, and here we are in 2021. We've done a few "lockdown videos" ourselves, played on one with Dave Mason and did one with the Doobies and Peter Frampton. And here we are . . .

And there's John McFee, the third principal in the present iteration of the Doobie Brothers and one of the family, who adds so much musically to everything we do, both live and in the studio. He can play anything with strings on it and play it extremely well! Guitar, both electric and acoustic, Dobro, pedal steel, great slide, and violin and cello. He has an extensive catalog of studio accomplishments with several artists, like Steve Miller, the Grateful Dead, Van Morrison, and Elvis Costello. He is also a great sound engineer and has some considerable producing credits as well.

It's been an incredible journey, one for which I would like to thank all the guys who've been in the band throughout the years who helped keep us going.

Our current lineup is John Cowan, who plays great bass and sings like a bird on any type of music from bluegrass to R&B (he is a member of the Bluegrass Hall of Fame); Marc Russo, who is a world-class sax player who has played with the Yellowjackets, Tower of Power, and Kenny Loggins and done tons of session work; Ed Toth (formerly of Vertical Horizon) on drums, who is also a world-class player with a great pocket feel that drives the band; Marc Quiñones on percussion, whom we got from both the Allman Brothers and later the Gregg Allman Band, and who is a well-known player in the world of Latin percussion with lots of session time under his belt; and our good friend and phenomenal keyboard player, Bill Payne, whom we've known since the early '70s, when he started playing on all the albums we did from *Toulouse Street* through *Stampede* and, years later, on *World Gone Crazy*. He was a founding member of Little Feat, who still gig occasionally, and has done years of sessions all over the world and toured with so many great artists, like Bob Seger, Linda Ronstadt, Jimmy Buffet, and many more. We are really fortunate to have such great players working with us!

Pat

We've been here on Maui now for twenty-four years. Seems like it went by in the blink of an eye. My kids are all grown now, and I have three grandchildren, Malu, Kolea, and Kukui, all from my youngest son, Pat, and his wife, Darci, better known as Shine. Pat has turned into a talented singer, songwriter, and guitar player. He recorded his first EP, *This Mountain,* and plays shows with his own band. Josh and Lindsey both attended college and excelled. Now Lindsey is married to talented photographer/artist Nadav Benjamin, lives in Portland, and works as a historical archivist, while Josh works with children as a special education instructor. I'm so proud of them all. The Doobies continue to play and record. We've done several albums and had a few personnel changes along the way. Tiran and John Hartman left. Keith Knudsen and John McFee came back. Sadly, both Keith and Mike Hossack passed away. We now work with one drummer, Ed Toth, who played with Vertical Horizon, a wonderful player and a great guy. We are so lucky to have Marc Quiñones from the Allman Brothers playing percussion, so we still have a big rhythm section. The amazingly talented John Cowan is still with us. What a voice, and an incredible bass player! Marc Russo has been playing sax with us for nearly twenty years now, I think. He came to us by way of the Yellowjackets and Tower of Power, an amazing player. After years of pestering him to play with us, we finally convinced Billy Payne from Little Feat to join the band. Absolutely my favorite keyboard player of all time. I love playing with John McFee. We just click musically. He never ceases to amaze me with his ability and versatility. We have been playing together on and off for, I think, forty-three years now. When you play with someone that long, you begin to be able to communicate with them on so many different levels. A really wonderful person and an outstanding musician. The same goes for Tommy. After over fifty years as friends and bandmates, we share a special bond. I can still see him the way I saw him that first time with Skip. Such a soulful singer and songwriter, with his own identifiable sound. A ripping guitar player who can crank it up and rock hard or pick up an acoustic guitar and play a beautiful ballad that touches your heart. Lifelong friends. I feel like the luckiest guy in the world to be playing with these guys.

As we draw to the end of our story, I feel like I need to give credit to some guys who really helped me to be more than I was when I started with the band. For years I worked overtime, hauling, setting up my amp every night in some club, then around 2:00 AM, tearing down, loading everything back into my car, and making my way home. Hard work, an extra two to three hours of labor depending on how far from home we were playing, and whether I had to haul it upstairs to play. Some of the clubs were up full flights of stairs. I was glad I wasn't the drummer! As we climbed our way up the ladder of success, we were able to coax others into helping with this backbreaking work. I'd like to pay homage to a few guys who deserve my gratitude, and respect. The first is Mark Brown. Mark came to work for us in 1972 at around the age of eighteen. He was a musician, and had virtually no experience on the road as a guitar tech. He basically invented what he thought he had to do. He more or less took care of all three guitar players; myself, Tom, and Tiran. Setting up three amplifiers, with backup amps, in case something broke down, tuning multiple guitars, changing strings, and sometimes driving a truck to the next show. He was on the stage for every show, making sure we had the right instrument for the song we were performing. Loading in, setting up, tearing down, on to the next show. We were able to hire other techs as time went on, but Mark was the go-to guy, simply indefatigable, an iron man. He was with us for about ten years, through many personnel changes. From Tom, Tiran, and myself, through Jeff Baxter, John McFee, and Willie Weeks. He never missed a beat, and always had a smile on his face for everyone. After he left to pursue other interests in 1982, he built three guitars for me, Strat knockoffs, which I still play to this day. They are well worn, but play, and sound as good as the day he made them. An incredibly talented artist/technician that I will always remember with fondness, and respect.

The other guy I want to talk about is Joe Vallee. Joe was my personal guitar tech for nearly twenty-five years. When the band reformed around 1989, we went through quite a few guitar techs. Nobody stuck around, or could keep their shit together, and had to be dismissed. I think around 1994 my wife, Cris, said, "You know my brother Joe repairs guitars, and has been teaching guitar building at the Roberto-Venn School of Luthiery in Phoenix. Maybe he would be interested in helping you out, at least temporarily?" I of course knew him, but hadn't really thought about him until she mentioned this. While we were playing in Arizona, I met with him. He told me he was interested, but needed to think about it. A few days later he called me, and said he'd like to give it a try. It was something he'd never done before, but I knew with his talent as a builder, and player (he's a great bass player), he could do the job. His first gig was *The Tonight Show* in 1995, the time when Hugh Grant was on with Jay Leno, just after his arrest with a prostitute ("What were you thinkin'?"). Just a little pressure having to jump in with millions of people tuning in. Like the pro he is, he made it happen without a hitch. Almost twenty-five years have gone by, and Joe is finally retiring to spend more time with his family, and re-dedicating himself to the art of guitar building. He built me the most beautiful guitar I own, a koa wood Stratocaster type, roughly based on Mark Brown's original design, but enhanced by Joe's own aesthetic vision. Another incredibly talented artist that took the time to share his many skills with the Doobie Brothers. Everybody loves Joe, and his presence can light up any room. His knowledge of sound, amps, guitars, and rock and roll history, is unparalleled. Joe is another tireless guy. His commitment to the band, the other crew members, and even many of the fans, who he grew close with, earned him their affection. He is one of my closest friends, and I'll miss him as we head into our Fiftieth Anniversary Tour. Thanks for all the good years, my brother.

Ed Ryan was our road manager for eighteen years; the best we ever had. An empathetic, funny, excessively organized individual. A musician, of course, he could play guitar, keyboards, and who knows what else? He always had it together, able to juggle ten different things at once. I always felt safe with him. He had worked with Van Morrison for many years, and if anyone knows Van, they know he can be a high-maintenance guy. He's a very complex artist. We had so much fun with Ed. He finally retired to spend more time with his family. Does this trend sound familiar? Anyway, I love Ed, and he and I keep in close touch. His kids grew up with ours, as did so many other children of the band, and our crew members. Doobie day care! He went from rock and roll to farming. Goats, chickens, orchards, country living, a great person.

Tyler Habrecht is another one of our crew I'd like to mention. Tyler started out as a drum tech. He is a very good guitar player, but somehow ended up on the percussion side of things. He has graduated to stage manager for the band, but does far more than that. He is an all-around organizer, and go-to guy for the whole crew, and really for the band as well. I can't remember exactly when he came to work for us; fifteen years ago, twenty?, seems like he's always been here. Along with John Perkins, our truck driver, another indispensable member of the Doobie family. John's been here for the last twenty-five years. John's never missed a show. Both he and Tyler are like brothers to me, and have kept this band together on, and off, the road. There are so many others who've been there for us, but I wanted to mention these guys, since to me, they've been truly pivotal in our career. We certainly are better off because of their spirit and contributions. We owe them so much.

Recently we hooked up with a fantastic producer, musician, and songwriter, John Shanks. We wanted to record some new material, and our managers, Karim Karmi and Irving

Azoff, asked John if he'd be interested in working with us. Both Tom and I really hit it off with John. He is different from anyone we have ever worked with. Besides being a great producer, he's an excellent guitar player and all-around great musician. Tommy and I wrote with him and came up with songs we are really enthusiastic about. We finished and recorded five songs initially and are working on five or six additional tracks. John is such a fun guy to write with. Both Tom and I were able to finish all the songs we worked on with John in record time. He just has great ideas and inspires you to work toward a vision that manifests itself as you progress, with a story that we both have experienced in some form or other. As of this writing, we are still waiting for a release date. Due to the COVID-19 virus that is now ravaging the nation, we have had to postpone shows, recording, rehearsals, and anything else that requires close contact with other people. Lord knows when we'll get back to work again, but that's another story.

I just want to thank you, dear reader, for picking up this book and following us on our musical, and lifetime, journey. It's been quite an amazing ride for me personally and has lasted much longer than I ever could have anticipated. So far, it looks like the train is still rolling down the track, though we're paused for a while at the station, waiting for the all-clear signal ahead. I know it's coming soon, and I'm anxious to get back out there in the world, where hopefully you all are safe and waiting for life to resume its more familiar cycle. Whatever our situation, I know we can all agree that life is a gift. No matter who or where we are, we are all part of a greater human family. Before

I was a musician, I was a fan. Music, for most of us, is a beautiful and almost inconceivable part of our lives. Sound vibration that reaches our ears and nervous system, sometimes taking us into exhilarating, delirious realms. Other times, we might experience sweet sadness or longing, extreme happiness, all the emotions available to the human spirit. Most often, there is some association involved, first love, a first kiss, first sexual encounter, an unforgettable party, you and your sweetheart's special song, a love lost, a sad experience, an angry encounter, disappointment. Whatever happens in life is usually accompanied by a song or tune that can re-create some of the feelings we may have experienced while it was happening. It's always amazing to me what happens when I hear a song with this strong association.

Truly a time machine that can take me anywhere, anytime I need to go. I can become someone else as well: a blues guy, a hipster, a cowboy, a bebopper, a rebel, a mountain man, or (my personal favorite) a rocker! Is this magic? Maybe . . . Whatever it is, I like it. And the best thing about it is, there's always music you've never heard before and a new experience waiting to be enhanced by a special song that, by fate, happens to be woven into the tapestry of the moment. Thanks for listening to the music and for being along for the ride. We wouldn't be writing this if it weren't for you.

AFTERWORD BY COWRITER
CHRIS EPTING

I grew up in the 1970s listening to the Doobie Brothers. I loved them, especially the first version of the band featuring Tom Johnston. Not that I didn't appreciate the Michael McDonald era, but what Tommy brought to the party, his hard-edged rock and rhythm and blues roots, was just more up my alley. That said, whenever I would go see the band live, I marvel at how Pat Simmons was able to help his band survive and evolve the way he did. Also, Pat's playing made me more interested in things like Americana, folk, and blues; his music actually educated me as a listener because it made me want to explore.

For whatever reasons, the Doobie Brothers never seemed to exist within the same conversations involving bands such as the Grateful Dead, the Allman Brothers, the Band, the Eagles, and other truly classic American rock and roll bands. From the critic's point of view, the Doobies were probably too commercially successful. That seemed to be held against them, which I always found kind of ridiculous. The fact that the Doobies found a way to connect with their fans, not just in an emotional way but also in a commercial way, to me, was something to be celebrated. Critics always seem to scoff at the way Michael McDonald "changed" the sound of the band instead of appreciating the fact that the band as an entity was so inclusive and open to new ideas that they actually allowed his talents to take root so that the world could appreciate what a great artist McDonald was and still is. As a music journalist myself, I will never understand why success is sometimes held against artists. Why is it such a bad thing if your music gets played all over the radio and you are selling out arenas and stadiums? When I first started talking to Tom and Pat about this project, I know that there was some hesitation to move forward. They both seemed to wonder if people would really care about reading their version of the band. Right there, I think that speaks to the humbleness and modesty with which these guys approach music. Over the decades, they have never really been identified as "front men" for their band, probably because the whole spirit of the band is about teamwork and family. Plus, the band has been a boot camp for so many fantastic players over the decades that the Doobie Brothers almost become defined by being a sum of its parts. Still, once we got talking about it, I think both guys started to realize and appreciate the fact that their story really does matter. They came out of a very fertile and progressive music scene in the Bay Area circa the late 1960s. Santana, Journey, the Tubes, and many others were emerging from the area that, just a couple of years earlier, had produced both Jefferson Airplane and Moby Grape, among others. Speaking of Moby Grape, one of the things I've really enjoyed hearing from everybody I spoke to for this book was just how much respect and appreciation they had for that wildly innovative, off-the-wall band, especially founding member Skip Spence. To a person, everybody acknowledged how the crazy, creative spirit of Spence helped inspire what would eventually become the Doobie Brothers. If you haven't heard the first Moby Grape album, I would invite you to stop reading right now and go listen. This book will make a lot more sense after you are familiar with the brilliance of that collection. I think it's safe to say that without Moby Grape the Doobie Brothers might have sounded a little bit different. But there still would have been a band. Both Tom and Pat may say how things were not focused back in the day or there really was no plan. And I believe them. But in their hearts and their souls, they were destined to do what they do.

At the end of the day, most great bands over time have two architects. Mick Jagger and Keith Richards, John Lennon and Paul McCartney, Bob Weir and Jerry Garcia, Robert Plant and Jimmy Page, David Gilmour and Roger Waters, Glenn Frey and Don Henley. For the Doobie Brothers, of course, it's these two guys, but as with those other bands, it takes nothing away from the other players. There's just something about the balance of a great band that seems to require two distinctly different yet equally talented personalities to fuse what they do together. It doesn't mean they have to be great friends or lifelong buddies. It just means when they get out onstage, they deliver what the people came for. In the case of the Doobie Brothers, they've been doing that now for more than fifty years for tens of millions of people all over the world. I was so happy and proud to see them inducted, at last, into the Rock & Roll Hall of Fame. Finally. They will be back on the road soon, because that's what they do. But once and for all, I hope we can all agree that this band has earned its place alongside the greatest bands in history. There's nothing they haven't done. There's no place they haven't been. There's not an audience they have not thrilled.

Thank you, Tom and Pat, for the music, for the friendship, and for the commitment to your artistic integrity.

THANK-YOUS

Pat

I would like to thank all the Doobie Brothers, past and present, for the music and friendship we have shared together through the years. The experiences and memories have been some of the greatest moments of my life. Truly a wonderful gift. Thanks to my beautiful family: my wife, Cris, for her love, patience, and advice; my children, Pat, Josh, and Lindsey; and our extended family. You have all been an inspiration, and I'm so proud of you all. Thanks to our management team, Irving Azoff, Karim Karmi, and Tim Jorstad. Thank you for your guidance and friendship. Thanks to Leslie Wiener for almost fifty years of financial advice, counsel, and wonderful friendship. Thank you, Chris Epting, for your talents and encouragement, and for helping us tell our story. You really came through. Lastly, thanks to all our fans, who stuck with us through the detours, kept listening, and supported our efforts. We would never have made it all this way without you.

Tom

I owe a special thanks to Pat Simmons for his friendship and all the music we've been playing together in one form or another since the beginning, in 1970. He's such a great player, songwriter, and singer, and the lynchpin that kept the band together through some volatile times. We've been through a lot together, and I'm grateful we're still doing what we love, playing music! Also a big shout-out to our crew, most of whom have been with us for many years: Tyler Habrecht, Chris (Hootie) Ledbetter, Jeremy Denton, Joe Vallee, and John Perkins.

I'd also like to thank my family. My wife, Diane, who has shared my life since 1982 and is the mother of our two children, always providing love and reason. My son, Christopher, who introduced me to being a father and taught me the gift of love and patience. And who now, with his wife, Kristen, has a son of his own. And my daughter, Lara, whose sunny disposition and exceptional gift of voice never cease to amaze me. Being a father has taught me a lot that is applicable in all facets of life, and I'm proud of Diane and both my children. The story continues.

I'd like to acknowledge our fans, who have stuck by us over this long career. You are the ones we look forward to seeing all across the world. Thank you for your unwavering support through all the versions of the Doobie Brothers! Both recorded and live. Without you, we wouldn't be here!

I'd also like to thank Irving Azoff and Karim Karmi for taking us on and advancing us to this level. And when this pandemic is finally brought under control, we will pick up where we left off. Of that I have no doubt.

Also special thanks to Chris Epting for his guidance and research in getting this book and us on the same page together and for providing more than a couple of memory jogs and great stories of other artists that we admired or were friends with, who shared the times when we were all coming up and making music!

Chris

Working with both Pat and Tom the last few years has been a fantastic experience. For their trust, friendship, and especially the music, I am deeply thankful to both of them for allowing me the privilege of helping to tell their story. Additionally, getting to know both of their families has also been a wonderful experience. To present and former band members and others, including John Hartman, Tiran Porter, Bill Payne, Michael McDonald, John McFee, Ted Templeman, and Dan Fong, thank you so much for your stories, reflections, and observations. To Karim Karmi and Tori Aiello at Full Stop Management, Anthony Mattero at CAA, and my literary agent, John Silbersack at the Bent Agency, thank you for all of your collective efforts in helping to make this book a reality.

CURRENT TOURING MEMBERS

- Patrick Simmons—guitars, backing and lead vocals (1970–82, 1987–present)

- Tom Johnston—guitars, lead and backing vocals, harmonica (1970–77, 1987–present)

- John McFee—guitars, pedal steel, violin, harmonica, backing vocals (1979–82, 1987, 1993–95, 1996–present)

- John Cowan—bass, backing vocals (1993–95, 2010–present)

- Marc Russo—saxophone (1998–present)

- Ed Toth—drums, percussion (2005–present)

- Marc Quiñones—percussion (2018–present)

FORMER MEMBERS

- Dave Shogren (d. 1999)—bass, keyboards, backing vocals (1970–71)

- John Hartman—drums, percussion (1970–79, 1987–92)

- Michael Hossack (d. 2012)—drums, percussion (1971–73, 1987–2012)

- Tiran Porter—bass, vocals (1972–80, 1987–92)

- Keith Knudsen (d. 2005)—drums, backing vocals (1973–82, 1987, 1993–2005)

- Jeff "Skunk" Baxter—guitars (1974–79, 1987, 1992)

- Michael McDonald—keyboards, lead and backing vocals (1975–82, 1987, 1992, 1995–96, 2019–present)

- Chet McCracken—drums, vibes (1979–82, 1987, 1995)

- Bobby LaKind (d. 1992)—percussion, backing vocals (1979–82, 1987, 1992)

- Cornelius Bumpus (d. 2004)—saxophone, keyboards, backing and lead vocals (1979–82, 1987, 1989–90, 1992, 1993, 1995)

- Willie Weeks—bass (1980–82, 1993)

- Dale Ockerman—keyboards (1988–95)

- Jimmy Fox—percussion, vocals (1989–91)

- Richard Bryant—percussion, vocals (1989–91)

- Danny Hull—saxophone, harmonica (1993–98)

- Skylark—bass, vocals (1995–2010)

- Bernie Chiaravalle—guitar (1995)

- Guy Allison—keyboards, backing vocals (1996–2015)

- M. B. Gordy—percussion (2001–2005)

- Ed Wynne—saxophone, trumpet, vocals (2002)

- Tony Pia—drums, percussion (2010–16)

- David Choy—saxophone (2002)

- Bill Payne—keyboards, backing vocals (2015–2021)

INDEX